The Sexual Dimension

The Sexual Dimension

A Guide for the Helping Professional

Herbert S. Strean

THE FREE PRESS
A Division of Macmillan, Inc.
NEW YORK

Collier Macmillan Publishers
LONDON

The Free Press
A Division of Macmillan, Inc.
866 Third Avenue, New York, N.Y. 10022

Collier Macmillan Canada, Inc.

Printed in the United States of America

printing number
1   2   3   4   5   6   7   8   9   10

Library of Congress Cataloging in Publication Data

Strean, Herbert S.
   The sexual dimension.

   Bibliography: p.
   Includes index.
   1. Sex.   2. Sex—Psychology.   3. Life cycle.
4. Sex therapy.   I. Title.   [DNLM: 1. Psychosexual
disorders—Diagnosis.   2. Psychosexual disorders—
Therapy. WM 611 S914s]
HQ21.S78   1983   613.9′5   83-47512
ISBN 0-02-932170-0

To my sons Richard and Bill—
with the hope that they will always
appreciate and enjoy the sexual
dimension of their lives

Contents

Preface ix

1   Sex and Society 1

2   An Overview of Psychosexual Development 11

3   Sex and the Mental Health Practitioner 30

4   Sex and Children 52

5   Sex and Adolescents 88

6   Sex and Marriage 123

7   Sex and the Single Person 151

8   Sex and the Aged 176

9   An Overview of the Sexual Therapies 197

References 216

Index 233

Preface

DURING THE PAST DECADE sexuality has "come out of the closet." People from all walks of life feel much freer than their forbears to bring their sexual conflicts and sexual unhappiness to the mental health practitioner. Not only is the social worker, psychologist, psychiatrist, and psychoanalyst now confronted with more men and women, children and adolescents, who want help with their sexual anxieties, their sexual inhibitions, their inability to enjoy sex or perform sexually, but, with increasing frequency, the physician, nurse, guidance counselor, teacher, or clergyman is asked to help individuals cope better with the sexual dimension of their lives.

As students and practitioners attempt to help their clients with their sexual problems, they are frequently confused by the vast array of techniques at their disposal. During the last several years particularly, theoretical perspectives such as system theory, role theory, and communication theory have appeared on the therapeutic scene along with behavior therapy, rational therapy, gestalt therapy, and numerous other systems of intervention. One result of this knowledge explosion has been that many practitioners and students have been overwhelmed with questions about what they are doing, why they are doing it, and where they are going.

My goal in this book is to make the underlying rationale of helping people with their sexual problems as explicit as possible. By synthesizing concepts from psychoanalysis and ego psychology as well as drawing from constructs of role theory and system theory, I have attempted to provide the basic skills required for the assessment and treatment of sexual problems.

During my thirty years as a practitioner, educator, and supervisor, I have observed two very common oversights in helping clients deal with their sexual problems. One frequent error made by many therapists is to view sexuality as essentially a bodily experience without recognizing that the way individuals function sexually is very much related to how much they like themselves and can love others. Often the practitioner fails to appreciate that people who cannot enjoy sex are plagued by anger, tortured by unacceptable fantasies, and cannot trust another person or allow another to trust them. When the whole person with his or her loves, hates, and ambivalences is neglected, when the individual's history is overlooked, and when the client's unconscious fantasies are not sufficiently considered, treatment of sexual dysfunctions is hit-or-miss. I believe that when the mental health practitioner treats sexual problems such as frigidity, impotency, premature ejaculation, lack of desire, or celibacy, it is important to be more than a technician who wants to fix a part of the body, much like a mechanic fixes a part of a car. Rather, to help a client genuinely enjoy his or her sexuality, the practitioner must relate to the client's complex person–situation gestalt, to the totality of the client's life.

The other oversight that I have noted among helping professionals is the failure to realize that many presenting problems of clients and patients in many settings are really sexual problems. Very often the man or woman who has difficulty succeeding on the job or elsewhere is really frightened of being sexually expressive and assertive. Frequently, marital arguments, when thoroughly studied, turn out to be fears of sexual intimacy. In my own practice and in the practices of those I have supervised, I have often observed that when the client is chronically engaged in a power struggle with a member of his or her own sex, he or she is frequently trying to ward off homosexual anxiety. Many children who are patients in child-guidance clinics or are seeing child therapists in private practice are really suffering from sexual problems. For example, the child who is afraid of heights is often frightened to become "sexually high" and the child who is phobic about fires is frequently trying to ward off unacceptably passionate fantasies. Those of us who work with senior citizens have often learned that an older person's chronic depression is very much related to his or her lack of a sexual partner. Likewise, people who are beset with addictions like alcoholism, gambling, or drug use are frequently utilizing these outlets as sexual substitutes, while many people who are overly involved in their work, in organizations, or in hobbies are seeking escape from their own sexual desires. It is these types of situations that I would like to examine in detail in this book.

What I also want to demonstrate in this text is that everybody—from the infant who is a day old to the senior citizen who is over ninety years old—has a sexual life. The baby at the mother's breast is not only getting nourishment but is also being sexually stimulated, and it is hoped, is getting sexually satisfied. If the mother of this baby is a mature and happy person, then there is a strong possibility that she, too, is deriving sexual satisfaction from the nursing. Children at play are often unconsciously enjoying the sexual contact involved in tag, wrestling, or football. Teenagers who "turn each other on" in philosophical debates and discussions are frequently stimulating each other in a disguised sexual manner. Work projects in the office can lead to conflict because the team members are sexually anxious with each other; similarly, successful partners in a work project often refer to their products as "babies."

In the ensuing pages I intend to expose and explore the unique sexual tasks, struggles, conflicts, and anxieties of all client groups: children, teenagers, adults, and senior citizens. Through case illustrations of real people, I will attempt to demonstrate how the client's history, fantasies, dreams, self-image, and self-esteem sharply influence his or her sexual life, for better or worse. Each chapter will not only take a close look at a particular client group with its unique maturational tasks, demonstrating through case vignettes how to make a dynamic assessment of sexual problems, but will also discuss therapeutic principles that are pertinent to helping people with sexual problems.

In order to help someone resolve sexual conflicts, the practitioner always needs to know how he or she is being unconsciously experienced by that person: i.e., the nature of the transference. Each client experiences the therapist through the lens of his or her own idiosyncratic unconscious—his or her unique history, unique fantasies, and unique internal conscience or superego. One of the best ways to help clients with their sexual problems is to show them over and over again how they relate to the therapist in the interviews. Does the client retreat? Does he or she make excessive demands? Is trust a problem? Perhaps competition is at work? These dynamic issues constitute much of the heart of all therapy—particularly, sexual therapy. As clients see what frightens them in the therapy, they can learn what is frightening in day-to-day sexual functioning.

Not only does the clinician have to be vigilant about the way he or she is being experienced in the therapy, but other issues are crucial as well. One way to dynamically assess a sexual problem is by considering what is transpiring in the client's internal and interpersonal life that *sustains* the problem. Is the impotent man so frightened of being assertive that only by unconsciously keeping his penis flaccid does he avoid danger? Is the nonorgastic woman so angry at men that by being unresponsive she is unconsciously expressing revenge? Do these clients have sexual partners who have been unconsciously chosen to aid and abet the continuance of their sexual problems? These types of questions will emerge in each chapter and it is hoped will be answered to the reader's satisfaction.

Another crucial dynamic factor in therapy which will be treated throughout this text is the clinician's feelings about and reactions to the client: i.e., the countertransference. It is difficult, if not impossible, to help clients if we do not feel comfortable with them. What do we do with our own sexual feelings and/or angry responses when we experience them toward our clients? Can we use these feelings therapeutically? If we are "turned off" by the client, maybe some of the factors at work in the client's therapy are operative in his or her day-to-day sexual life.

In sum, this book is an attempt to help the mental health practitioner and other professional personnel such as physicians, nurses, and clergymen to assess and treat sexual problems of children, teenagers, and adults of all ages. My primary thesis is that the sexual dimension of clients' lives must be viewed as part of a larger gestalt— their histories, dreams, fantasies, and other parts of their dynamic unconscious. I further contend that for such people to mature sexually, they need a corrective emotional experience with a dynamically oriented therapist who relates to their transference reactions, history, defenses, despair, and internal and interpersonal conflicts.

Chapter 1, "Sex and Society," will take a look at sexuality in our contemporary culture. Chapter 2 will consist of an overview of psychosexual development. Chapter 3 will more sharply define the role-set of the practitioner of the 1980s who is helping people with their sexual problems. Chapters 4–8 will deal with the assessment and treatment of various client groups who have sexual conflicts. In these chapters there will be many case illustrations of sexual conflicts in children, adolescents, married adults, single adults, and the aged. Finally, chapter 9 will present an overview of the many sexual therapies that are being utilized today. In the chapters on married and single adults, some of the discussion and case material, as well as some of the references, are drawn from a previous book, *The Extramarital Affair*, published by The Free Press in 1980.

I would like to thank the many students, practitioners, clients, teachers, and colleagues who have contributed ideas and case examples to this book. I am also grateful to Joyce Seltzer, senior editor at The Free Press, for her encouragement and constructive criticisms. Finally, I would like to thank my wife, Marcia, and our two sons, Richard and Bill, for their patience and forbearance in constantly listening to "Daddy's daily seminars on sex."

Graduate School of Social Work
Rutgers University
New Brunswick, N.J.

Chapter 1

Sex and Society

THE PAST DECADE has witnessed rapid, perhaps revolutionary, changes in sexual behavior and sexual attitudes (Karasu and Socarides, 1979; Gochros and Kunkel, 1979; Hunt, 1974). Premarital cohabitation and sexual intercourse, instead of being shunned, have been gaining increased acceptance by parents, college officials, and even the courts. "Swinging," "switching," and "group sex" among the married are far from taboo in many sectors of American life. Homosexuality, formerly considered morally and legally reprehensible, is now legitimized as a "life style," and no longer deemed as psychopathological by the American Psychiatric Association. Many dynamically oriented therapists advocate premarital and extramarital sex as avenues to mental health, and some have even opined that such sexual activity will enhance ego functioning and sexual maturation.

Changes in sexual behavior have induced modifications in therapeutic approaches to resolving sexual problems. The growing popularity of sensitivity groups, "touching" encounter groups, "hugging" therapy groups, and nude marathons reflects the pervasive influence of societal values and practices on psychotherapeutic modalities (Strean, 1976).

1

A superficial glance at just a few of society's major institutions leaves no doubt that our overt attitudes and overt sexual behavior have been drastically modified. In 1944 Professor John Honigmann, writing in the *Journal of Criminal Psychopathology*, stated that "sexual interaction in the presence of a third party would unquestionably be considered obscene in our society and indeed, our cultural norms would scarcely tolerate such a situation even in the scientific laboratory" (Honigmann, 1944, p. 721). Yet two decades later Dr. William Masters and Mrs. Virginia Johnson were observing couples having intercourse in the laboratory and recording their physical and emotional responses (Masters and Johnson, 1966). In contemporary movies the nude human body is constantly exposed and sexual intercourse is frequently visible. Furthermore, acceptable language in the movies, theater, and literature has changed radically. Words like *fuck*, *cock*, *cunt*, and *prick* are frequently utilized with limited objection from viewers and readers. Describing the sweeping changes in our sexual mores that evolved during the 1970s, Morton Hunt writes: "Even in respectable literary works, descriptions of sex acts ceased to be indirect and poetically allusive, and became clinically graphic. Writers such as Philip Roth, John Updike, and Jean Genet included scenes of masturbation, fellatio, cunnilingus, buggery—oh yes, and intercourse—of such explicitness that Lady Chatterley seemed second cousin to Heidi" (Hunt, 1974, p. 7).

In order to appreciate our age of "sexual liberation," it may be helpful to view it within a historical context. What were the sexual attitudes and sexual practices of our forefathers?

A Brief Historical Review of Sexual Attitudes and Practices

Historical overviews of sexual attitudes and practices (Hunt, 1959; Licht, 1932; Vanggaard, 1972; Dickes, 1979) have pointed out that in pre-Christian times sexuality was accepted as a biological necessity and was overtly practiced, in a manner quite different from our own. The Greeks, for example, had several classes of women who sold their sexual favors openly and without interference from the state. The lowest class, the *pornae*, were prostitutes in brothels. Higher in rank were the *auletrides*, who not only gave of themselves bodily but sang, danced, and played musical instruments for their men. The highest rank were the *hetaerae*, highly educated women who functioned as intellectual companions as well as mistresses. Many of the *hetaerae* owned their own homes and enjoyed considerable social status, and according to Hunt (1959) many had a social status considerably higher than that of a legitimate wife.

The open acceptance of sexuality in Greece included homosexuality as well as heterosexuality. Pederasty was an accepted practice and was regulated by law (Dickes, 1979). Solon, who established the decrees that governed much of Greek society, forbade slaves to have sexual intercourse with freeborn boys; this activity was reserved for the wellborn. Usually, the homosexual relationship was between an older man and a boy, and the Greeks regarded it as an important factor in the development and education of their wellborn youths. Such relationships were conducted in a formal manner, requiring the consent and approval of the boy's father. Following this approval, a public announcement was made of the intention to have the boy live with an older man as his lover. The parents were then no longer held responsible for the boy inasmuch as his lover became his guardian and teacher. A highlight of the sexual relationship was anal penetration, because the Greeks believed that the boy would absorb the good qualities of his guardian (Vanggaard, 1972).

Bisexuality was also characteristic of the Romans. Julius Caesar, when young, perfumed himself and denuded his body of hair. He openly practiced homosexuality, and was at one period of his life called the "queen of Bythynia" because he slept with the king. It is of interest that the term *queen* is still utilized today to denote the feminine male homosexual. Caesar was called *queen* because he was the passive partner in the act, this being considered a sign of submission and therefore of weakness. Remaining bisexual, Caesar was sexually competent with women as well as with men. The Romans called him the lover of any and all women as well as a mistress to many men. Bisexual behavior was not considered unusual in Rome, and the respect for Caesar the general was not affected by his sexual behavior (Dickes, 1979).

By 100 B.C. Roman wives were taking lovers freely. Their lovers entered their homes, and "any gentlemen could and did pursue a wife, provided she was not his own" (Dickes, 1979, p. 245). The poet Catullus, for example, openly conducted a love affair with Clodia, the wife of a provincial governor, and no one seemed to object.

Sexual practices and attitudes were drastically modified with the evolution of Judeo-Christian prohibitions and pronouncements; these dicta affect us to this day. Masturbation was condemned and the pleasure of coitus was denounced, while the value of abstinence was extolled. St. Paul's denigration of sexuality was typical. He stated that it was a sin to touch a woman whether one was married to her or not. The celibate marriage was considered holy, and the erotic elements of marriage were viewed with disfavor. The Council of Trent, in 1563, declared that celibacy was better than marriage and the virginal state was ideal for women (Licht, 1932).

Although many other vagaries of the sexual drive have been observed throughout history, it is important to note the subtle but continuing influence of romantic or courtly love on sexual behavior. Developed in the twelfth and thirteenth centuries among the nobility of France and later encouraged throughout Europe by the wave of romantic individualism that swept the continent, romantic love is characterized by total fealty to and idealization of the beloved, and particularly by asexuality. The chivalrous romantic lover, although always intensely idealizing his beloved, never demonstrated his passion physically, even by a kiss or a hug (Montagu, 1956).

The courtly ideal derives from the medieval cult of the Virgin and persisted in the writings of the early English Puritans, notably John Milton, who described intense relationships that combined a high degree of idealization, dedication, selflessness, and tenderness (Hunt, 1969).

Romantic love as described in literature was not always requited and often was not even acknowledged. This is best exemplified in the relationships between Cyrano de Bergerac and Roxanne. Far from confessing his devotion to Roxanne, Cyrano wooed her successfully for another man. When romantic lovers do have sexual contact, the contact is usually limited in frequency; physical distance and legal and moral constraints serve to keep them separated.

In courtly love nakedness and petting were occasionally but ambivalently acknowledged, and echoes of this attitude can still be observed in some premarital conduct of the twentieth century, e.g., "It is OK to pet above the waist." No basic changes in romantic attitudes transpired until the Reformation, when Martin Luther approved of marriage for the priesthood and condemned celibacy, stating that the best way to deal with temptation was to indulge in moderate enjoyment. He averred that sexual impulses were natural phenomena and not due to demonic forces (Vanggaard, 1972).

John Calvin, a contemporary of Luther's, held to the old traditions of asceticism. He arranged to have public laws enacted to punish those who permitted themselves sexual pleasure. John Knox and others also adhered to this Puritan doctrine, which was espoused primarily by the middle classes. The aristocracy remained more hedonistic, and these two opposing trends have tended to continue, thus expressing society's ambivalence toward gratifying sexual impulses (Dickes, 1979).

The contradictions in our culture's attitudes toward sex persisted throughout the nineteenth century and became quite extreme. Marital sexual activity received approval, but the mere mention of sex in the presence of ladies was unacceptable. Sex could not be referred to even by innuendo; even the leg of a chicken was considered too suggestive, and a lady was not offered one at dinner (Hunt, 1959). Some librarians, in their attempts to avoid anything indicative of sexual contact, separated books by male authors from those written by women. Dickes says: "We may be inclined to laugh at these foibles, but we behave in a similar manner [today]. People 'sleep together' and go to 'powder rooms,' 'smoking rooms' or to the 'john.' We do not mention the natural functions involved" (1979, p. 247).

As we have already noted, the changes in sexual attitudes and sexual practices in our current culture have been considerable. Some authors even regard the emerging sexual behavior of this century as revolutionary (Crist, 1971; Robinson, 1972; Hunt, 1974). What is truly revolutionary about the twentieth century approaches to sexuality are the discoveries of Freud and his colleagues about the psychological aspects of the sexual drive in children, teenagers, and adults. Freud is the acknowledged pioneer in introducing a scientific approach to the study of sexual behavior and its motivations. He also conclusively demonstrated that sexual dysfunctioning has its roots in the individual's dynamic unconscious and personal history (Fine, 1979a; 1981; Dickes, 1979; Karasu and Socarides, 1979; Wiedeman, 1975). Freud, although not exempt from biases toward women (Freeman and Strean, 1981) was able to point out that women are not just passive, submissive objects of men's passions, but have sexual wishes of their own which should be gratified. As we will discuss in subsequent chapters, Freud's notions of psychosexual development help us understand in depth why a person may or may not enjoy the sexual dimension of his or her life.

The last three decades have produced a great deal of data that stresses a scientific approach to sexuality, rather than a religious or moral one. First came the Kinsey report on men (Kinsey et al., 1948), followed by the report on women (Kinsey et al., 1953). The physiological studies of Masters and Johnson (1970) enlightened us about bodily changes during sexual intercourse. Many surveys have been

published which demonstrate an increase in the prevalence of intercourse among teenagers (Zelnik and Kantner, 1971), and many high
schools are now teaching young people about contraception (Offer,
1971).

While it is clear that rapid social change during the last few decades has provided modifications in sexual practices and in sexual attitudes, we nonetheless have to ask: "Are people in our current society
more sexually satisfied?" "Is rapid change in social, sexual, and ethical roles extracting a price from Americans?" How are we to understand the sexual dimensions of their liberalized lives and perceptions?"

Sexual Life in the 1980s

According to a recent epidemiological study of stress in the United
States presented by Dr. George Serban of New York University at the
American Psychiatric Association's annual meeting (Serban, 1981)
the majority of men and women in our culture are experiencing anxiety and a large percentage are suffering depression concomitant with
changes in their sexual roles. Serban further reported that most people are not comfortable with "the new sexual permissiveness as well
as with the tolerance of pornography and homosexuality." He
pointed out that stress seems to permeate the whole organization of
the life of the individual. In interviews with 509 men and 499 women
representing a nationwide probability sample, Serban's team found
that about 60 percent of the women and 52 percent of men had moderate to high anxiety, and that 41.3 percent of the women and 34.2
percent of the men had high degrees of depression. Only 23.6 percent
of the married women—compared with 37.9 percent of the men—felt
content with their marriages. Almost 40 percent resented their
spouses moderately to very much.

One of the conclusions of Serban's comprehensive report is that
"although the pressure for remolding the sex roles has grown due to
economic and technological pressures, most people appear to feel it is
an imposition alien to their needs and a threat to their sense of sexual
identity as male and female" (p. 3). In order to master their stress,
many people are turning to what Serban described as "more primitive forms of coping," including religious beliefs and such adjuncts
of magical thinking as the use of horoscopes and lucky numbers.

With rapid social change being one of the most conspicuous features of twentieth-century culture, most social scientists have de-

scribed members of our society as increasingly narcissistic, neuroti-
cally ambitious, and hateful (Hendin, 1975; Fine, 1981). Although
everyone is constantly titillated by increased sexual opportunities,
many people do not feel sexually relaxed or sexually competent. In
countless ways the battle of the sexes has intensified in the 1980s. Divorce is frequent, and as the Serban study reflected, many married
people are engaged in oneupmanship and other forms of power struggles. Some groups in the women's movement argue that a woman who
commits herself to one man is collaborating in her own oppression
(Durbin, 1977) and that traditional marriage is a form of serfdom or
slavery (Smith and Smith, 1974). Many writers emphasize masturbation or lesbianism as acceptable routes to sexual gratification for
women, and some (e.g., Hite, 1976) find these alternatives in some
ways superior to heterosexual intercourse. Marriage as seen by the
popular writer Jane Howard has become "a chancy, grim, modern
experiment instead of an ancient institution" (1978).

Because of the blurring of gender roles, husbands and wives are
unsure about what the rules and regulations of married life should or
can be. Every day another book or article appears that attempts to
help people conduct heterosexual transactions, particularly the inevitable fights in married life. The proliferation and popularity of
books such as *The Intimate Enemy*: *How to Fight Fair in Love and
Marriage* (Bach, 1969) are testimony to the fact that the norms pre-
sumed to govern marital behavior are shifting and vague in most individual's minds. Sexual differences have become blurred, as seen in
the growing similarity of the sexes in dress and grooming. A booth at
an amusement park recently bore the sign, "Guess Your Sex."

Men and women, children and teenagers, in the 1980s are constantly being stimulated by the lure of many potential pleasures.
Eroticism in both advertisements and the popular media is flooding
the market, promising increased happiness and self-esteem to those
who heed the message. When appeals to narcissism, excess, and omnipotence are ubiquitous, frustration tolerance tends to decline. People want what they want when they want it and are furious when they
do not get it. The newspaper columns of Ann Landers, Rose Franz-
blau, and Joyce Brothers are full of complaints by unsatisfied lovers
and spouses who resent their unfulfilled states. Rape is on the increase, sexual violence is pervasive, and the battered wife now has a
counterpart, the battered husband. In a recent book, *Wife Beating:
The Silent Crisis*, Langley and Levy (1977) reported that one fifth of
the married women in America beat their husbands, but that few of
the men would admit it.

In the 1980s many individuals have been led to believe that life can be ecstatic and that one can be loved and admired most of the time provided that one learns the right methods to achieve the promised state of bliss. Increased sexual and social opportunities as well as the constant stimulation by the media have increased most people's sexual expectations. Many people are unhappy in their sexual relationships because they are convinced that much more gratification is available somewhere else (Strean, 1980).

Herbert Hendin (1975), a psychoanalyst who has studied the impact of cultural forces on individual behavior, has dubbed our current era "The Age of Sensation." According to Hendin, we are living in a time when people are exclusively concerned with their own desires and find it extremely difficult to love another human being. Obviously, when people cannot easily love they cannot easily make love. Hendin contends that the high rate of divorce and disruption in family life reflects the cultural trend toward replacing commitment, involvement, and tenderness with self-aggrandizement, exploitation and titillation.

Psychoanalyst Reuben Fine (1975a) has referred to our society as "a hate culture" and has pointed out that most individuals harbor a great deal of distrust and suspicion in their interpersonal relationships. Competition is more valued than cooperation, and there is more self-centeredness than genuine concern for others. In a hate culture, sexual interaction will reflect what is dominant in the society: frustration, anger, competition, and self-centeredness.

Although the mental health practitioner of the 1980s has a clientele who can talk more easily about sexuality than was possible in the past, the practitioner is also confronted with many people who have intense sexual conflicts. Men of all ages are reporting that they are bothered by potency problems, and women of all ages report that despite frequent sexual activity they are not enjoying themselves (Frosch et al., 1979). While women clients will mention their increased sexual freedom, frequently they will also discuss their shame at being unorgastic or not multiply responsive. Perhaps occurring more commonly, after being involved in therapy for a while, many women will discuss their profound sense of sexual guilt in an era of sexual liberation.

A psychiatrist and psychoanalyst specializing in the treatment of women with sexual problems, Dr. Natalie Shainess (1979), has pointed out that the sexual standards of today are set by business and commerce, which is why so many people believe that pleasure can be mechanically induced. She further points out that our media have helped us distort sex so that we erroneously conclude that sex can be separated from the individual's beliefs, personal myths, emotions, and attitudes toward others, as well as the presence or absence of a degree of self-esteem.

Just as instant coffee is popular today, so is instant sex. According to many writers (Karasu and Socarides, 1979; Gilder, 1973; Shainess, 1979) sex has not only become more mechanical, but is increasingly a vehicle for the expression of aggression rather than love. The tendency today to engage in instant sex and only later to learn something about the partner is one that seems to create distrust between people and to destroy mutual appreciation. It decreases the motivation and capacity for mutual cooperation. It fosters retreat—sometimes temporary, sometimes of a more permanent nature, depending on the degree of hurt experienced (Shainess, 1979).

In reflecting about people of the 1980s, it would appear that their pervasive sexual problems are part and parcel of their personality problems and conflicted interpersonal relationships. That is why the professional who wishes to help individuals cope better with their sexual conflicts must relate to the child or adult's total and complex personality dynamics. It is the major thesis of this text that sexual problems cannot be viewed as separate from the psychodynamics of the individual who has those problems. If we do not relate to the entire personality gestalt of the client, we may become mechanics without empathy and clinicians without expertise.

One of the trends in today's society is a denial of unconscious processes. Freud tended to reify dimensions of the personality—e.g., the ego, id, and superego—and therefore his theories of personality and the unconscious may no longer be acceptable to many, but the existence of unconscious processes, particularly in sexual behavior, cannot be denied. The conspicuous feature of human sexuality is that it is governed less by hormonal influence, statistics, changing sex roles, and other factors, no matter how important these factors might be, than by unconscious (and conscious) psychological events occurring at the level of the cerebral cortex (Karasu and Socarides, 1979; Shainess, 1979).

If sexual behavior is primarily a motivated field, how do we understand what motivates our clients and patients? In his *Three Essays on the Theory of Sexuality* (1905) Freud demonstrated that the sexuality of men, women, and children is strongly influenced by their developmental experiences. Whether or not an individual is able to enjoy a sustained and loving sexual relationship depends on how well he or she has resolved the psychosexual tasks appropriate to the various stages of childhood.

The fate of a person's sexual responses is decided long before he or she engages in sex. The human psyche is formed early in childhood and the result is enshrined in the person, often without the individual's conscious knowledge. To understand what motivates people to sexually behave the way they do, we need to understand the vicissitudes of their psychosexual development. Perhaps only with the exception of rape and incest, there are few victims of sexual disasters; the misfortune is usually unconsciously arranged and self-perpetuated (Bergler, 1963). Let us now turn to a review of psychosexual development—the major determinant in our clients' sexual functioning.

Chapter 2

An Overview of Psychosexual Development

The Oral Stage (Trust vs. Mistrust)

In order to participate in a sexual relationship and derive gratification from it, one must be able to trust another human being and feel that one is trusted. How comfortable one is when involved in an intimate sexual relationship, and how expressive and spontaneous one is, derive in many ways from experiences during the first year of life. Erik Erikson (1950) called the first year of life the "trust-mistrust phase" because he was able to demonstrate that if the child has had a consistent, warm, empathetic relationship with the mother during the first year he or she develops an "inner certainty" and a trusting attitude which helps immeasurably in the enjoyment of an intimate sexual relationship.

The first phase of maturational development has also been referred to as the "oral period" (Freud, 1905) because the needs and interests of the infant center around the mouth; to be fed and made comfortable through the nursing are overriding wishes at this time. The feeling of being wanted, loved, and played with is an important part of the infant's diet, and the intake of nourishment and the intake and acceptance of good will should proceed simultaneously (English and Pearson, 1945).

One of the major characteristics of the oral phase of development is a strong sucking impulse. As we will discuss in more detail in subsequent chapters, if the child has been well gratified at the breast and/or bottle, he or she can later enjoy the oral dimensions of sexual foreplay—kissing, fellatio, cunnilingus, expressing love verbally, etc.—and if the child has not been consistently gratified he or she will be repelled by kissing and other oral forms of sexual activity. Just as the child who is frustrated at the breast or bottle will express discomfort and hostility by biting or withdrawal, the adolescent or adult who has not had an enjoyable first year of life will tend to make "biting" remarks, "chew out" the partner, or ignore the partner altogether.

In many ways the tenderness and bodily closeness in sex recapitulates the closeness of the early oral period. Lovers frequently refer to each other in oral terms ("cookie," "honey," "sweetie pie") and often affectionately call each other "baby" or "babe." Frequently the individual who cannot trust another human being in a sexual relationship has been extremely frightened and frustrated during the first few months of life. Being intimate with another human being usually conjures up unconscious associations to the early nursing period. A person who has angry memories of Mother will probably displace these hostile feelings onto the sexual partner and distrust the partner. Frequently the man or woman who suffers from an alcohol addiction is one who cannot trust another human being. He or she feels more comfortable sucking on a whiskey bottle than kissing or hugging—which stimulate feelings of anxiety and fears of abandonment. This is why alcoholism in many instances may be viewed as a sexual problem: the client fears oral contact in an interpersonal relationship and substitutes a bottle for a sexual partner.

Men or women who perceive sex as a battle of wills often have strong feelings of murderous rage toward their first interpersonal partner, their mother. Such people are unable to trust a sexual partner because they have never overcome the trauma that resulted from their first and most crucial human ecounter.

Frustrations During the First Year of Life

The small infant is dominated by the "pleasure principle" and therefore wants what he wants when he wants it. However, he is inevitably going to be rebuffed. For example, the infant may desire continued sucking when his biological equipment makes weaning more appropriate. He may want to be carried when he has the capacity to crawl. As mental health practitioners have long recognized, weaning and other frustrations are prerequisites for healthy maturation, for they help the child to develop new skills for living in an imperfect world.

If a child has been indulged and not appropriately and consistently frustrated, he will tend to approach a sexual relationship as a demanding baby. This individual will probably be very narcissistic and view himself as the center of the universe. Consequently he will be unable to empathize with his partner's desires, for in his mind only he exists. Often the individual who runs from one sexual partner to another and is never satisfied is really an insatiable baby who yearns for the omnipotence of his infancy. Also, many unhappily married people (who usually feel sexually frustrated) contend that their spouses do not have the capacity to be twenty-four-hours-a-day parental figures and are furious at them for not anticipating their primitive wishes and gratifying these wishes pronto. If someone has not been physically and emotionally weaned as a child, and therefore has not been helped to experience frustration as a fact of life, this individual, when not catered to later on in a sexual relationship, can have temper tantrums, and may even physically hurt the partner, much as a baby bites and hits whomever and whatever is in sight when his demands to be immediately gratified are denied. Some of the people who participate in sadomasochistic sexual orgies are angry individuals who are utilizing sex to discharge the violence and desire for revenge that they consistently feel. They feel violent and revengeful because their narcissistic and omnipotent wishes are never being fully gratified; like babies, they feel that they deserve to be treated as if they were kings and queens.

When the developing child begins to realize that he is not omnipotent and cannot control his universe, he tends to project his desires onto his parents and believe that they have the power to do almost anything. This conviction can persist beyond early childhood, so that the sexual partner is believed to be an all-powerful god. When one ascribes unrealistic power to his sexual partner, he begins to feel powerless himself, is easily intimidated, often feels hurt and criticized, and is baffled when his sexual partner is unable or unwilling to gratify his every whim and ease every dissatisfaction. These dynamics are frequently part of the picture in men's impotence and women's inability to have orgasm.

If the sexual partner is invested with a great deal of omnipotence, emotional or physical distance from the partner induces the same

kinds of emotional responses that are observed in an infant when separation occurs. Psychiatrist John Bowlby (1969) has described the sequence of protest–despair–detachment when a child is threatened
with loss of his mother. Many older people demonstrate the same
emotional reactions when confronted with the possible loss of their
sexual partner, even if the loss is a temporary one. It has often been
observed that when adults think their love relationships are about to
break up they react with loss of appetite, insomnia, depression, and
desolation (Strean, 1980).

Some authors have contended that the child's early intense attachment to the mother is one reason that monogamy has existed as an
ideal in people's minds (Spotnitz and Freeman, 1964). According to
the psychoanalyst Melanie Klein (1957), a child who experiences the
mother as cruel and unloving is likely to have a dual image of "the
good mother" and "the bad mother," which may persist throughout
life.

All love relationships for both sexes tend to recapitulate the early
mother–infant interaction to some extent. The oral phase of development seems to establish a lasting association between affection, the
need for others, and oral activity. If children have received consistent
warmth from an empathetic mother, later they will be more inclined
to trust themselves and their partners in a loving relationship
(Erikson, 1950). However, if the first year of life has been characterized by inconsistent mothering and abrupt weaning, the adult will be
most suspicious of the sexual partner, feel strong hostility toward him
or her, and anticipate rejection. Often, individuals who are chronically suspicious of their sexual partners and preoccupied about the
partners being sexually involved with others were children who did
not experience their mothers as consistently available and consistently
loving.

When individuals can trust themselves and their world, they are
less inclined to be narcissistic and omnipotent in a love relationship
and therefore a partner will be able to appreciate them more.

The Oral Period and Symbiosis

Research by Mahler (1968, 1963, 1952) and Brazelton (1969) has documented a phase of development during the first year of life called
"the symbiotic phase." At this time, during the latter part of the first
year of life, the infant perceives himself and his mother as one. He

believes that his ideas and her ideas are identical and he also believes that he and his mother share the same hurts, joys, wishes, and pains.

Many, if not most, lovers and spouses unconsciously aspire to recreate the symbiosis of infancy and never want to leave each other. When symbiotic wishes are very strong, then sexual difficulties are inevitable. The person with strong symbiotic wishes fears that he or she will be gobbled up in sex and will have no separate existence as an individual. Fearing merger, the symbiotic man or woman often avoids sex altogether.

Another negative consequence of sustained symbiotic wishes is that the man or woman cannot tolerate the ending of a sexual encounter. Apprehensive about something that appears like death, he or she will try to avoid sex as much as possible.

If a child has been helped to give up symbiotic wishes within a mutually gratifying mother-infant relationship that is characterized by consistent warmth and empathy, the child will be led to seek out emotional attachments to other people for the rest of his or her life. If the child's first emotional attachment has been gratifying, he or she will have resolved the first psychosexual task and therefore will later have the potential to enjoy mutually gratifying love relationships.

The Anal Stage (Autonomy vs. Self-Doubt)

During the second year of life the child is ready to leave one level of adjustment and explore a higher one. Providing the infant has received adequate physical and emotional gratification in the nurturing process of the first year and has also been appropriately weaned, he or she can move from making the mouth the center of life's activities, become less concerned with exclusively incorporating what others have to offer, begin to derive satisfaction from mastery of impulses (e.g., in toilet training), and increase the range of intra- and interpersonal experiences.

Although we expect children to expand their interests and show more impulse control during the second year of life, this does not imply that the activities of the oral period have ceased; the activities and needs of the oral period continue in some form throughout life (English and Pearson, 1945).

If tasks at higher levels of maturation activate anxiety, the child or adult will return to less mature satisfactions. When this occurs, we speak of *regression*. For example, a child who cannot cope with the demands of toilet training might regress to orality by compulsively sucking a thumb. Similarly, the adult who cannot cope with anxieties activated by sexual intercourse might compulsively and exclusively engage in oral sex such as fellatio and cunnilingus.

It is difficult for the child to mature. The baby, who during the oral period of development has been "all id," i.e., living a life of consistent and constant gratification, is not eager to change. As a matter of fact, the baby strongly resists growing up—and this is eminently understandable. For a whole year the infant has been the recipient of bounties, and then, suddenly, during the second year of life, a dramatic change occurs. Instead of being a receiver, the baby is asked to be a giver. Instead of being temporarily responsible, he is asked to take on some commitments. This is why anybody who has had some experience as a psychotherapist or counselor recognizes that people cannot quickly give up old gratifications regardless of how self-destructive and dysfunctional these satisfactions are. The compulsive masturbator, the child molester, the rapist, will all recognize even before they meet the therapist that their forms of sexual gratification get them into a great deal of interpersonal and intrapsychic conflict; nonetheless, rarely can such individuals cease and desist from their immature sexual activity, no matter how strongly motivated they are to do so.

Ambivalence and Conflict

A great deal of ambivalence is characteristic of children during the learning and training period of the second year. They want to please their parents and live in peace with them, but they also want to express their hatred of the parents' impositions and controls. Children's attempts to control their impulses so as to preserve love relationships with parents often take the form of games and rituals, such as the familiar chant "If you step on crack, you'll break your mother's back." In this game children express their wish to defy Mother and at the same time their ability to control this wish so as to retain her love.

Learning to meet the environment's demands for cleanliness is not an easy process. It is quite frustrating for the child to learn to regulate bowel movements and excrete them in a toilet. Many parents, failing to understand their child's normal resentment of the new restrictions they must impose, attack the child for rebelling. Thus power struggles often occur at this time between the parent, who wants the child to be toilet trained, and the child, who wants freedom of expression. The child often withholds from the parent what the parent wants; he rebels against the pressure to do his "duty."

The power struggles that exist among sexual partners, particularly between marital partners, derive in large part from unresolved difficulties of the anal period. Many a lover or spouse experiences giving sexual satisfaction to the partner as "doing one's duty," feels humiliated by it, and like the child who resents feeling subordinate to a seemingly tyrannical parent, wishes to defy and rebel. Refusal to participate in sex that is initiated by the partner, threats of separation, or extramarital affairs are often the adult expression of an unresolved anal conflict: a need to spite the partner, who is unconsciously viewed as a parental figure.

If a child has been trained prematurely and/or harshly, he frequently becomes an intimidated adult with a harsh superego, or conscience. He then feels that he must perform regardless of what his inclinations and preferences are. As an adult this individual feels an enormous obligation to please the sexual partner but unconsciously resents it. Usually the individual is not spontaneously loving the sexual partner but is angrily "doing his duty" for fear of punishment if he does not conform.

In contrast to the child who has been punitively and rigidly trained is the one who has been indulged and not expected to master the tensions of toilet training and other learning situations. As an adult he "shits all over others" and is rarely mature enough to genuinely cooperate with a sexual partner. He expects the partner to indulge him, cater to him, and submit to his narcissistic wishes. In sex he finds it difficult to empathize with the partner and does little or nothing to bring the partner pleasure. Sex exists only for him; in his mind the partner, like the parent of the past, has no need except the obligation to minister to him.

Anality and Distortions of Sex

Many individuals—children, teenagers, and adults—have a distorted view of sex, as if they were submitting to the demands of an arbitrary parent. To them sexual relations are not occasions for mutual pleasure but are seen as "putting out" and being exploited. Like the child who refuses to defecate or urinate in the toilet because, in his mind, "it's all for my parents," such a person sees "nothing in sex for me." Adults who have not resolved conflicts of the anal period feel that sex is "dirty" like urine or feces. It is as if they are urinating or defecating on or in their partner, or as if their partner is defecating or urinating in or on them.

Many sexual problems of adults are related to unresolved problems of toilet training. Not only are the organs of excretion the same as or close to the sexual organs, but many people are brought up with the idea that sex is a form of evacuation. Many young children who have observed the primal scene describe it as "Father pissed in Mother's peepee place." As adults, such individuals may be unable to separate the feelings of shame and guilt connected with the toilet from the sex act.

Because bowel and urine training is the first strong demand for control which the parents place on the child, conflicts are inevitable. How these conflicts are resolved will, in many ways, determine whether the individual will be a cooperative sexual partner or one who is defiant, obstinate, and rebellious.

Erikson (1950) describes the conflict of the second year and part of the third year of life as one of autonomy versus shame and doubt. If the anal period has not been too conflictful, the individual will be able to give and take in a love relationship. He or she will not be troubled by shame and doubt and therefore will feel autonomous without having to cope with feelings of revenge, spite, or exploitation.

Mahler (1968) in her discussions of the growth and development of the infant, describes an important task during the second year of life as being "separation-individuation." If the child feels like a separate individual apart from but loved by his parents, he is free to enjoy his capacities. The adult who is able to see himself and his sexual partner as separate, nonsymbiotic individuals is usually freer to enjoy his own sexual desires and those of his partner.

The Phallic-Oedipal Stage (Initiative vs. Guilt)

As the child gradually resolves the conflict between the urge to express his instinctual wishes and the desire to maintain the security of his relationship with his parents by conforming to some of their demands, he becomes less narcissistic. At about the age of three, the youngster should begin to give love as well as receive it. Initially children love both parents indiscriminately, but between the ages of three and six they turn their affection with greater intensity to the parent of the opposite sex and compete with the parent of the same sex (Freud, 1905).

Although there is ongoing debate as to whether the oedipal conflict is a biological phenomenon or evolves because of familial and social arrangements, the evidence seems clear that it is found in all human beings and in all cultures. The anthropologist Malinowski (1922), who studied familial patterns in several cultures, concluded that the oedipal conflict is a universal phenomenon.

Because the nuclear family is virtually an ever-present institution in most societies (Murdock, 1949), the sexual partner who seems to be the most accessible is the parent of the opposite sex. Against such a choice the incest taboo has been set up by all known cultures.

The Oedipal Conflict in Boys

From birth onward, a little boy is primarily dependent on his mother for comfort and security. Although the object of love, the mother, does not change during the oedipal period, the nature of the boy's relationship to her does change. He continues to value her as a source of sustenance and security, but at the same time he begins to feel wishes of a romantic and sexual nature. In much the same way that he notices his father loving his mother, the boy between three and six years of age wants to be his mother's lover. As he competes with his father, the father becomes a dangerous rival for the mother's affections. Because of the boy's competitive fantasies concserning his father, the boy fears the father's disapproval, anger, and punishment. Also, he usually feels guilty about the sexual wishes directed toward his mother.

Because of the boy's wishes to surpass and supplant his father, the boy feels uncomfortable around his father and fears that his father will hurt him. From dreams and fantasies of adult men and from the play and dreams of boys, it is quite clear that the boy unconsciously fears his father will castrate him for his oedipal wishes. This fear becomes reinforced when the boy observes the absence of a penis in his mother, sister, or girl friends. Often the boy erroneously believes that these females have been castrated and that the same catastrophe can befall him. It would appear that the mythical Oedipus displaced his castration anxiety onto his eyes and lost them as punishment for his sexual and competitive wishes and actions. Similarly, the oedipal boy reasons, "An eye for an eye, a tooth for a tooth." This talion principle is frequently revealed in the nightmares of children and adults who have strong guilt feelings about their oedipal wishes. In their dreams their teeth are being forcibly extracted or are falling out.

Fear of retaliation for his hostile feelings is only one part of the oedipal conflict that creates anxiety for the boy. Because the boy needs and loves his father, he often feels "bad" for wishing to displace him. Inasmuch as the boy fears his father's retaliation and concomitantly loves him, he submits to Father for a while and psychologically imagines himself as Father's lover. He becomes ingratiating and compliant with him. Unless the boy is helped to feel less guilt and less fear of punishment for his oedipal wishes, he can remain fixated in this position and have difficulty relating to women; he may become a latent or overt homosexual.

A common means of handling the oedipal conflict is by repressing hostile wishes and displacing them to other objects such as nonparental figures or animals. This is what usually occurs in the phobias of children between the ages of three to six. They fear attack not by the parent but by a "bogeyman" or burglar. In this way they preserve the love relationship with the parent of the same sex by taking the oedipal battle elsewhere. As adults, particularly after enjoying themselves sexually, they fear attack or criticism by a boss or some other authority like a policeman. Sometimes they just contemplate that some disaster will befall them but do not realize that they are unconsciously asking for punishment for their oedipal wishes.

Contributing further to the boy's oedipal conflict is his small size compared to his father's. Inasmuch as Father is such a powerful adversary, the boy begins to wonder whether the battle is really worthwhile enduring. Aiding and abetting these doubts is the fact that the mother usually is not seduced by her son's amorous advances and does not move away from the father. After a while, the boy feels like a loser and does not wish to chance defeat any further. Feeling inadequate in the face of a very tough battle, many boys compensate by trying to exhibit their toughness through the use of toy guns and other phallic symbols or by playing at being "Superman" or "Batman." If they do not resolve their feelings of inferiority toward their fathers, they continue to try to be supermen in later life by competing with other men for women and by boasting of their sexual "scores." Occasionally they become Don Juans and behave in a compulsively promiscuous fashion in order to diminish their strong feelings of inadequacy.

Many men experience sexual problems due to unresolved oedipal conflicts. Because they often fantasize the wife or sexual partner as the incestuous mother, sex becomes forbidden, and impotence can be the result. A man may experience a successful and gratifying sexual experience as a hostile triumph over his father and unconsciously arrange for punishment by making his wife or sexual partner his conscience and provoking her into an argument. Or he may renounce his wife or lover as he renounced his mother during the stressful oedipal period of his boyhood, and go out with "the boys" and join them in lambasting their wives. Because of their oedipal conflicts, many men can derive more satisfaction from male confreres in bars and meetings than they can permit themselves to receive from women.

The Oedipal Conflict in Girls

Although there are many similarities in the oedipal conflicts that boys and girls experience, there are differences as well. The girl's oedipal conflict is usually more difficult for her than the boy's is for him. In contrast to the boy, who continues to rely on his mother as a source of love and security, the girl, in directing her libido (sexual energy) toward her father, becomes a rival of the parent who has been her main emotional provider. Inasmuch as the dependency gratification coming from the mother has usually been great, the girl is caught in a powerful dilemma: whether to give up the dependence on Mother which has been so gratifying or to try and maintain it while simultaneously risking its disruption as she pursues Father.

Unresolved oedipal conflicts in a woman create, of course, conflicts in her sexual relationships. If the woman is still unconsciously clinging to Father, she may experience sex and intimacy as incestuous and therefore forbidden and deserving of punishment. The punishment may take the form of frigidity and/or sadomasochistic battles with men. Some women can never sustain a sexual relationship with a man because they are still looking for the Prince Charming of their dreams, i.e., their fantasized father. Some women, like oedipal men, may experience sexual fulfillment an an oedipal victory, feel guilty about their fantasized triumph, and regress to latent homosexuality, spending their time with and energy on women and enjoying being derogatory toward their male sexual partners and other men.

As we discussed earlier, all children have omnipotent fantasies and want what they want when they want it. Therefore, all boys fantasize about having the privileges and pleasures of women. They want babies, breasts, vaginas, etc. Similarly, when the girl turns toward Father, she has fantasies of wanting a penis. It is part of Father, whom she treasures, and also, like all children, she wants to own everything in sight, particularly if it belongs to somebody else.

While there are some writers who contend that penis envy is a biological phenomenon, many contemporary therapists and psychoanalysts believe that it is a by-product of culture, exacerbated by a male-dominated society. Some feminists argue that girls and women covet a penis because they desire the special status and privileges that its possessors seem to enjoy. Penis envy, whatever its source, is usually buried in the unconscious and becomes manifest only through its derivatives: for example, low self-esteem; lack of assertiveness; inability to initiate sex; or reaction formation, a defense mechanism which operates by accentuating the qualities that are the reverse of low self-esteem, lack of competitiveness, and inability to initiate sex. In a sexual relationship, a woman with unresolved problems of penis envy may either take a very subordinate role with her husband or lover or may constantly deride him (Marasse and Hart, 1975).

Recent research by Galenson and Roiphe (1979) has tended to demonstrate that the emergence of genital awareness and special sensitivity, along with the consequent sense of castration and loss, takes place in girls toward the end of the second year, at least two years earlier than Freud had anticipated. Boys and girls are socialized into their respective sexual roles from day one; consequently, it should not surprise us that quite early in life a girl is keenly aware of her uniqueness as a female.

The maturational dilemma to be resolved in the oedipal period for both boys and girls, according to Erikson (1950), is taking initiative versus feeling guilt. Children who feel guilt about their sexual fantasies and activities may become docile and passive. However, if the phallic-oedipal period has been essentially conflict-free, the maturing child will enrich his or her capacity to achieve and to love. Such a child will be able to form an enjoyable, trusting attachment as a carry-over from the oral stage, to be cooperative and yet feel autonomous because the anal stage was successful, and to admire the beloved persons of the opposite sex and take initiative with them.

The Latency Stage (Industry vs. Inferiority)

If the child has resolved most of his oedipal conflicts, he is able to move from the close and intense tie to his family toward the social world of his peers for many of his emotional outlets. While he cannot feel safe and secure in the school, neighborhood, club, or gang without the continued protection and guidance of his parents, the child between ages six and ten should gradually be able to become part of a group. Feeling some security in his own identity as well as reinforcement from his parents, the youngster should be increasingly capable of foregoing childish impulses and empathizing with the needs and wishes of others (Josselyn, 1948).

The period from age six to ten has been called "the latency period" because the intensity of the child's instinctual impulses is temporarily subdued. The child during this time, impelled by what he feels are the dire consequences of his oedipal wishes, attempts to renounce his erotic attachment to the parent of the opposite sex and also to reduce competition with the parent of the same sex. At this time the child diverts his libidinal energies into socially acceptable channels such as Boy Scouts and Girl Scouts, clubs, gangs, and other peer activities. The degree of withdrawal from sexual preoccupation during the latency stage depends on the sexual climate of the particular culture in which the child is being socialized. Consequently, the degree of sexual activity in latency varies widely (Roheim, 1932).

As the Oedipus complex is gradually outgrown, early in the latency period (age six or seven) the child has his first love affair with a youngster of the opposite sex. This is observed in most children and recalled by many adults. It would appear that almost no one can give up an important love object except by substitution of another. From Mother the child moves to Father. From Father the child moves on to another child, with whom he forms a love relationship that is similar to the love relationship of his parents, as he perceives it. A child who does not experience this first love affair with a peer has not succeeded in liberating himself from his parents, with serious consequences for later personality formation (Fine, 1975a).

During the latter half of the latency period (eight to ten years of age), most boys and girls confine themselves to same-sex groups and often express much contempt toward members of the opposite sex. Much of the sexual antagonism of this period can be better understood if we consider where the latency child is maturationally. Rather than acknowledge that he feels sexually inadequate, rather than admit his attraction to members of the opposite sex, which might reactivate the power of his sexual impulses, the child proclaims to his sexual counterpart, "I don't love you, I hate you!"

When oedipal anxieties are intense and sexual feelings are experienced as forbidden, the latency child often avoids close one-to-one relationships. He may utilize the gang or group as protection. If his anxiety is not resolved, as an adult he will frequently want to escape from intimate relationships with the opposite sex and instead will become active in political, social, or professional organizations. Group activity is much safer than man–woman interaction, which conjures up oedipal associations. Frequently, married couples or men and women living together who are involved in switching and swinging are individuals who cannot tolerate the anxiety they feel in a one-to-one relationship with its oedipal overtones.

An intimate relationship such as marriage is very similar psychologically to the latency period because in both cases the individual is required to take on many new responsibilities. The child who enters school, like the adult who enters marriage, has to share more than he did before rather than be concerned exclusively with his own interests and desires. Like marriage, school and club affiliation in latency requires frustration tolerance, mutuality, compromise, negotiation, and problem solving. Many adults handle their marital frustrations in the same manner that the latency child deals with his unacceptable impulses—by "squealing" on another who is doing the very thing he wishes to do but finds forbidden. Thus many husbands and wives enjoy collecting injustices and point out how and why their partners are "unfair" or "not playing the game." A favorite preoccupation of some married individuals is to find out who is the "cheater" among them and gossip about that person. This achieves the same psychological purpose for adults as similar activity does for latency children. Discussion of somebody else's sexual or aggressive activity is stimulating for the discussants, and concomitantly, because someone else is the culprit, the conscience, or superego, is placated.

The maturational task of the latency period is to resolve the conflict between "industry" and "inferiority" (Erikson, 1950). Adults who have resolved the tasks of this state feel relatively sure of their internal resources. Feeling confident and not inferior, they are freer to love and enjoy their sexuality.

Adolescence (Identity vs. Identity Diffusion)

After a period a relative quiescence, the child moves into puberty and adolescence. *Puberty* refers to the glandular changes that take place from about age eleven or twelve to about age fifteen. *Adolescence* connotes a phase of development beginning approximately at the time puberty commences and lasting until age eighteen or nineteen.

Adolescence, although a social and cultural construct in part, is always characterized by psychological changes in mood, role, and peer activity, and by modified relationships with parents and other important adults.

Anatomical, physiological, emotional, intellectual, and social factors combine to make adolescence a turbulent and unstable stage of development. As hormonal changes define the onset of puberty, the adolescent storm begins, and sexual and aggressive drives express themselves with greater intensity. Teenagers want to be treated like independent adults in many ways, yet with so many changes occurring, they feel a strong yearning for parental direction. Consequently, teenagers are extremely ambivalent, prone to mood changes and angry tirades, impulsive and unpredictable.

Adolescents are usually quite egoistic, and yet at no time in later life are they capable of so much altruism and devotion. They form the most passionate love relations only to break them off as abruptly as they began them. They can oscillate between blind submission to some self-chosen leader and defiant rebellion against any and every authority (A. Freud, 1937).

Very few teenagers consciously realize what makes their burgeoning sexuality so anxiety-provoking. Their strong yearnings to hug, touch, and explore friends' bodies and their own conjure up memories of where and when these activities largely took place for the first twelve or thirteen years of life—with mother, father, and siblings, Much of the teenager's self-consciousness surrounding bodily contact stems from concern about whether he or she is a young child again. Particularly among boys, verbal and physical expressions of affection are often considered signs of weakness and/or unmasculine behavior. One of the most painful conflicts for many teenagers is the dilemma between wanting to give and receive sexual stimulation and have emotional contact with another person, on one hand, and the need to repudiate this wish, on the other, because emotional and physical closeness is frequently experienced as childlike dependency that must be derogated (Blos, 1953).

The intensification of the sexual urges during adolescence threatens the barriers previously established against the incestuous impulses of the oedipal period. Many young people fall in love with a movie hero or heroine, a teacher, or a sports idol. Sexual impulses receive some gratification in fantasy, but because the beloved is beyond reach the adolescent does not have to confront the demands of an intimate relationship that is real.

Because of the resurgence of oedipal fantasies during adolescence, the young person again feels rivalrous with the parent of the same sex. This usually manifests itself not only in regard to the parent but also in relationships with other figures of authority. Frequently the young person attempts to minimize the importance of the parent of the opposite sex by deriding and deprecating that parent.

Just as the oedipal youngster often finds his rivalry with the parent of the same sex too intense and defends himself by means of an inverted Oedipus complex, a transient phase of homosexuality during adolescence can frequently be noticed. Friendship frequently disguises the homosexual element, but it is not uncommon for young people of the same sex between twelve and fifteen years of age to experiment sexually with each other.

Inasmuch as adolescence recapitulates all the previous stages of psychosexual growth, if young people do not resolve the conflicts and face the tasks of this period they will find it difficult to function in an intimate sexual relationship. They will feel rebellious when they are asked to cooperate and they will assume a pseudo-independent facade to deny their dependency: If they have not resolved oedipal rivalries and incestuous wishes—or, as Erikson (1950) has pointed out, if they have not mastered the tasks of "identity versus identity diffusion" and "intimacy versus isolation"—they will be troubled by emotional conflict in their adult life.

Mature Sexuality

By the time an individual has reached the age of eighteen or nineteen, he or she should be able to enjoy a mutually gratifying relationship with a member of the opposite sex. A period of free sexual experimentation in adolescence is optimal for the individual's development. The anthropological evidence is overwhelming that this makes for healthy growth (Fine, 1975).

The period of experimentation during adolescence should be followed by an intimate relationship with one person of the opposite sex. This sexually intimate connection should include a mutual interchange of feelings, hopes, attitudes, memories, and everything else that makes a relationship worthwhile. Here, for the first time, the person can feel that he or she is an adult (Erikson, 1950; Fine, 1975a).

In any sexual relationship, the history of individual psychosexual development is recapitulated in condensed form. Each person follows an inner script, and that is why handbooks on sexual technique have only very limited value. If the individual, as a child has successfully progressed through the various psychosexual stages, he will be able to form an attachment and trust himself and his partner in it. The hypothetically mature person will want to cooperate with his partner and will feel autonomous as he does so. He will admire his sexual partner without feeling any loss of self-esteem. He will be able to initiate lovemaking without feeling uncomfortable because he has a sense of identity. The mature person will be able to let himself be passive without feeling threatened and will enjoy sexual intimacy and devotion without feeling self-sacrificial about it. He will enjoy giving and receiving in sex because symbiotic wishes, hostilities, and destructive competition are all at a minimum.

Only a minority of individuals can engage in an intimate sexual relationship in which they freely admire the loved one without finding the attachment threatening. While many individuals will aver that they enjoy a gratifying sexual relationship with a partner with whom they are always bickering, it is important for the practitioner to understand that the sexual pleasure and the interpersonal fracases cannot be viewed separately. Many people have to fight and to suffer before and after enjoying sex. If the fighting and suffering did not take place, neither would the enjoyment. Similarly, many married couples have virtually no sexual relationship but do have a consistent and friendly interaction. Again, it is important for the therapist to recognize that only mature people who have resolved psychosexual tasks can concomitantly enjoy sex and love, which includes being loved in the day-to-day interpersonal relationship. If a couple gets along well without participating in sex, the initiation of sex would probably disturb their interpersonal relationship.

Virtually every person who is a client of a mental health practitioner is not able to love maturely. The person is either not enjoying sex or is suffering in interpersonal relationships. Love, as most psychotherapists have observed, can be expressed in a variety of neurotic forms (Fine, 1975a).

Immature Forms of Love: A Summary

Love as Dependency

Here the individual is consistently submissive to the loved one, saying overtly or by implication "I will do anything for you; just love me in return." There is a strong quest for a symbiotic relationship reminiscent of the oral period. Usually this person cannot enjoy sex unless he is being constantly admired and reassured, and he may get depressed or angry when such support is not forthcoming.

Sadistic Love

Many individuals who feel vulnerable and weak can only enjoy a sexual relationship if they turn their partner into an abused victim. Co-operating with the partner is experienced as a form of humiliating submission; consequently, the sadistic person is forever trying to get his partner to suffer, feel weak, and become the powerless child that he himself unconsciously feels he is.

Another reason the sexual partner is debased emanates from the oedipal conflict. Children frequently find it difficult to believe that their parents willingly engaged in sex; hence they split people into the asexual and the sexual—the loved mother (father), who is chaste, and the hated mother (father) who is sexually promiscuous (Klein, 1957). An adult who has not resolved this issue may need to have an extra-marital partner, who is experienced as a sexual object, since he needs to perceive his spouse as asexual and hence deserving. A spouse who manifests sexual interest or excitement is debased and derogated.

Love as a Rescue Fantasy

Many men and women can enjoy themselves sexually only with a person whom they regard as unhappy. This form of neurotic behavior derives from the child's perception that the parent of the opposite sex is a victim of his or her spouse. For example, if a boy feels his mother is brutally forced to have sex with his father, in adult life he will be attracted to women whom he feels are suffering with brutal male partners; he will want to rescue these women from their horrible situation.

Love for Virgins Only

While buttressed by cultural mandates, the inability to love anyone but a virgin derives from an oedipal conflict in which the boy or girl (more often the boy) splits an internal image of the mother into the "loved mother" and the "hated mother" and can only love a nonsexual mother figure. This neurotic anxiety makes it impossible to love anyone but a virgin, and in some cases people also forbid themselves to love anyone who has been previously married.

Homosexuality

Although homosexuality is regarded as a life-style by many professionals and laymen, those who subscribe to a psychosexual perspective on the human being view it as an expression of incomplete maturation. Homosexual men or women cannot accept and usually fear their own gender, and they unconsciously identify with the opposite sex. As case illustrations and discussions in later chapters will point out, the homosexual is coping with strong quantities of hostility and anxiety, and is quite terrified of the opposite sex.

Compulsive Sex

Individuals who engage in compulsive and joyless sexual activity with members of the opposite sex are attempting to prove, to themselves or others, that they are not homosexual. Through their active engagement in compulsive sexual activity, they are denying their homosexual fantasies.

Regardless of frequency, sexual activity that is pleasurable should not be regarded as Don Juanism or nymphomania.

Love for the Unattainable Object

Many individuals still seek the perfect romantic partner. The more unattainable the love object, the more lovable he or she seems. This neurotic modus vivendi usually evolves from an unresolved childhood conflict in which the unattainable object is a substitute for the fantasied mother or father of the past. As soon as the individual succeeds in attaining the love object, it loses its fascination and a deep disillusionment sets in.

This and all the other immature forms of love make for unfulfilling and unhappy sexual relationships. As we assess and treat people with sexual problems, their immature forms of love, which evolve from unresolved psychosexual tasks, will be very pertinent.

Chapter 3

Sex and the Mental Health Practitioner

WHILE THE LATER CHAPTERS focus on the assessment and treatment of
the particular sexual problems of children, adolescents, and adults,
this chapter deals with the more general issues and principles involved
in helping people resolve their sexual conflicts. Three phases of the
therapeutic process are discussed: the helping interview, the psychosexual assessment, and treatment skills.

The Helping Interview

The basic medium of exchange between a practitioner and a client
who has sexual difficulties is the helping interview; in most instances
it is the exclusive medium of exchange. It is through empathetic interviewing that the applicant seeking to enter therapy is helped to become a client; an assessment of the client's psychosexual functioning
evolves largely through an examination of data from the interviews;
and intervention with and for the client is provided by therapeutic interviewing.

The interviewer behaves in a manner that reveals very little but encourages the interviewee to reveal a great deal (Garrett, 1951; Ka-

dushin, 1972). This affords the client the opportunity to feel, perhaps for the first time in his life, that another person is devoting exclusive attention to him—to his wants, fears, conflicts, and pressures. Particularly for individuals with sexual problems, who are so frequently convinced that they must bend over backward to please their partners although there is nothing much in it for them, it is extremely important to feel that the helping person is devoting exclusive attention to them.

An old axiom of psychotherapy is that clients must feel free to be themselves and manifest their customary ways of relating if the outcome of an interview is to be successful. The practitioner's biases should not interfere with or in any way affect the manner in which the client behaves.

Particularly in the treatment of sexual problems, practitioners will constantly be engaged with individuals whose ways of conducting their lives are different from their own. When a client's sexually sadistic or masochistic wishes, homosexual fantasies, or extramarital affairs emerge in interviews, it is important for practitioners not to praise, condemn, or reassure, but to help clients explore what is occurring in their internal and interpersonal lives that drives them to behave the way they do. Unless practitioners are comfortable with themselves as they hear clients' material, they can become unempathetic and be emotionally unavailable, subtly disapproving, or falsely reassuring.

Mr. Aronson, a thirty-five-year-old high school teacher, in his first consultation interview at a mental health clinic told the interviewer that he was very embarrassed about discussing his problem. The intake worker responded by saying that she understood most people's problems and would help him no matter what the difficulty was; she encouraged him to feel free to "let go." After a long, uncomfortable silence during which he was sweating profusely, Mr. Aronson said, "Well, I might as well come out with it. I'm having an affair with one of my students. I'm old enough to be her father. I'd like to stop, but I can't." The interviewer told Mr. Aronson that she knew she could help him stop the affair if he would see her weekly at the clinic. She further told him that he shouldn't feel upset about his situation because others had been in it and they'd come out of it all right.

Mr. Aronson gave some history of his marriage, his relationship with his children, and his past quite cooperatively. He agreed to come for another interview the following week and thanked the intake worker for her help.

Mr. Aronson canceled his appointment and did not respond to the worker's many attempts to get him back to the clinic. He was adamant about not returning for further help.

The above case illustration is quite instructive, for it demonstrates how reassurance and promises of cure make a client suspicious of the worker and alienates the client from the helping process. When Mr. Aronson stated that he was embarrassed to discuss his problem, it would have been more helpful to reply that this often is the case when people seek help and to then ask him what he was worried about right now. By asserting her own competence the intake worker very well might have made Mr. Aronson feel more anxious and more inadequate, compared to her, than he had been before. It was too difficult for him to "let go." When Mr. Aronson guiltily and embarrassedly told the worker about his affair with the student, the intake worker failed to understand that promising to help him stop the affair alienated him further. Although many clients assert that they want to stop certain sexual practices—e.g., affairs, compulsive masturbation, homosexuality—it is always important for the practitioner to realize that these clients are deriving gratification from their sexual practices and are unconsciously reluctant to give up what they are doing. Furthermore, while clients want expert help, they resent "know-it-alls" who promise quick cures; these therapists are realistically suspect.

When the worker does not reassure, but listens; does not promise, but tries to understand; does not advise, but tries to empathize and identify with the applicant, there is more possibility for the applicant to become a client who will return for help.

Miss Beck, a twenty-four-year-old secretary, sought help because she was unable to "make contact with men." She reported that almost every time she was on a date she felt "tongue-tied," "anxious," and "very unattractive." In her interview with her male therapist, she found it difficult to reveal herself and kept questioning whether she was a good therapeutic candidate. She said that many of her friends had tried therapy and it did not work. The therapist noted to himself that Miss Beck's reluctance to talk to him and her desire to maintain a distance from him paralleled what transpired in her relationships with men; then he said, "I get the feeling that I make you uncomfortable and it's difficult to talk to me." Miss Beck visibly relaxed, chuckled a little, and remarked, "Well, you are a man, too." She went on to talk about her relationships with her father and two older brothers, and gave many examples of feeling rejected and unwanted. When the therapist suggested that perhaps Miss Beck felt he was not very eager to work with her she answered, "Yes, I think no man wants me. Is that my doing?" The therapist said, "It's something you might wish to explore further with me." Miss Beck did become involved in therapy.

In assisting clients to cope better with their sexual and interpersonal problems, one of the major tools at practitioners' disposal is to carefully observe how clients relate to them. As we learned in the case of Miss Beck, she related to the therapist with the same feelings of apprehension and tentativeness that were apparent in her interactions with all men. When the therapist tactfully and empathetically suggested that he was making her anxious, she could feel understood and then reveal more of herself. To be able to reveal more of herself was psychologically equivalent to becoming more sexually intimate with the therapist—something that was usually quite terrifying to her. It will be noted that in this interview the therapist spent a lot of time listening without promising. He tried to understand without advising. Feeling the empathy and identification with her, Miss Beck could return for more therapeutic assistance.

Beginning practitioners, in their genuine zeal to ameliorate their clients' distress, too often rush to solutions without first obtaining a sound understanding of the individuals and their situations. Such a procedure can be destructive; it is hardly ever helpful. To tell a couple to try a new form of communication, or an adolescent to try a new form of sexual experimentation, without getting a full understanding of the client's intrapsychic and interpersonal conflicts will rarely help. All clients have conflicting wishes, loves, and hates, desires to seek and avoid intimacy, and ambivalence about themselves and others. Consequently, to prescribe a course of action prematurely, before allowing clients to talk about the many sides of their problems and of themselves is to silence parts of them. This can only lead to resentment and depression, which may induce a client to drop out of the therapy.

Listening

A good interviewer is a good listener. While most practitioners concur with this statement, it usually takes many years of experience for the professional to truly believe this. To become convinced that listening is a crucial variable in the helping process one has to see over and over again that when an individual is given the opportunity to have a concerned listener attend to his thoughts, feelings, ideas, and memories, his tensions are reduced and energy previously utilized to repress disturbing feelings and thoughts becomes available for productive and enjoyable sexual and interpersonal functioning.

It should be remembered that most people who become clients do so because there is no one in their immediate environment to hear them out. Most listeners, on hearing someone else describe a sexual or interpersonal conflict, feel obliged to advise, or offer notions and experiences that worked for them, or they change the subject. They fail to realize that one of the most effective means of being helpful is to permit the interviewee plenty of latitude to voice what is on his mind (Barbara, 1958).

Psychologist Carl Rogers (1951) described effective, nonjudgmental listening as offering the client "unconditional positive regard." When the client feels that he is regarded positively by the interviewer, he begins to regard *himself* more positively.

Nineteen-year-old Craig had fifteen sessions with a woman therapist and reported in his sixteenth session that his presenting problems of premature ejaculation and depression had disappeared, at least temporarily. When his therapist nodded with an accepting smile, Craig said, "You know, you don't do a hell of a lot here, but it helps." (Thirty seconds of silence ensued.) "As a matter of fact, you *do* do a hell of a lot here," Craig said assertively. "You let me be myself and that makes you a special person. You never interrupt me or try to persuade me . . . I like you."

By offering Craig an experience with a nonintrusive, warm listener, *who let him finish his thoughts*, the therapist was helping Craig vicariously have sex with her, without feeling controlled or manipulated. Feeling accepted unconditionally, he could begin to like himself more. Liking himself more, he could relax in sex and be more potent.

The Practitioner Talks

Although therapeutic techniques will be discussed in more detail in a later section of this chapter, it will be helpful here to briefly review some pertinent interventions which usually enhance almost any therapeutic interview.

One of the central procedures in good interviewing is posing pertinent questions. To elicit historical data from the client in order to arrive at a comprehensive psychosexual assessment usually requires well-framed questions. Questions can also be asked to help the client explore and reflect upon his role in his interactions and upon the fantasies and wishes which propel his difficulties. A question that truly engages a client will be one that clarifies ambiguities, completes a picture of the client's situation, draws out more detail in his thinking, and elicits affective responses (Kadushin, 1972).

In order to experience a question as timely and important, the client has to feel that if it is answered in full it will enhance him in some way. Questions that can be answered with "Yes" or "No" usually do not help the client ease distress, explore his life more fully, or increase his understanding. Asking a client "Are you happily married?" leaves him little opportunity to reflect on his marriage, examine his role in it, or discharge his complaints. However, if the interviewer asks "Could you tell me about your marriage?" there is more chance for meaningful data to be elicited.

Questions have to be brief and unambiguous, but, of equal importance, the client must feel that they evolve from the interviewer's empathy and identification with him.

Empathic questions can supplement good listening and can contribute to the interview's success.

Mr. and Mrs. Diamond, a couple in their early forties, had been involved in marital counseling for about twenty sessions. Although they both acknowledged that they had an enjoyable sexual relationship, they wanted counseling because they were always bickering. During the course of the treatment the therapist noted that almost every time either spouse mentioned something that was mutually pleasurable the other would disagree and an argument would ensue. So the therapist asked, "What is it about enjoying each other that bothers both of you? Do you realize that you argue after anything enjoyable between you is mentioned?" The Diamonds were stunned and remained silent for about a minute. Slowly they both began to reflect on the question. Each brought out that in their families of origin, pleasure was taboo. Each also talked about experiencing enjoyment as something defiant and rebellious. The question unleashed painful memories for both the Diamonds, but they could use it to eventually diminish much of the sadomasochism in their interaction.

In addition to listening attentively and asking well-timed questions, the interviewer comments at appropriate times. Like questions, comments should be brief and clear (Fine, 1971). Furthermore, the interviewer's use of language should take into consideration the client's social, economic, and cultural circumstances. Terms like "hostility" and "interaction" may be more meaningful to a middle-class literate adult than they would be to an ill-educated, lower-income teenager.

Inexperienced therapists are usually too eager to clarify, advise, or interpret in order to convince themselves that they are competent professionals. As we have reiterated, the good interviewer is a good listener and one who asks well-timed and well-formulated questions. When he comments he is taking a stand. Consequently, the practitioner should be very sure that the observation is correct and that the client is ready to accept it. Often a therapist may be correct in discerning a client's "performance anxiety in sex" or "ambivalence toward his sexual partner" or "underlying passivity"—but a client who is not ready to hear this appraisal will fight the help that is offered.

Two useful rules in deciding whether or not to comment are: (1) When in doubt, don't! (2) Comment—i.e., clarify, suggest, or interpret—when the client is almost ready to make the statement himself. Continued listening punctuated with occasional questions is rarely destructive to clients, but premature interpretations or other such comments can activate anxiety and increase defensiveness. It requires patience, tact, empathy, and restraint to wait for the appropriate time to interpret something to a client of which he is only partially aware.

After twelve interviews in which unemployed, impotent, and alcoholic Mr. Ender had constantly talked of his shyness and indecision around women and had given many instances of it, his woman therapist said, "You seem to be afraid of asserting yourself toward women. What do you suppose the danger is?" Mr. Ender anxiously smiled and said, "I'm afraid I'll offend them with my temper and that's why I keep it under control. If I didn't keep myself quiet, I'd be outlandish because I have a lot of hateful thoughts toward a lot of broads." When Mr. Ender discussed his hateful thoughts during several more interviews, it turned out that the women he was most intimidated by "make me feel like I'm a small boy next to a big mama." Later the therapist could interpret the anxiety that contributed to Mr. Ender's problems by saying "You seem to protect yourself from your aggression by *making yourself* a small boy next to a big mother. No wonder you are so scared of women. You feel one-quarter of their size." Mr. Ender corroborated the therapist's interpretation with many instances of feeling like a small boy in the present and in the past. He went on to say to the therapist, "Sometimes I think I cater to you too much."

When the practitioner, as in the above example, has enough data and the themes of the client's life situation are very clear, comments can be made to clarify, suggest, or interpret this material. Therapists who work at the client's pace will find that their comments are frequently accepted and used for growth.

The Psychosexual Assessment

If the practitioner is to be of help, he must obviously understand what is troubling the client and what seems to be contributing to his problems. The assessment represents the thinking of the therapist about the facts presented by the client. It is a professional opinion that is influenced by the frame of reference that he uses to guide him in understanding the meaning of the facts (Strean, 1978).

In a psychosexual assessment, the practitioner makes judgments about the interaction between the client's intrapsychic, interpersonal, and sexual experiences. The psychosexual assessment is not a "one-shot deal" but is an ongoing process throughout the life of the treatment. The therapist is constantly trying to determine the meaning of the client's symptoms and dysfunctional interpersonal and sexual behavior.

The Client's History

The details of the client's psychosexual history are crucial in the formulation of a psychosexual assessment. As any dynamically oriented therapist knows, symptoms by themselves offer little clue as to what they mean to the client and what purposes they serve. It is only when the client's psychosexual history is available to us that we can know what the symptoms are all about. For example, we may learn that Mr. Jones's impotence evolves from his inability to trust because he experiences his sexual partner as the ungiving mother of his oral period. On the other hand, as we subject Mr. Smith's psychosexual history to examination, we learn that his impotence has more to do with his inhibitions about taking initiative. Each time he does so, he is in unconscious competition with his father. Fearing his aggression, he holds back sexually.

An examination of the client's history often reveals the answers to many therapeutic enigmas.

Miss Friend, a single woman of twenty-four, appeared to be warm, engaging, high-achieving, and very successful in her work in advertising. Although she found herself to be well liked by men and liked them, as soon as she became involved with them sexually, "all hell would break loose." She would become involved in intense power struggles and would resent what she called "putting out."

As the therapist and Miss Friend reviewed a part of her history, what emerged was a chaotic toilet-training phase. "Mommy and Daddy made me work hard and insisted I 'put out' all the time," Miss Friend angrily declared. She added, "I can get along with anybody but when they tell me what to do, I feel like a kid on a potty who must give the other person what he insists on having." Later in treatment she referred to the sexual movements in sexual intercourse as similar to "bowel movements" and felt that sex for her seemed so much like the "squeezing I had to do on the toilet."

When the practitioner utilizes the psychosexual history, he begins to appreciate how the sexual dimension of the client's life enters into seemingly nonsexual problems like alcoholic, drug, and gambling addictions.

Mr. Gold, a forty-two-year-old married man, sought help for his alcoholism. As his current circumstances unfolded and his history was explored, it became quite clear that he was unconsciously making his wife his mother of the past. Guilty and anxious about his unconscious incestuous fantasies, he avoided his wife emotionally and sexually, and joined other men in bars to complain about their wives. When he felt close to his masculine compatriots, homosexual fantasies would surface and he would be acutely anxious. To "drown out" his homosexual fantasies, he drank until he felt "numb."

By linking the client's symptoms to his history we can rather clearly see how a seemingly nonsexual problem can derive from the client's sexual conflicts, as was true in Mr. Gold's case. Psychosexual assessments of other clients in later chapters will make this notion quite apparent.

Unconscious Wishes

The psychosexual assessment should also point out the unconscious gratification and unconscious protection that sexual and interpersonal problems offer the client. Very rarely does the client recognize (and all too often the therapist fails to note) that virtually every chronic marital complaint is an unconscious wish. Inevitably, the husband who complains that his wife is sexually and emotionally un-responsive unconsciously wants her to be that way. Her warmth would scare him. Similarly, parents usually get some unconscious gratification and protection from their child's symptoms. Although parents will be consciously disturbed about a child's compulsive exhi-bitionism, voyeurism, masturbation, or other symptoms, a closer ex-amination of the parent-child interaction and of the parents' inter-views with the therapist will usually demonstrate some unconscious collusion on the parents' part. Many mental health practitioners have now recognized that when a client habitually complains about some-thing within himself and/or in somebody else (e.g. spouse, lover, par-ent, child, boss) he unconsciously wishes the very thing about which he complains.

Harvey Harris was in therapy because he was sexually impotent. At his first consultation interview he said he was driving his wife crazy by his inability to satisfy her and feared that she would leave him.

After a few months of therapy, Harvey became more potent with his wife. One night, after a mutually satisfying experience, Maxine turned to Harvey and asked, "How come your penis is so much smaller than most guys'?"

Using his wife as a punitive superego, Harvey then attacked himself again and told his therapist he was not good enough for Maxine. It took many months for Harvey to realize that he *unconsciously wanted* and *unconsciously needed* a wife who experienced him as weak and that she *unconsciously wanted and needed* to weaken a man.

In doing conjoint marital or conjoint sexual counseling, it is im-portant in the psychosexual assessment make it clear how the partners are in unconscious collusion to sustain their difficulties (Strean, 1980).

Although Al and Barbara Isaacs had similar educational and social back-grounds and shared many interests and values, there was always a great deal of tension in their interaction. When Barbara desired sexual relations, Al was usu-ally impotent; when Al was potent and took some initiative sexually, Barbara resented his "ineptness." She also complained about Al's "arrogance" and said he constantly "put her down." Al complained about Barbara's persistent efforts to "castrate" him.

As a youngster Al was very much attached to his mother and was very com-petitive with his authoritarian father. He had conscious wishes that his father would die. When Al was thirteen his father did die, of a heart attack, and Al blamed himself for the death. He became very depressed and withdrew from most people, including his mother.

Barbara, as a child, was her father's favorite and had a strong erotic attachment to him; her relationship with her mother was very ambivalent. She consciously felt that her sexual feelings toward her father upset him and unconsciously experienced his death as punishment for her sexual fantasies.

Although Barbara and Al complained about each other, *unconsciously* both wanted an asexual spouse to defend against the anxiety that stemmed from their incestuous wishes.

Ego Functions

In making a comprehensive psychosexual assessment and planning treatment it is helpful to know something about how the client's ego functions. The ego, which develops out of experience and reason, is the executive of the personality; it mediates between the inner world of the id (the drives) and the superego (conscience) commands. The ego also mediates between the demands of the outside world and the person's inner wishes. Some of the functions of the ego are judgment, reality testing, frustration tolerance, and relating to others (sometimes called "object relations"); the ego also erects defenses against anxiety. By assessing a client's ego strengths and weaknesses the therapist can determine how well he or she is adapting, because the more severe the client's disturbances the less operative are the ego functions and vice versa.

One of the most important ego functions, to which the therapist should give much attention, is how the client defends against anxiety. When an impulse such as a sexual wish or an aggressive thought is activated, and the person feels that further acknowledgment of the impulse will conflict with ethical mandates or other superego commands, he or she erects defenses against experiencing the impulses.

When the ego senses that acting on an impulse or even just feeling it will create danger, the ego produces anxiety. The anxiety serves as a signal of the impending danger and is able to offer opposition to the emergence of unacceptable impulses. Such opposition is referred to as "defense" or as the "defensive operation of the ego" (Brenner, 1955).

In all defense mechanisms (repression, denial, reaction formation, projection) there is always an attempt to repudiate an impulse (A. Freud, 1937). In response to the id's "Yes" the ego defends itself and says "No," to avoid the danger of the forbidden impulse coming to consciousness.

By assessing the client's habitual use of defenses, we learn what inner impulses he or she really fears.

Mrs. Joseph, age forty-five, was in marital counseling because of lack of sexual desire and constant sado-masochistic battles with her husband.

In the treatment situation Mrs. Joseph spent considerable time discussing her work as a salaried crusader against vice. She severely criticized "burlesque queens," who are always exhibiting themselves, and prostitutes, "who make money out of sex."

In her treatment Mrs. Joseph learned that the very impulses she was condemning were wishes of her own which she found unbearable. As an anti-vice crusader she "made money out of sex" but projected her wishes and guilt onto prostitutes. By making dramatic speeches criticizing "burlesque queens" she was also exhibiting herself, but again she was denying her own desires and projecting them on to others.

Seemingly irrational, provocative behavior that appears disruptive to interpersonal relationships can often be understood and related to with empathy if the observer is aware that all human beings defend themselves from ideas, thoughts, and feelings that arouse anxiety. When defenses of repression, reaction formation, or regression are viewed as protective maneuvers that clients (and all individuals) summon up when they are in danger, behavior that at first appears puzzling begins to become more understandable.

Superego Functions

Another dimension of the psychosexual assessment is an appraisal of how the client's superego functions. The superego is the judge or censor of the mind, and is essentially the product of interpersonal experiences. It is divided into two parts, the conscience and the ego ideal. The conscience is that part of the superego which forbids and admonishes "Thou shalt not!" The ego ideal is the storehouse of values, ethical imperatives, and morals. It commands the person in the form of "Thou shalt!"

Therapists sometimes overlook the fact that a client with a punitive and exacting superego also has strong wishes propelled by the id (sexual and aggressive drives) that cause great anxiety. Like Mrs. Joseph in the last case vignette, the individual with unacceptable wishes arranges for the superego to constantly admonish "Thou shalt not enjoy pleasure!" By staying away from potentially pleasurable situations, the individual does not have to face the sexual and aggressive fantasies that are in conflict with the superego's commands.

Part of every good psychosexual assessment is a determination of the level and quality of the client's superego functioning. For example, if clients are very strict with themselves and others, an understanding of their superego development and functioning will help in determining the strength or weakness of capacity for sexual pleasure and of such ego functions as self-image and interpersonal relationships. Similarly, when clients are destructive, manipulative, and damaging to others, an understanding of the development and functioning of the superego will guide the practitioner in making psychosexual assessments and formulating treatment plans.

Reactions to the Therapist

As has already been implied, an excellent way to assess how the client relates to others and to determine his habitual defenses, his capacity for intimacy, his self-esteem, and his sexual identity is to carefully observe how he relates to the therapist. The nature of his sexual conflicts and other interpersonal difficulties become clearer as the therapist carefully observes if the client wants to cooperate or is defiant, is evasive or direct, is personal or impersonal, is spontaneous or controlled. Assuming that the therapist does not control the client but lets him be himself, the client's attitudes will in many ways suggest his vulnerabilities, conflicts, and strengths.

Treatment Procedures

Although some features of therapeutic intervention have been discussed in the section on the helping interview, there are a few other aspects of such work that it would be useful to address in this section.

Just as a good psychosexual assessment involves an understanding of the client's id wishes, ego defenses, superego admonitions, unconscious investments, and modes of relating to the therapist, so a client cannot be substantially helped in treatment unless he becomes aware of childish wishes, faces persistent superego admonitions, and recognizes how he is distorting the present and perceiving it as if it were part of his past. If dysfunctional attitudes and behavior are to be significantly altered, the client must become sensitized to how he is unconsciously arranging a good part of his own misery (Strean, 1979).

It has already been explained that most clients welcome the idea of saying what comes to their minds to a quiet, attentive listener who asks pertinent questions and makes timely comments. Eventually, however, for many clients the therapy can become painful and can create anxiety. As the client discovers parts of himself that have been repressed, particularly sexual impulses that cause embarrassment, he may feel guilt and shame. Then he may become silent and evasive or want to quit the therapy altogether.

Resistance

When the client stops talking about himself and ceases to examine himself, he is engaging in a kind of behavior referred to as "resistance." Resistance is any action or attitude of the client's that impedes the course of therapeutic work. Inasmuch as every client, to some extent, wants unconsciously to preserve the status quo, all treatment must be carried on in the face of some resistance.

What are referred to as defenses in the client's daily life—e.g., projection, denial, repression—are resistances in therapy. If, for example, a client has a tendency to project his anger onto his spouse and other individuals, in therapy he will try to avoid examining his own angry thoughts and feelings and will report how his wife, friends, and relatives are hostile to him. From time to time he will also accuse the therapist of being contemptuous toward him.

If we view the client's sexual and interpersonal problems as part of his habitual modus vivendi, which he wishes unconsciously to maintain, no matter how dysfunctional, then we would expect him to resist self-observation and change. For example, if the client has strong passive sexual wishes which scare him so that he has to defend against these wishes, he will begin to resist the therapy as he starts to feel passive in the therapeutic situation. Similarly, if a client has to defend against homosexual fantasies and wishes by being compulsively heterosexual, he will probably resist any examination of what he feels propels his promiscuity. Celibate men or women will probably resist a discussion of why they do not permit any sexual gratification, while swingers will become equally frightened if they consider what motivates the swinging.

Resistance is not created by the therapy. The therapeutic situation activates anxiety, and the client then uses habitual mechanisms to oppose the therapist and the therapy (Greenson, 1967). In helping clients resolve their sexual and emotional problems, the practitioner will find that resistance takes many forms. The following discussion takes up a few of the common forms of resistance and suggests some of the ways in which the client can be helped to overcome them.

LATENESS. As has been implied several times, a therapist working within a psychosexual perspective takes the position that behavior in and of itself does not tell very much. A resistance like lateness to appointments with the therapist can have different meanings for different clients, as the following vignettes indicate.

Mr. and Mrs. Klein, a couple in their early thirties, were seen for marital and sexual counseling. After six sessions with their therapist, during which they expressed a lot of contempt for each other, they began to arrive ten to fifteen minutes late for their appointments. When the therapist noted this consistent lateness, at first they denied that it had any significance. However, when the therapist suggested that coming to the interviews must be bothering them because they probably wanted to avoid discussing something with each other and/or with him, the Kleins were eventually able to examine some of the reasons for their lateness. With help from the therapist, the Kleins recognized that both were very dissatisfied with each other's role in lovemaking but were frightened "to level" with each other because they felt that if they were direct with each other they would make their relationship worse. Said Mr. Klein, with Mrs. Klein agreeing, "Criticisms damage, and we'll destroy each other. I'm not ripe for that."

Eventually the Kleins could learn that criticisms "did not have to kill" and that they could inform each other empathetically what they each wanted in sex.

The Kleins' lateness was an expression of their fear of aggression and of their separation anxiety. But lateness can have other meanings.

Mr. and Mrs. Lorman, a couple in their early forties, were also involved in marital and sexual counseling. After about ten sessions with the therapist, which they both agreed were constructive and helpful, the couple started arriving late for their appointments. When they were confronted with their lateness, both of them did acknowledge that the therapy was making them uncomfortable.

On the therapist's noting that the Lormans were coming late after they both verbalized positive feelings toward each other and said that the counseling was helpful, Mrs. Lorman stated, "Now we're supposed to have sex and I still hate that idea!" Mr. Lorman voiced similar fears about sex and wished "to postpone making love."

The Lormans' lateness was an expression of their resistance to sexual intimacy. As they felt increased warmth toward each other, their sexual desires became more intensified and this frightened both of them. Paralleling their desire to ''postpone'' sex was a wish to ''postpone'' intimate discussions in the therapy by coming late.

SILENCE. Usually, when a client is silent, it means that he or she is consciously or unconsciously reluctant to communicate sexual or aggressive thoughts, feelings, or memories. The client is frightened about how he or she will appear in front of the therapist.

Ms. Moore, aged twenty-five, was in treatment with a male therapist because of her "inability to relax and relate to men." Although she was able to discuss her problems quite freely during the first several interviews, after she recalled some memories involving sex play with a male cousin she became silent. When the therapist asked, "What might be making you avoid me at this time?" Ms. Moore said, with some hesitation and embarrassment, that she was afraid the therapist might try to seduce her as her cousin had, so she avoided talking to him.

As often happens in treatment, when sexual issues are discussed the client becomes stimulated by the talks. If sexual stimulation activates anxiety for the client, as it did for Ms. Moore, silence can be used as a resistance to prevent feeling further stimulation.

RELUCTANCE TO PAY FEES. Since money plays such a significant role in our society, it will be inevitably used to express resistance in treatment. Often, when clients have some resentment about the treatment and/or are competitive and in a power struggle with the therapist, they may consciously and unconsciously withhold payment of their fee.

Fees can also be used to express seductive desires and wishes to manipulate the therapist.

Mrs. Norton, a wealthy client in her fifties, "bought her friends" by giving them gifts and holding big parties. Although loved by most of her family and friends, she sought treatment because of depressed feelings, low self-esteem, and lack of sexual desire. In her relationship with her male therapist, she felt insufficiently appreciated and wanted more praise, more encouragement, and more advice. When the therapist did not gratify Mrs. Norton's requests but tried to subject them to examination, she resisted exploring her wishes. Instead, she made an offer to the therapist. She pointed out that because she had a high income and did not need all of her money, she wanted to pay the therapist a higher fee. She felt that the therapist could use some of the money that she did not need.

Rather than accept or reject Mrs. Norton's offer, the therapist explored with her the meaning of her proposal. At first angry and then more thoughtful in subsequent interviews, Mrs. Norton eventually said, "I want to buy your love. In some ways I'm making you a whore, though. That feels like fun but it is so embarrassing."

There are an infinite number of other ways that clients can resist therapy. They can spend their sessions blasting a lover or spouse for sexual ineptitude. They can damn the therapist for not "coming up" with anything worthwhile and criticize him or her for being an impotent person. They can resist facing their distress in their current sexual relationships and overemphasize the past. They can idealize the therapist and avoid self-examination.

What is important for the practitioner to keep in mind is that when an individual enters into a relationship with a therapist, part of that individual unconsciously works against progress. All clients, no matter how much they consciously want their lives to be different and regardless of how much they are suffering, still fear change. Resistances are facts of therapeutic life, and understanding the unconscious reasons for their unique expression is crucial to both client and therapist.

Transference

Anyone who is engaged in helping others make changes in their sexual and interpersonal lives recognizes that in the face of all logic and reason, the client may often behave in a most obstinate manner. In addition to the fear of change, therapeutic progress is always hindered by the client's major resistance, transference—the feelings,

wishes, fears, and defenses that influence his perception of the therapist. Transferential reactions are unconscious attempts by the client
to recapitulate with the therapist types of interpersonal interaction
similar to those he experienced with significant persons in the past.
Every client in a helping situation, no matter what the subject of discussion is, experiences the therapist not only in terms of how he objectively is but in terms of how he wishes him to be and fears he
might be.

If the therapist does not understand how he is being experienced
by his client, he will not be very helpful. Each client responds to interpretations, clarifications, confrontations, and questions not only
in terms of their content, but also in terms of his transference to the
therapist. If he loves the therapist, he will be inclined to accept therapeutic interventions; if he hates the therapist, even the most neutral
question such as "How do you feel?" will be suspect. Finally, if the
client has mixed feelings toward the therapist, he will respond to virtually all interventions with ambivalence.

One of the tasks of the therapist is to help the client see how and
why he experiences him as he does. Why does the client act like a
compliant child and accept everything the therapist says? Or why
does he argue with the therapist every time he says something? Why
is the therapist's silence experienced by one client as rejection and by
another as love?

One of the ways that the client can gain some inner conviction of
his own role in sexual conflicts is by recognizing that he experiences
the therapist the same way he experiences a lover or spouse. This will
occur more readily if the therapist does not impose his own values on
the client's productions and does not side with either the client or his
sexual partner. The following case example demonstrates this point
quite poignantly.

Mrs. Joyce Olsen, a twenty-seven-year-old married woman, had been in treatment for about eight months when she blurted out in a session that her husband, Calvin, was "a cold, insensitive, unfeeling ox who is afraid of intimacy."
On her birthday she complained, "All Calvin got me was some stinky perfume.
He's afraid to have me smell nice 'cause then he'll feel close and that scares
him!"

After discharging a great deal of anger, Joyce began to cry. In between her
sobs she said that she was very capable of an intimate relationship with a man
but that Calvin would not or could not reciprocate her wishes for "closeness,
tenderness, and warm sex." Then Joyce fell silent for several minutes. When the

therapist asked what she was thinking about during the silence, Joyce said, "I'm feeling very close to you now. I feel you understand me. I feel warm inside . . . I have a fantasy that your arm is around me and I thought it might be nice to lie on a couch with you." (A minute of silence.) "Now I have a fantasy of throwing a chair at you. You affect me too much, you bastard! Go away."

Joyce Olsen was afraid to feel close to her male therapist and protected herself from warm, sexual feelings toward him by fantasizing that she would hurt him with a chair. Psychologically, this was precisely how she coped with Calvin; she attacked him in order to ward off close feelings toward him. When, later in treatment, Joyce expressed the wish to seek out another therapist although she still felt very close to her regular therapist, she was able to understand some of her motives for arranging the extramarital affair in which she had been involved for several months.

Joyce's case illustrates that when a person complains that the spouse is emotionally or sexually inhibited (and the spouse very well may be) the complainant unconsciously wants it that way. That the complaint is a manifestation of an unconscious wish is verified when the same phenomenon is observed in the client's transference relationship with the therapist.

The intimate relationship of client and therapist is one in which the client *depends* on the therapist. This invariably activates feelings and thoughts that the client experienced in respect to others on whom he depended in the past. These feelings and thoughts are always present in any interpersonal encounter and cannot be obliterated, avoided, or neglected in a helping relationship. Transference reactions are normal in any interaction and become intensified in helping situations. If the client has experienced those who nurtured, advised, and educated him as essentially positive and well-meaning, he will in all likelihood experience the therapist in the same way. However, usually there are residual mixtures of love, hate, and ambivalence toward parents and others in all individuals, and every therapist will be the recipient of all these feelings.

When the therapist recognizes that transference always exists in all the relationships that clients have with him, he can look at his therapeutic results more objectively. If the client wants him to be an omnipotent parent to whom he can cling, then he will fight interventions aimed to help him become more autonomous. If the client unconsciously wants the therapist to be a sibling rival, then he will use the therapist's intervention to continue his sibling fight. Because the client views all the therapist's interventions through the lens of his transference, the therapist must explore with the client why he wants to make the distortions he does, and what gratification and protection this provides for him.

A very common use of transference is the client's projection onto the therapist of unacceptable parts of his psychic structure: id wishes, ego defenses, and superego mandates.

Mrs. Potter, thirty-seven, was seen in treatment for marital difficulties. She was a very constricted woman with a powerful superego and therefore could not permit herself much pleasure. During treatment she transferred many of her unacceptable id wishes to her woman therapist. She told the therapist her fantasy that the therapist "probably had many extramarital affairs," "enjoyed getting beaten up by a man," and "took hot showers with him." The therapist neither accepted nor denied Mrs. Potter's transference projections, but encouraged the client to fully explore her fantasies. Mrs. Potter was eventually able to identify with the therapist's nondefensive attitude and face some of her own sexual fantasies, which had been deeply repressed.

Quite often, the client projects his own superego onto the therapist and expects punishment from him. During the course of this process, a consistent comparison of the projection with reality serves to break down the superego in the course of time (Fine, 1971).

Twelve-year-old Ralph came to therapy with a variety of academic and interpersonal problems. A few weeks after he started treatment, he told the therapist that he had stopped masturbating. When the therapist wondered out loud why Ralph had done that, Ralph replied that it was a bad habit and that the therapist would condemn him for it. Ralph went on to discuss his fantasies about going blind and getting pimples from masturbation. All of these fantasies were manifestations of Ralph's punitive superego. In treatment he had to learn that the therapist was quite different from his parents. He, the therapist, did not feel that sex was something bad; it was something to be enjoyed.

Transference, it should be restated, exists in all relationships. There is no such thing as a client who has "no transference" or in whom transference fails to develop. As clinician and client accept transference as a fact of therapeutic life, they gain an appreciation of the client's conflicts and aspects of his history that are contributing to his dysfunctional sexual and interpersonal behavior.

Countertransference

Countertransference is the same dynamic phenomenon as transference, except that it refers to those unconscious wishes and defenses of the therapist that interfere with his objective perception and mature treatment of the client. Frequently, the client represents for the therapist an object of the past onto whom past feelings and wishes are projected. Countertransference reactions arise because of the therapist's inability to deal maturely with aspects of the client's communications that impinge on problems of his own. For example, if a therapist has unresolved problems connected with his own aggression, he may need to be ingratiating with the client. Similarly, if a therapist is threatened by his own unconscious homosexual feelings, he may be unable to detect homosexual implications in a client's material or may perceive them where they do not exist.

POSITIVE COUNTERTRANSFERENCE. Therapy usually proceeds well when the therapist likes the client. If the therapist does not care for his client, the latter will sense it and not make good use of the therapy. While a positive countertransference is a desirable attitude, like a positive transference it must be studied carefully (Fine, 1971). When the therapist is overidentified with the client, he begins to overlook the client's contributions to his own problems. This can strengthen the client's self-pity and intensify his wishes to be an omnipotent and indulged child.

Mr. Shine, a thirty-five-year-old married man, was seen in treatment for sexual and marital difficulties. In his presentation of his marital difficulties Mr. Shine described his wife as tyrannical and overpowering, while he described himself as warm and conciliatory. The therapist joined Mr. Shine in his attacks on his wife under the guise of "helping him assert himself better." What was overlooked in the treatment was Mr. Shine's strong masochism, repressed sadism, passivity, and desire to be dominated. Only when the therapist realized his countertransference problems could he help Mr. Shine see how he was both inviting and sustaining a sadomasochistic relationship with his wife.

NEGATIVE COUNTERTRANSFERENCE. Sometimes therapists and clients forget that a therapist is a human being and is more like his clients than unlike them. Inasmuch as therapists always have vulnerabilities of their own, from time to time they may feel angry at a client. It is often difficult for therapists to acknowledge their hostility toward their clients because angry feelings are considered a liability by most professionals. Frequently hostile feelings manifest themselves in disguised and subtle forms. Two of the most common expressions of disguised hostility are the use of the clinical diagnosis as a countertransference expression and alterations of therapeutic plans and techniques (Fine, 1971). When the clinical diagnosis is used in the service of countertransference, the therapist may use a label to put distance between himself and the client, sometimes rejecting the client altogether and saying the latter is untreatable. Sometimes the labels "sexual psychopath," "polymorphous perverse character," or "sexual addict" are used for the purpose of subtly expressing contempt toward the client.

When the client does not respond to questions, confrontations, advice, or interpretations, there may be a tendency for the therapist to express hostility not only by using labels in a way that is not benign, but by applying "innovative" procedures. These procedures often turn out to be sadistic attacks. Drugs, shock therapy, and backward isolation can be administered when the client rejects the therapist's efforts.

Mrs. Thomas, a forty-year-old mother and a client at a child-guidance clinic, refused on many occasions to take the therapist's advice. The angry therapist diagnosed Mrs. Thomas as "severely masochistic" and under the guise of "innovative" techniques became quite cruel to her. Contending that Mrs. Thomas's assertiveness should be liberated, every time the client said she was disgusted with herself the therapist replied, "Yes, you are disgusting." When the client said that the therapist's techniques were not helpful, she was told that she wasn't a helpful patient.

The therapist did everything but face with Mrs. Thomas her wish to defeat her own therapy. Instead, she tried to cope with her own countertransference reactions by using hostile techniques that only induced a deeper feeling of despair in the client.

Countertransference, like transference, exists in all helping relationships. Just as there is no such thing as a client who has "no transference," there is no such thing as a therapist who has "no countertransference." A practitioner who acknowledges countertransference as a therapeutic reality is in a good position to help clients and not be influenced by his or her own irrational loves, hates, and ambivalences.

Chapter 4

Sex and Children

Infantile Sexuality

One of the major contributions of dynamic psychology to the helping professional is the notion of infantile sexuality. Until the early part of this century it was alleged that children had neither erotic desires nor sexual fantasies. Sexuality, it was thought, suddenly appeared at puberty. Apparently the idea of a child having a sexual life was so upsetting to earlier generations that a child found masturbating or expressing sexual curiosity was severely admonished and often even punished by physical abuse (DeMause, 1981).

While most individuals living in the 1980s can acknowledge that a child has sexual interests, it is still difficult for some to realize that there are sensual pleasures in the oral period, i.e., nursing and sucking, and that the pleasures of the child in urinating and defecating have a sexual or sensual component. A narrow perspective on sexuality usually comes from confining the thinking about sexual expression exclusively to the genital region (English and Pearson, 1945).

As demonstrated earlier, all affectional ties have sexual origins and there is no sudden leap from childhood innocence to adult sophistication. Erogenous zones such as the mouth, the anus, and the skin arouse pleasure in the early years of life and continue to do so throughout life. They are not suddenly stimulated because a marriage has been consummated nor do they cease to be a source of pleasure when a marriage is terminated. Their demand for pleasurable gratification has to be reckoned with at all ages, and if this process is "sexual" in a grade school or high school student it must be considered "sexual" in the infant as well (Ross, 1979; English and Pearson, 1945).

Although the discovery of infantile sexuality was initially met with disbelief, it is now recognized that this phenomenon has profound implications for the capacity to give and receive love as well as to express oneself sexually; and it is at the core of neurotic and other psychological difficulties. While there is no one causal relationship between childhood experiences and adult sexual experiences (Hartmann, 1958, 1964), many psychologists and psychoanalysts contend that the origin of all love is that of the mother for her offspring and that "this love is the basis of the love of man for woman, woman for man, both for their society, love of others, and the passion of the mind" (Ross, 1979, p. 52).

Those who have researched childhood maturation or have done therapeutic work with children offer us more than enough data to justify abandoning the notion of "the original sin" of sexuality (English and Pearson, 1937; Cohn, 1943). Furthermore, we also now know with certainty that children are hampered in their sexual and emotional growth when parents and significant others do not give the sexual dimension of the child's life the attention it deserves.

Answering Children's Questions on Sex

There are now numerous books and pamphlets which prescribe methods of helping children appreciate and enjoy their sexual wishes and erogenous zones. While providing correct facts on sexuality to a child is essential for the child's maturation, one important source of sexual information that has not been sufficiently appreciated is the quality of the relationship that children observe between their parents and the quality of the relationship children experience with them.

A child will be more inclined to enjoy his own sexuality if he frequently witnesses his parents enjoyably hugging each other, touching each other, and being physically affectionate with him. Conversely, if these interpersonal experiences are missing, he will probably have sexual conflicts. Love and sexuality can only superficially be learned from a textbook; children must observe love and sexuality consistently being expressed if they are going to be able to love and enjoyably express themselves sexually.

When a child observes parents hating each other, all of the well-answered questions on sex cannot serve as an appropriate buffer to ward off the uncomfortable notion that warm intimacy between the sexes is most difficult to achieve. Furthermore, a child who experiences parents constantly arguing with and tormenting each other often feels forced to take sides with one of them. If the child sides with the parent of the same sex, his heterosexual growth becomes blunted; if he sides with the parent of the opposite sex, he becomes very guilty, is always on the lookout for retaliation, and once again, his sexual growth is marred. Studies of one-parent families and dysfunctional families consistently expose the fact that when a child does not have two parents who genuinely love each other and demonstrate it physically, the child's own sexual identity is disturbed and his capacity to enjoy himself sexually is reduced (Ackerman, 1958; Neubauer, 1960; Strean, 1970).

In addition to witnessing their parents enjoying each other, children if they are to sexually mature and love their sexual partner, must experience warm physical affection from both parents. As already indicated, sufficient and continuous pleasurable physical contact between infant and parents is essential for the child's optimal development. Not only is this physical contact necessary for emotional and sexual development, but it is crucial for the development of perceptional, motor, linguistic, and social skills (Bowlby, 1969; Greenacre, 1971; Mahler, 1968; Ross, 1979). Spitz (1945) has dramatically shown how infants may literally get sick and die if they are not loved.

Although emphasis has been placed on the importance of observing and experiencing pleasurable relationships as a crucial source of sexual information for children, nonetheless parents and others have to deal concretely with answering children's questions on sex. Once again, the content of the answers is of less pertinence than the atmosphere that exists and the emotions that are expressed when the adult answers children's queries. If the adult is anxious, frightened, angry, or embarrassed, the manifest content of his or her answers will be less influential than the atmosphere in which they are given. As in all educational experiences, the student must feel understood by the teacher; if empathy is absent, learning about sex will, at best, be a didactic experience which will not appreciably influence the child's sexual and emotional life.

It is important for parents to realize that questions should be answered frankly as they arise. What parents sometimes overlook is that children need and want very little information at any one time. Very frequently parents distort the needs of a child and think they are obligated to give the child a two-hour seminar when he asks where children come from! Often, all a child needs to be told is that a baby grows inside the mother's body. That answer may satisfy the child for weeks or even months, until he is ready for more information (English and Pearson, 1945).

Although this chapter will later discuss in more detail how the professional can assist parents in coping with their children's sexual concerns and conflicts, a word on the subject is appropriate here. Parents who are working on their children's problems with a professional frequently identify with the professional's attitude and perspective and recapitulate this perspective with their own children (Feldman, 1958; Strean, 1970). Consequently, when a parent raises questions on how to respond to a child's sexual concerns it is important that the practitioner answer truthfully and without anxiety.

Sometimes adults think that "a little knowledge is a dangerous thing" and that children will use sexual information in a destructive or self-destructive manner. Mental health practitioners have noted that only when the parents themselves have distorted notions on sexuality and unconsciously transmit them to their children will the children use the sexual information in an immature manner (Sternbach, 1947).

If the child's relationship with his parents is positive and his questions about sex have been answered frankly and without hesitation, then he will ask more and more questions about sexuality. As the child asks more detailed questions, he needs more detailed answers. The body parts should be called by name—e.g., vagina, penis, anus—and the child should be told what takes place when men and women have sexual intercourse. It is important for the child to hear that when the man's penis is put into the woman's vagina this is a mutually pleasurable experience. The birth process should also be discussed with the child, who should be informed how sperm is deposited into the womb and there is united with the woman's egg to grow into a fetus and eventually a baby.

While simple and frank statements are usually not shocking to a child unless the parent is anxious or shocked, much more is going on in the child's mind as he or she discusses sex with a parent. Usually the child's questions about sexual intercourse and the birth of babies evolve during the oedipal period, when the child is competing with the parent of the same sex and is sexually interested in the parent of the opposite sex. This "mind set" has to be considered as the parent and child discuss sexual matters.

Alfred, age six, had a good relationship with both of his parents and showed normal oedipal concerns. One day he asked his father for several details about sexual intercourse. When his father answered his questions truthfully and talked of inserting his penis in Alfred's mother's vagina, Alfred rather angrily asked, "Did *you do* that with Mommy?" When his father said "Yes," Alfred remarked with a twinkle in his eyes and a challenge in his voice, "Then, *you are* a mother-fucker!"

In part, Alfred was using his discussions with his father to compete with and deride him. Unless the practitioner helps the parent recognize some of the interpersonal issues at work when children discuss sexual matters, the conversation can deteriorate into something negative.

Mrs. Bell, age thirty-two, tearfully reported to her therapist that she was unable to cope with her five-year-old daughter's questions on sex. Although Mrs. Bell had answered her daughter Barbara's questions truthfully and kindly, Barbara insisted that she wanted to see "how intercourse happened." She told her mother that she was a mean mother and that she, Barbara, didn't care what her mother said, she was going to sneak into the parents' bedroom and watch them have sex. Furthermore, Barbara averred, "When you fall asleep, I'm going to shove you out of bed and be with Daddy alone."

Barbara, like Alfred, was using her discussions to act out oedipal conflicts. What Mrs. Bell needed from her therapist was some understanding of Barbara's oedipal conflicts. Barbara, like most girls her age, wanted to replace her mother and be alone with her father, and when she realized that her parents understood this wish and would not punish her for it, her provocativeness diminished.

Very often children ask questions on sex in a very provocative manner because they unconsciously want to be punished for their sexual curiosity and sexual excitement. They are guilty about their erotic desires for the parent of the opposite sex and frightened of their competitive wishes concerning the same-sexed parent; their hostile manner in asking questions is unconsciously designed to provoke an oedipal fight. It is important for parents to become aware of the latent issues in sexual discussions, e.g., oedipal competition, seductive wishes, and guilt. For example, when a child insists that the stork brings babies and rejects sexual facts that a parent has presented, it is incumbent on the practitioner to help the distressed parent become sensitized to the interpersonal issues that are part of the parent-child discussions on sex.

Occasionally parents, under the guise of appearing sexually liberated, walk around the house in the nude. Usually they rationalize their stance by pointing out that they are trying to sexually educate their children. Child therapists and other professionals have consistently noted that parents who frequently walk around in the nude are unconsciously trying to seduce their children by exhibiting themselves. Usually in such a situation there is not a good sexual relationship between the parents and the child is being used as a sexual substitute.

From the point of view of a child's mental health the growing sexual maturity, constantly being exposed to the parents' nudity is contraindicated. It can foster excessive anxiety, stimulate more competition than is tolerable and induce more sexual stimulation than the child can endure.

The Role of the Parents in Children's Sexual Problems

In the remaining portion of this chapter we will take a look at a variety of children's sexual problems that come to the helping professional. Some of these problems emerge as overtly sexual, such as compulsive masturbation, while in other situations the sexual dimension is somewhat covert, such as in certain learning problems. In the assessment and treatment of children's sexual difficulties, most clinicians would agree that the role of the parents is crucial. Not only must the therapist understand how the parents have contributed (and are still contributing) to the child's difficulties, but some treatment or counseling of the parents must also be arranged if the child's therapeutic gains are going to be sustained. Although there will be reference to work with parents throughout the chapter, it is important to examine specifically some of the unique features of the parents' role in the etiology and treatment of the child's sexual difficulties.

Until the late 1930s the parents' contribution to the child's therapy was to present the child's problems and history to the therapist as they saw them and then be relegated to the waiting room for the duration of the child's treatment.

Child therapists by the 1940s began to realize that a child had un-conscious meaning to parents and that their own anxieties and fanta-sies influenced the growth and development of the child. Profession-als learned that a child's sexual and interpersonal problems were often, if not always, unconsciously induced and sustained by the par-ents and that therapeutic modifications in the child's behavior, no matter how positive, adversely affected the parents' psychological equilibrium.

First mothers were helped to become clients and their participa-tion in the treatment process helped the child's therapy. When the mother's wishes and fears were addressed, the child's therapeutic gains did not threaten her so much. However, as mother and child im-proved in their internal and external functioning and modified their transactions with each other, the father often felt excluded and be-came threatened by their changes (Burgum, 1942; Beron, 1944). While it took much longer for child-guidance personnel to help fa-thers become clients, by the mid-1960s many fathers were actively participating in their children's treatment (Grunebaum, 1962; Strean, 1970; Grunebaum and Strean, 1970).

A psychosexual perspective on child pathology alleges that if a child has sexual problems, one and probably both parents have unre-solved maturational conflicts of their own which the child reactivates (Despert, 1965; Feldman, 1958; A. Freud, 1951). For example, as an infant expresses himself during the trust-mistrust, oral phase, the parents' unresolved problems with dependency, giving and taking, and bodily contact will come to the fore and very much influence how they cuddle, feed, and nurture the child. Similarly, if the parents have unresolved problems with sexual intimacy or sexual identity, these problems will emerge in the parent-child relationship and will hamper the child's further sexual and emotional development.

Usually when a parent describes a child's problem to the thera-pist, he is referring unconsciously to something unresolved in him-self. For example, when a parent says, "Johnny is afraid to ask ques-tions about sex," the chances are quite strong that the parent is anxious about answering questions on sex. Similarly, when a parent says, "Mary keeps coming into our bedroom and won't stay out," the parent is, in all probability, experiencing some ambivalence about Mary coming into the bedroom and is therefore uncertain and un-comfortable about what to say or do with Mary.

If the practitioner realizes that a parent, in discussing features of a child's life, is also unconsciously referring to the child within himself, the practitioner will then relate to the parent's anxieties. This approach frequently helps a parent to become a client in his own right.

During an interview at a child-guidance clinic, Mr. Colm, age thirty-six, reported that his son, Robert, did not want to come for treatment. Robert had been referred for treatment by school officials because he had rather consistently lifted up girls' dresses and tried to take down their panties. When the child-guidance worker asked Mr. Colm what he thought bothered Robert about coming to the clinic, Mr. Colm replied that Robert "doesn't like to talk about himself. He has some hesitancy about revealing himself to a stranger." Asked what he thought Robert's hesitancy was about, Mr. Colm said that any relationship was threatening to Robert because he "wants to preserve his privacy." When the worker asked Mr. Colm which parts of Robert's life he thought Robert would not want to reveal, Mr. Colm said that *he* was too embarrassed to talk about it. After a long silence he said, "I'm not sure what embarrasses Robert. I guess in many ways we are one and the same."

In the above example it is quite clear that when Mr. Colm was talking about Robert's fears of exposure he was talking about himself. Although the statements about Robert were accurate, Mr. Colm was implying that he was unconsciously aiding and abetting Robert to identify with his father's own inhibitions. Just as Robert eventually learned in his therapy that he compulsively wanted to expose girls' genitals to avoid looking at the naked girl in himself, in later therapeutic work Mr. Colm recalled how, when he was Robert's age, he could never get undressed in front of boys in locker rooms "because they'd see how effeminate I am."

When the practitioner recognizes that a child's sexual problems are frequently mirror images of the parents' conflicts, he realizes that advice to the parents will not usually be effective unless their unconscious contribution to the child's conflicts and their need to sustain them are respected and addressed.

Whatever a parent's reason for coming for help with difficulties, "sooner or later we become aware that a parent, too, is emotionally disturbed now or was disturbed as a child, and that his or her difficulties are very similar to the child's. The more we study the parent, the more we see the similarity of the disturbance" (Feldman, 1958, p. 23).

Clinicians have noted that parents of sexually provocative children usually offer them subtle rewards for their behavior and help them behave as they themselves behaved or would have liked to behave. It has also been observed that parents of sexually inhibited and passive children characteristically prevent assertive behavior in their children because such behavior induces anxiety in them. Such parents withdraw friendliness and other forms of positive recognition except on those occasions when the child inhibits himself or submits to parental dictates (Sternbach, 1947). The child becomes unwilling to relinquish neurotic or acting-out pleasures because he is so frequently the recipient of love premiums when he demonstrates his sensitivity and acquiescence to parental desires.

Paul Drake, age eleven, was referred for therapy by guidance personnel from his school because he was very passive and effeminate, and his reading level was very much below his capacity.

As reports from Mrs. Drake were carefully reviewed and as her interaction with Paul was observed, it became quite clear that almost every time Paul asserted himself Mrs. Drake would squelch his spontaneity and finish his sentences. Paul, in effect, was obeying an unconscious mandate from his mother, namely, "Don't assert yourself! Don't be too individuated! I am your mouthpiece and in many ways your eyes and ears, too!"

When Paul started therapy, Mrs. Drake made strenuous efforts to sabotage it. She spoke negatively to everyone of the boy's therapist and told Paul that he was not being helped. When Paul actually did improve his reading, Mrs. Drake made her most determined effort to stop the treatment.

As work with Paul and his parents continued, the social worker was able to conclude that Paul was extremely frightened of his own aggression and independence. To assert himself was—in his mind—to destroy his parents, and this thought overwhelmed him. It was much easier for him to be passive, effeminate, and ineffectual; this made him nonthreatening to adults and in this way he could maintain their love. In many ways, not being a good reader protected him.

Mrs. Drake was extremely frightened of having an assertive, independent son and had to castrate him psychologically. When Paul appeared potent, as he did when he started to read at a higher level, this activated enormous anxiety in his mother and she tried to undo his progress. She was, in effect, afraid of an erect penis, and the therapist learned later that Mr. Drake was an extremely poor reader himself, thus confirming the worker's notion that Mrs. Drake wanted the males in her life to be weak. Paul unconsciously realized this, and in many ways identified with his weak father.

Parents who have conflicted relationships with their children unconsciously reward them for maintaining a regressed position which they, the parents, enjoy vicariously. A parent may unconsciously prohibit a child's further psychosexual growth, not out of malice, but because such growth would activate the parent's unbearable anxiety. Unprepared for emotionally healthy living because he himself has been improperly nurtured, the parent maintains a relationship with the child that is dynamically similar to the one he experienced in his own childhood.

Mrs. Epstein, age twenty-nine, was referred to a child-guidance clinic by her physician because her daughter, Michele, was constantly constipated, and was untrained for bowel and urine control. Mrs. Epstein insisted on examining Michele's feces almost daily and discussed bowel training with anybody who would listen to her. When the intake worker at the clinic asked Mrs. Epstein what concerned her so much about Michele's defecating, she eventually responded, "It gives me a feeling of . . . importance . . . I dread the day when I'll have to discuss sex, boys, and all that stuff with her. I want to keep her young, I guess."

Parents in Treatment

As has already been indicated, whatever a parent's reasons for coming for help with a child's difficulties, sooner or later it becomes apparent that the parent, too, is emotionally disturbed now or was disturbed as a child, and that his or her difficulties are very similar to the child's (Feldman, 1958). Consequently, in helping a parent resolve difficulties in interaction with a child, it is important to ascertain which life tasks the parent needs help with and then offer him or her the appropriate therapeutic relationship that he or she needs to overcome maturational hurdles. A parent's treatment, in effect, is very similar to a child's, because usually both require similar attitudes on the part of the practitioner, who functions in many ways as a parental figure.

Early in the child-guidance movement there was a notion, still somewhat prevalent today, that if parents were simply told what they were doing that interfered with a child's mature functioning, they would behave differently. However, the dynamically oriented clinician now realizes that if a parent's own wishes, anxieties, defenses, and history are not taken into consideration and related to therapeutically, the parent cannot alter attitudes or behavior in relation to the child.

It is naive to assume that telling a seductive parent to stop seducing a child means that she or he will do so. Parents can modify their maladaptive behavior only when they experience less anxiety, and

usually this can be achieved only through a corrective therapeutic relationship that motivates them to become more mature.

A dynamic orientation to the treatment of parents is predicated
on the notion that parents who are unequipped to meet their children's particular maturational needs have not received appropriate
parenting themselves. For example, parents who cannot offer consistent limits or provide appropriate sex information were probably deprived of these important nutrients by their own parents. It is the
practitioner's task to give parents psychologically what they did not
receive in their past. The practitioner, in effect, becomes the symbolic parent that the parent never had.

Mr. Fulton, age forty-five, did not seek help directly. Unknown to him at first,
and later against his wishes, Mrs. Fulton applied to a mental health center for
guidance in relation to their only son, Lloyd. Twelve-year-old Lloyd was a neurotic child who had several phobias, compulsively masturbated, was withdrawn, could not tolerate competition or aggression, and was extremely passive
and very compliant.

Mrs. Fulton and Lloyd were involved in treatment for about six months
when Mr. Fulton became threatened by Lloyd's developing interest in sex and
his overall increased assertiveness. On the telephone he said to the therapist, "I
am coming down to bawl you out. You don't know what you are doing."

Mr. Fulton arrived ten minutes late for his appointment, and on entering
the office took the therapist's seat and announced, "I'm going to tell you a
thing or two." He went on to criticize the therapist, saying, "You are corrupting
Lloyd's mind by talking about all that sex stuff. Instead of talking about jerking
off with the kid, just tell him to stop!" He went on to tell the therapist that
"there are many things wrong with the way you guys run your business." The
therapist told Mr. Fulton that he was eager to learn about his mistakes, where-
upon Mr. Fulton vented a great deal of anger. He pointed out that Lloyd had to
be dealt with very strictly or else "he would not be kept in line." He further remarked that "sex for children is a lot of hokum and nobody should be molly-
coddled. That's what you do to my son." With encouragement from the therapist, Mr. Fulton offered several suggestions on how young boys should be
treated. At the end of the first interview the therapist told Mr. Fulton that he
welcomed the conversation and invited him back for another interview the following week.

Mr. Fulton arrived on time for his second interview. He proceeded to damn
the worker and his profession once more. He suggested to the therapist that he
"get out of the field and learn how to make money like I do." In succeeding
interviews, but with a more subdued tone, Mr. Fulton continued to give advice
on the treatment of people in general and the approach to Lloyd in particular.

By the sixth session Mr. Fulton told the therapist that he could have his seat back, and thanked him for "taking all my advice and guff." He went on to say that a big change had come over Lloyd recently. "I started to listen to his point of view and it really works." Mr. Fulton followed this up with a requestion for therapy for himself.

Unconsciously Mr. Fulton was recapitulating with the therapist what Lloyd was doing at his stage of treatment—acting out hostility toward a parental figure. Just as the therapist demonstrated a method of dealing with Mr. Fulton's infantile demands and fantasies, so Lloyd eventually became the recipient of a new mode of parental responsiveness.

It will be noted that at no time did the therapist try to point out to Mr. Fulton the illogic of his approach to Lloyd. He did not tell Mr. Fulton that Lloyd needed encouragement to ask sexual questions and permission to be assertive, for this would have fallen on deaf ears. Mr. Fulton wanted to fight with the therapist, and therefore the therapist had to first help him ventilate his anger without censure.

Prior to his meeting the therapist, Mr. Fulton had to try to suppress Lloyd's assertiveness and sexual curiosity because of his inability to cope with his own sexual conflicts and assertion problems. When Mr. Fulton had an experience with a father figure who helped him with his own aggression and sexuality, he became less fearful of Lloyd's expressions of the same drives.

As Mr. Fulton's treatment continued, it became clear that he had introjected an image of a tough, intimidating father that compelled him to act the same way with Lloyd. Otherwise, he would have hated himself for being a "softy." Because the therapist was not defensive about his own gentleness and permissiveness, Mr. Fulton could permit himself to be softer with Lloyd.

In sum, the therapist tries to sensitize himself to the parent's maturational conflicts and note where the parent has been improperly nurtured. It is the practitioner's responsibility to provide a corrective experience for the parent so that he can climb the psychosocial ladder and mature. In doing so, the parent can then help his child do likewise.

Children in Treatment

We are now ready to examine some of the more common sexual problems that children present to the helping professional. As has already been indicated, some of these difficulties, such as problems in sexual identity are manifestly sexual, while in other conflicts, such as certain learning problems, the sexual dimension may be more obscure. In focusing on the diagnosis and treatment of specific sexual problems of children, the discussion will also refer to some of the dynamic issues involved in work with their parents.

Problems in Sexual Identity

One of the most frequent referrals to the clinician who works with children is the boy or girl who has problems with his or her sexual identity. The boy with such a problem emerges as a passive, effeminate, youngster who is often scapegoated by his peers. He is usually inhibited when it comes to asserting himself and he fears normal competition with peers. Frightened of his aggressive impulses, he usually submits to most authorities. Often he has learning problems and is terrified of achievement. More than occasionally, he has strong fantasies of being a girl and in play will assume a maternal role. The idea of having a penis and competing with other boys is repugnant to him. A girl's life seems more appealing.

A girl who has problems with her sexual identity repudiates the feminine role. Often she prefers to wear boys' clothes and compulsively champions traditional activities of boys. Derogating other girls, toward whom she is often contemptuous, she feels that only a person with a penis has value. She does not like her vagina, gets no pleasure from it, and tries to deny is existence.

When the family constellations of these children are examined, we inevitably find that the parents are unconsciously encouraging the children to repudiate their natural identities and to assume the role of the opposite sex. The parents have problems with their own sexual identities and cannot accept the normal spontaneity and inclinations of the boy or girl. Usually there is considerable marital conflict, and the child frequently observes that the parent of the same sex is depressed and tense.

Where problems of sexual identity especially emerge are in one-parent families. In 1905 Freud, in his *Three Essays on the Theory of Sexuality*, pointed out that the loss of one parent, whether by death, divorce, or separation, often induces the remaining parent to absorb all of the child's love. The boy or girl frequently becomes a substitute for the lost spouse and finds his or her natural sex role overwhelming. In his study of Leonardo da Vinci, whose illegitimate birth deprived him of a father's influence until perhaps his fifth year and left him open to the tender seductions of a mother whose only solace he was, Freud described a type of male homosexuality in which etiological factors were the maternal seduction of a son because of the libidinal shift from husband to child and the absence of a paternal influence on oedipal development (Freud, 1905). Neubauer (1960), in his paper "The One-Parent Child and His Oedipal Development," stressed the pathogenic potential of the situation in which there is an absent parent and underlined the profound conflicts in sexual identification and superego formation found in the children he studied. Current writers have reported similar findings (Cooper, 1977; Wallerstein and Kelly, 1980).

Whether the child with problems in sexual identity is from a one-parent family or not, treatment is usually not easy. The parents, who have strong wishes to preserve the status quo in respect to their children, are frequently reluctant to release the children for treatment and also fear examining their own conflicts. Furthermore, the children unconsciously feel obliged to obey their parents' mandates and resist treatment themselves.

In working with the parents of these children, the helping professional has to be very tolerant of their resistances to treatment. Often they wish to debate the merits of treatment, provoke the clinician into a battle, and then withdraw from the therapeutic situation. Because they are very suspicious of the therapist who treats the child, it is usually helpful for the child's therapist to also be the parents' therapist.

Mrs. Zion, age forty, had divorced her husband when she was thirty-five and the man had subsequently died. Although her marriage was always stormy, domestic harmony was completely unknown shortly after the birth of their son, which occurred three years after the Zions were married.

Mrs. Zion was advised by her son's guidance counselor to seek therapeutic help for him. According to teachers' reports Robby, age thirteen, appeared withdrawn, showed little spontaneity, and spent much time immersed in fantasy talking to himself. His characteristic way of relating to his peers was to be the "fall guy"; he submitted to their wishes when they suggested that he insult a teacher, lift a girl's skirt, or swear. Although the counselor suggested the idea of therapy for Robby as a possibility, Mrs. Zion responded to his proposal as if it were a court summons.

In her initial interviews, Mrs. Zion was very quick to defend her son: "He has had a hard life and you can't expect too much from him. He has no father and I'm his whole life. I try my best to cheer him up and when he's lonely I get into bed with him. The people at the school are making too much of a fuss out of this." When the therapist empathized with Mrs. Zion's plight and suggested that she felt misunderstood and attacked by the school, Mrs. Zion condemned the school for "making me think that my Robby is a problem." She damned psychotherapy and said that she could take care of Robby by herself. She further exclaimed, "I love my boy and nobody will take him away from me!" When the therapist pointed out that Mrs. Zion was worried that he would take Robby away from her, Mrs. Zion remained silent for a few moments and then burst into tears. "People just don't understand," she sobbed. The therapist said that he would like to understand.

For several sessions Mrs. Zion went on damning educators, therapists, and others. When this was not challenged, Mrs. Zion began to speak of her own history. "I've had to fight my way in life. Nobody cared about me. I had to marry the man my parents wanted, not who I wanted." The therapist took note of Mrs. Zion's experiences of being frequently squelched, ordered around, and defeated—which she felt was being repeated with the therapist. She responded during her fifteenth session, "Oh, I forgot to tell you, I let Robby join the Y on his own. I think it's good for him to do things on his own."

In subsequent interviews Mrs. Zion reported that Robby wanted to start seeing the therapist, and eventually he did.

As is the case for treatment of the parents, therapy with the type of child we are considering is fraught with many difficulties. He or she frequently resists the therapist's help. If the professional does not get into a power struggle with the child, the child may slowly identify with the professional's perspective of self-examination and begin to face his or her insecurities about problems of sexual identity.

Robby, the son of Mrs. Zion in the above case illustration, in his initial interviews was very argumentative. "Look," he said to the therapist, "I've got your number! You think you can straighten me out? Well, you're mistaken! I've got a good deal all the way around and I don't care what the school says. You can't win!" When the therapist casually remarked that since Robby seemed to have been capable of defeating anybody who bothered him, it was a safe bet he could defeat the therapist, too, Robby was silent for a moment and then said, "I'll get you yet!"

Since Robby's resistance to treatment was not attacked, the therapeutic encounter did not appear too forbidding to him. He could come for his sessions because "there was nothing else to do." But in interview after interview he tried to provoke the therapist: "I tell my mother what a jerk you are and she's beginning to agree." "You're so dumb, you couldn't harm a flea."

After seven months of treatment on a regular basis, Robbie tried a new tactic. During one of the sessions when Mrs. Zion was seeing the therapist, Robby rapped on the door and demanded to see his mother immediately. Although Mrs. Zion was ready to acquiesce, the therapist stated, "I am with your mother alone now and we can't be disturbed by you." Mrs. Zion initially felt that the therapist was being cruel, but when he maintained a nondefensive attitude and attempted to explore her reaction she began to recall how Robby would interrupt her conversations with her husband and other men, and how he frequently entered the parents' bedroom with no limits imposed on him.

In Robby's next interview he yelled and screamed at the therapist for not sharing his mother with him. "You want my mother all to yourself, don't you?" he belligerently queried. "At times I do," the worker replied. Though Robby spent several hours castigating the therapist for being so unfair, he finally modified his tone. "You're trying to be like an old man to me and show me that I'm a lad. You're a knucklehead but sometimes I see your point a bit."

Robby's perception that the therapist was "trying to be like an old man" to him was a correct one. In working with a child who has problems of sexual identity, the clinician should try to help the child identify with a parental figure who focuses on the child's conflicts and distresses. When the initial resistances to treatment are lessened, the child can then share his or her fears in assuming the appropriate sexual role and focus with the therapist on the gratifications involved in keeping an immature sexual role. Robby was eventually able to look at his actual fear of being a boy among other boys and a boy among men. He could realize that his pseudo-aggressive behavior was a protection against a wish to be "a pampered baby" or "a little girl who Mother would just love and not ask anything of me."

Usually it is helpful for the child who feels uncomfortable with his or her sexual role to see a therapist of the same sex, and one, of course, who feels comfortable in being a man or a woman.

Yetta, eleven years old, was referred for help by school officials because she was very belligerent toward schoolteachers and toward her female peers. She was very contemptuous of traditional feminine activities such as cooking, baking, and child-rearing and championed football, wrestling, and boxing. She cursed a great deal and occasionally stole athletic equipment from stores.

After deriding and attempting to battle her female therapist for several months, one day she said to her, "You know, you are soft but bright, warm but strong, pretty but not weak." The worker had apparently demonstrated by her own behavior that one did not have to be a man to achieve and be competent.

Respecting the worker, Yetta could then go on to talk about how much she felt like a second-class citizen next to her brothers and how much she felt both of her parents valued boys over girls. She cried as she told her social worker how her mother never spoke to her about menstruation, masturbation, or sexuality in general, and how her father only rewarded her if she excelled in traditional male activities. Eventually Yetta was able to talk about a fantasy that her vagina was a wound and that at birth she had been castrated. Sharing her vulnerabilities with her therapist and not being censured, she could slowly give up her defense of defiance, and begin to associate with girls and feel more equal to boys. Of course, her parents needed a great deal of help in understanding why they both had to repudiate femininity.

Learning Problems

The most frequent referral to child-guidance personnel is the child with learning problems. Unfortunately, many helping professionals are oblivious to the sexual dimension of learning problems and focus too exclusively on the child's cognitive deficits. Learning, if it is to be an enjoyable and fulfilling experience, like enjoyable and fulfilling sex, necessitates a mastery of the psychosexual tasks of development that were reviewed in chapter 1.

In order to learn, a child has to ingest information that is palatable to him so that it can be enjoyably digested. If life at the breast or bottle during the oral period was unsatisfying, the child feels that taking in food for thought will be equally unsatisfying and threatening. Furthermore, if anybody, child or adult, is to learn, he must be able to trust his teacher. Many children with learning problems have never resolved the problems of the trust–mistrust phase of development and experience their teachers as ungiving, hostile, mother figures whom they must avoid. Many a child who cannot read or listen in class is unconsciously saying to his mentors, "Your ideas are like sour milk. I must vomit up what you give me."

Learning and training, as we know, begin long before a child goes to school. If "do's and don't's" are harshly or abruptly provided, the child will feel rebellious when asked to do something and/or will feel intimidated and overpowered (Kesten, 1970). Also, if parents have been reluctant to impose limits on their child, the youngster may emerge as an uncontrolled, narcissistic baby who only wants to be gratified. Many youngsters approach the learning situation as if they were on the potty. They refuse to "put out" for their teachers because they experience them as parents who are arbitrarily or prematurely ordering them to defecate or urinate. By the same token, there are children with learning problems who have never been appropriately toilet-trained, and in the classroom these children are unruly, and want "to shit all over the place."

Many academic failures emerge because children must stifle their normal curiosity. Often learning is unconsciously equated with preoccupation about forbidden sexual matters such as intercourse, sexual differences, or parts of the anatomy. Just as many children have felt forced to close their eyes and ears to sexual stimulation, they erect barriers to being stimulated intellectually.

To master an educational task, a child must be able to like his or her aggression and be able to compete. Many a girl or boy experiences academic achievement as an oedipal victory and must punish himself or herself by being a failure (Berman and Eisenberg, 1971; Halpern, 1964).

Willie, age ten, was referred to an educational counselor because he was unable to read. Although his IQ was in the normal range, he functioned as if he were a dull child. He feared participating in athletics and was panicky when it came to asserting himself. His family dynamics revealed that his mother was frightened of male assertiveness and his father was a very frightened and passive man who felt easily defeated.

In his play therapy with the counselor, Willie was extremely unverbal and inhibited. He often sat quietly and just stared at the window. When his counselor remarked to the boy that he was quiet and seemed frightened during therapy, Willie said that he didn't like to talk or "do anything much." He said his father was the same way. As treatment moved on, Willie and his therapist were able to learn that Willie was very frightened of surpassing his weak father. In games with the therapist, as soon as Willie would be on the verge of winning he would retreat.

Willie's counselor realized early in the treatment that his client's learning problems were a direct expression of his oedipal conflicts and decided that the best way he could assist Willie was to help the boy beat him in competitive games. Consequently, he showed Willie how to be the winner with him in chess, checkers, and Monopoly.

As Willie learned that he could beat a father figure without killing or being killed, his assertiveness increased, he began to read, and his functioning in school improved.

Although Willie's parents were frightened when they experienced his increased assertiveness and wanted to withdraw him from treatment, the therapist was eventually able to help them with their fear of their own aggression, and of course, Willie's too.

As has been noted, many children who have lived in homes where sexuality is a taboo subject carry this notion over to the learning situation.

Veronica, age five, came into treatment because almost every time her teacher would introduce an idea she would cover her eyes and ears. Although the teacher was a sensitive and patient person, she was unable to help Veronica lessen her fears.

Interviews with Veronica's parents revealed not only that Veronica was very phobic about dark rooms, subways, and heights, but that both of the parents were sexually repressed. When Veronica asked questions about how babies were born, pregnancy, and sexual differences, the parents told her that she would have to wait until she got older before she could get the answers.

In the treatment situation, Veronica related to her woman therapist very guardedly. When her fears of talking to or playing with the therapist were verbalized, Veronica was reassured and began to play a game called "I've got a secret." In this game Veronica wanted the therapist to guess what her secrets were. As the therapist would make a guess and say, for example, "Maybe your secret is how babies are born?" Veronica would giggle, aver that this was not the secret, and then go on to ask for sexual information. As this game was continually played, Veronica's inhibitions slowly dissolved. She began to see the therapist as a benign and loving superego who was giving her permission to have her own sexual wishes and be sexually curious.

It turned out that the parents were both products of sexually repressed homes and needed the same type of treatment that Veronica was receiving. They were seen in therapy together and shared with Veronica's therapist their anger in being sexually squelched, their own unanswered questions, and their fears of being sexually expressive. As they became able to accept with more tolerance their own childhood sexual wishes, they could become more tolerant of Veronica's sexual curiosity.

While there are thousands of youngsters like Willie and Veronica who are in treatment for learning problems, only a small percentage of them are receiving the appropriate therapy. All of the tutoring in the world will not appreciably help a child whose learning block evolves from unconscious sexual conflicts, and many learning problems of children are symptoms of sexual and other emotional conflicts. In a recent study, *Learning to Read*, Bruno Bettelheim and

Karen Zelan (1981), after much thorough research, concluded that children do not reverse letters, stumble, substitute, or block when reading aloud because of dyslexia or hyperkinesis or any of the other so-called neurological disorders (which are actually far rarer than they appear to be, according to the authors), but because of unconscious wishes that create anxiety. Bettelheim and Zelan were able to convincingly demonstrate that it is far more useful to acknowledge the unconscious cause of a reading error than it is simply to correct the child. Again and again the authors found that if the child's unconscious wishes were recognized in an uncritical manner, then the child would correct the mistake spontaneously.

As more educators and child-guidance personnel relate to the unconscious sexual and aggressive wishes involved in learning problems, children who cannot succeed in the classroom will have more of a chance to do so.

Phobias

Just as the sexual dimension has been frequently overlooked in the etiology of learning problems, it has also remained obscure, although less so, in the diagnosis and treatment of many children's phobias.

A phobia is an irrational fear of a person or an object. In a phobic situation there is no realistic reason for the child to become afraid, but he can tremble, panic, shudder, or vomit when confronted by the object or situation which stimulates unconscious sexual wishes that scare him and for which he feels he deserves punishment. For example, the child who is phobic about the dark is frequently wrestling, when in a dark room, with such sexual fantasies as incestuous oedipal desires, impulses to masturbate, voyeuristic or exhibitionistic urges, or wishes rape or maim. These wishes, which are forbidden, create anxiety, and the phobia helps the child avoid facing them.

The etiology of children's phobias was first described in 1909 by Freud in his *Analysis of a Phobia in a Five-Year-Old Boy*. Little Hans, a five-year-old boy, was so paralyzed by his phobia of horses that he was forced to stay at home and not risk going outdoors for fear that he would be confronted by the animals. Freud and Hans's father discovered that Hans's horse phobia emanated from the child's oedipal wishes—his strong erotic attachment to his mother coupled with his wish to displace his father and penetrate his mother with his own "widdler." Because Hans was convinced that his sexual desires for Mother and competitive drives directed against Father were taboo, he had to pay a penalty, namely, castration at the hands of his father. Unable to cope with his strong ambivalence toward his father, Hans repressed the hateful feelings, displaced them onto horses, and then feared the horses' hostile retaliation rather than that of his father.

When Hans assimilated and integrated interpretations focused on his oedipal difficulties, he recovered and was able to go outdoors again. Recognizing that his father would not punish him for his sexual and aggressive wishes, he became less anxious, and the energy utilized to repress his impulses was liberated so that he became freer to resume his energetic life.

The assessment and treatment of Hans's phobia has remained a paradigm for dynamically oriented workers in the clinical field. When the clinician who is confronted by a phobic child asks "What sexual temptations and unconscious wishes for punishment are at work here?" many obscurities become clarified and many treatment plans become better organized. For example, although the "school phobic" youngster is often one who has unconscious hostile wishes about one or both parents and is afraid to leave them, lest they die in his absence, this child may also have forbidden sexual fantasies about a teacher or a schoolmate and therefore must avoid school. A child who is phobic of the playground or some other recreational spot may fear being aroused by the play, which is experienced by him as sexual stimulation.

All children in growing up tend to have transient phobias. The most common phobias involve burglars, monsters, witches, and animals. The reason most, if not all, children experience these phobias is because they represent, in symbolic form, anxieties emanating from the universal oedipal conflict. A burglar often symbolizes the parental figure who is sexually tempting but who will also punish the child for his or her sexual and competitive wishes. This is usually the explanation for monster and witch phobias, as well. Animals symbolize the child's animal wishes (unrestrained sexual and aggressive impulses), and if the child fears being hurt by an animal this fear is a manifestation of the child's conviction that he or she should be punished for such wishes.

Childhood phobias disappear only when the child's sexual conflicts diminish. They cannot be willed away, nor can the child be talked out of them. Often it appears as if the child just made up his mind to give up the phobia, but this is not the case. For example, when a child takes his toy gun and in play shoots the tiger that troubles him, and then his phobia of tigers disappears, it is important to recognize that now the child is feeling stronger and more courageous in acknowledging and playing out his hostility toward his father.

The practitioner should also keep in mind that parents and children are often misled into believing that the cause of the child's phobic anxiety is a recently viewed movie or TV program.

Each time after he saw a movie, Tom, age four, developed an acute panic attack, trembling and vomiting. His parents sought therapy for him because they felt helpless in coping with Tom's intense distress. The social worker learned during the initial consultation interview with the parents that the movies Tom had viewed—Snow White and the Seven Dwarfs, Jack and the Beanstalk, and Cinderella—all had phallic-oedipal themes. The movies would not have affected Tom so acutely unless he had been in the throes of an intense conflict about his love and hatred for his father and his erotic wishes toward his mother. When he was able to play out family scenes in his therapy and found his sexual and competitive fantasies less ominous, he became freer to watch TV and movie programs that had oedipal themes.

As with any sexual problem that a child experiences, the parents are also experiencing a conflict similar to the one troubling their phobic child. In the case of Little Hans, the parents themselves had sexual problems which interfered with their marital relationship and which were also communicated unconsciously to Hans (Strean, 1970). In working with a phobic child, it is always important to keep in mind the unconscious forbidden wishes of both child and parents.

Sally, age six, had an intense phobia of dogs. If one appeared anywhere near her, she ran away in desperation. The onset of the phobia did not appear with any confrontation with a dog. Rather, one day while sick with a cold Sally became convinced that there was a dog under her bed. No amount of reassurance could reduce her feeling that a dog would bite her.

Inasmuch as Sally's intense fear of dogs continued, the parents sought out a child therapist. As her history unfolded and the family dynamics were exposed, it became clear that Sally, an only child, was attracted to her seductive father and was very competitive toward her mother. Although she had many loving feelings toward her mother, Sally also wanted to hurt her. In her play therapy Sally had the girl doll bite the mother into several pieces.

Sally's conflict was exacerbated by being ill with a cold because while she was in bed she received the tender ministrations of her loving father. But a more basic cause of the phobia was the parents' poor marital relationship. Both parents resisted intimacy with each other and both tended to turn to Sally for solace. It was living in this atmosphere that created Sally's intense phobia.

It was only as Sally became able to express in play her animal wishes to bite and destroy her mother that her phobia of animals diminished. Furthermore, in confessing her erotic feelings toward her father to a female therapist who did not censure her, Sally was helped to feel less intimidated when with her mother; consequently, she feared less retaliation from a dog. Finally, the parents needed help with their marital problems before Sally could really relax with herself and her own wishes.

The closer the terror of the phobic object (whether it be a dog, a cat, or a horse) approaches something real—i.e., dogs may bite, cats may scratch, and horses may kick—the less serious is the phobic problem. However, when the phobic object does not exist in reality, as with a strange nonexistent animal like a dinosaur, then the child's anxiety is probably quite intense. In virtually every instance of a phobia the choice of the phobic object is somewhat accidental—e.g., the child happened to be exposed to a dog or horse—but the formation of the phobia is always a result of the projection of the child's sexual conflict and has very little to do with the phobic object itself (English and Pearson, 1945).

Compulsive Masturbation

Masturbation, the stimulation of one's own genitals in order to produce pleasure, is a universal and normal phenomenon. Under present cultural conditions it is normal not only in childhood but also in adolescence, and even in adulthood as a substitute when no sexual partner is available (Fenichel, 1945). When the practitioner finds that a client did not masturbate as a child, he usually also learns that the client was overwhelmed by a great deal of fear and guilt.

Before the end of the first year of life children discover that the genital area is sensitive to touch and capable of pleasurable responses. For this reason children will play with themselves at various times.

Dreams of adults and children indicate that masturbation is regularly equated with play. The play of children at first has the function of achieving mastery of internal stimuli; later it anticipates possible events, preparing the child for future excitement. Similarly, masturbation can serve as a means of learning to master the experience of sexual excitation (Wermer and Levin, 1967; Fenichel, 1945).

Masturbation does not produce neurotic problems; however, it may be a sympton of neurosis when it is compulsive. Compulsive masturbation occurs in a child, much as in an adult, when interpersonal gratifications are at a minimum. The child usually feels unloved and has to love himself to be gratified. Often the youngster, by habitually touching his genitals, is reassuring himself that indeed he is a sexual and therefore a worthwhile person. Often the constant manipulation of the genitals can serve to ward off tension created in other areas of living. For example, a child may be swamped by strong hostile, even murderous thoughts. To avoid focusing on these forbidden and frightening ideas, he may masturbate. Furthermore, the child who feels that he may be hurt for his aggressive thoughts might masturbate to assure himself that his genitals are still there.

As already indicated, masturbation does not create a neurosis. However, what frequently creates guilt and anxiety are the fantasies that accompany masturbation. Often these fantasies are disguised oedipal wishes for which the child feels guilty.

A child's guilt about masturbation can be intensified by parental reactions to it. Some parents, like Little Hans's mother, threaten bodily harm when they see a child masturbate (Freud, 1909). Other parents really believe (because of their own unresolved masturbatory conflicts) that masturbation is wicked, dirty, shameful, and will ruin health. These parents need help in understanding that masturbation "can be accepted along with accepting the child's need to nurse, to suck, to evacuate, to eat, to ask questions, and that far from being any special problem it is one that responds as well as the others to the intelligent combination of gratification and direction" (English and Pearson, 1945, pp. 83–84).

In working with a child who is compulsively masturbating, it is important for the practitioner to help the child get in touch with the disguised wishes and anxieties that propel the compulsion. This is indeed the task in helping a child or adult get rid of any compulsion or obsession.

Ralph, age eleven, among other difficulties was compulsively masturbating. His hand was continually on his crotch and he played with himself wherever he was—at meals, in class, in gym, everywhere. As his guidance counselor investigated his history and family dynamics, it turned out that Ralph was an unwanted child who was the youngest in a family of seven children. His mother was frequently ill and his father spent many hours away from the home. Ralph's siblings had very little to do with him.

It became very apparent that Ralph's most important source of gratification was playing with himself. He felt extremely anxious when with children or adults, constantly fearing rejection. What came out in his work with his guidance counselor was that he had strong murderous feelings toward most people, and one major reason for avoiding interpersonal contact was his fear of retaliation.

In his treatment, Ralph was quite resistive for a long time. He avoided the counselor's attempts to involve him in games or to encourage him to partake of refreshments. The counselor would comment frequently that Ralph disliked and wished to reject him, and Ralph was eventually able to acknowledge his distrust and anger toward all adults. As he voiced his anger and found it accepted by the counselor, Ralph slowly made tentative attempts to involve the counselor in a relationship.

As Ralph became able to interact more enjoyably with the counselor, he masturbated less frequently. As he started to trust his counselor, he slowly came to trust teachers and peers. Because his parents refused to come in for any interviews, Ralph needed the relationship with the counselor for over three years.

When a girl does not feel sufficiently appreciated as a girl and has been negatively compared to brothers and other boys, her compulsive masturbation may serve the purpose of reassuring her that she has something which is worthwhile that can give her pleasure.

Phyllis, age ten, was referred for therapeutic help because she was "always masturbating," according to her mother. She was essentially withdrawn from her peers, and her sense of social isolation was compounded by her classmates' derision when they saw her masturbating.

The youngest child in her family, she was constantly demeaned by both her parents because she was "just a girl," while her older brothers—three of them—were constantly praised for their athletic skills and other achievements.

Unappreciated, full of anger and self-hatred, Phyllis had very low self-esteem and a poor body image. In her treatment with a woman therapist, she communicated little and played in a very constricted manner. Since the therapist patiently respected Phyllis's resistances, Phyllis was able to eventually become more involved in play and conversation. However, in the competitive games she played with the therapist, such as checkers and chess, she always arranged to lose.

As the therapist helped Phyllis ventilate her anger for being treated like a second-class citizen and supported her strengths—artistic talents, literary interests, and writing skills—her self-esteem increased and she became less withdrawn from her peers. As she received more gratification from her interpersonal relationships, her compulsive masturbation subsided.

Enuresis

Enuresis is a condition in which the child who has been toilet trained wets himself during the day or in bed during the night. Inasmush as toilet training is not expected to be completed until the fourth year, any involuntary wetting before that time cannot be termed enuresis.

Although enuresis may be caused by many factors—such as lack of training or revenge when the child is angry ("pissed off") at the parents for some reason, e.g., the birth of a sibling—one of the major contributory factors is sexual conflict.

Frequently, in boys and girls who are sexually stimulated but do not masturbate to the point of orgasm the enuresis serves as an orgastic substitute (Sternbach, 1947).

In some girls who are strongly competitive with boys and men, the enuresis comes at the climax of a dream in which they want to urinate in the same manner as boys. Often these are girls who feel keenly disappointed by their fathers and want to give up being feminine.

Boys who are enuretic are frequently passive and effeminate and have retreated from competing with Father for Mother. These boys are so passive that they invariably say that "the bed got wet" and take no responsibility for their situation. They feel castrated and in sleep regress to the psychological position of a child who has not been toilet trained.

When enuretic children reach puberty and masturbate to the point of orgasm, the enuresis usually stops. However, some children are so frightened that they will be punished for their masturbation that they stop masturbating. When masturbation ceases there is a halt in psychosexual development and the child regresses to the stage of interest and pleasure in urination (English and Pearson, 1945; Fenichel, 1945).

One of the reasons that many children have difficulty with urinating or defecating is that the organs involved in these processes are either the same as or close to the organs involved in direct sexual pleasure. Many a child (and many an adult) equates urinating or defecating with sexuality, and if they are guilty about their sexual wishes they cannot urinate or defecate in front of others or cannot ask to be directed to a bathroom. Many children do not use public toilets because they fear they will get "germs," i.e., get punished for their sexual "crimes." When children have so much conflict about eliminating, they must consciously suppress this function during the day, and only at night, when they are asleep and certain surperego restraints are less influential, can they urinate or defecate.

Because enuresis is an emotional problem caused by problems in sexual identity and inability to discharge sexual impulses, treatment should be addressed to these issues. It should *not* be directed toward stopping the enuresis, which is only an expression of an emotional conflict. Although charts, bells, and restriction of fluids may at times stop the wetting, they are completely useless in helping the child resolve the underlying sexual problems. What is called for is treatment which helps the child face his or her fears of the opposite sex and reluctance to be a member of his or her own sex.

Polly, age eight, was referred for therapy because of her enuresis, phobias, and inability to work up to par academically. Although she had been toilet trained at age four and remained trained until seven, for close to a year since that time she had been enuretic almost nightly.

When she was seven Polly's parents separated, and they later divorced. She lived alone with her mother and saw her father on weekends. Father was living with another woman.

In her treatment with the therapist, Polly slowly was able to verbalize a lot of anger toward her father, "for leaving me." She said that "if he really loved me, he wouldn't have left." Polly's play therapy revealed strong erotic interests in her father, ambivalence toward her mother, and wishes to castrate and maim her father for his departure.

As Polly continued to enact her conflicts in play therapy, she had the girl doll stand up to urinate and gave her a penis. As she talked about her own wish to be a boy, she pointed out that if she were a boy her father would have loved her more and would not have left home.

When the therapist related to Polly's repudiation of her femininity, she learned from Polly (and it was later corroborated by Polly's mother) that as a smaller child she had been stimulated by her father, had become frightened of her own excitement, and had felt weak and helpless next to her father. She found her feminine feelings hard to acknowledge and felt a boy's life could be better.

As Polly began to identify more with her female therapist and discussed her fears of being a girl and her envy of boys, her phobias and enuresis eventually disappeared.

It should be reiterated that the cessation of bed-wetting is not a reliable guide to the progress of therapy. There are parents and even therapists who regard the enuresis as the main symptom and therefore want treatment terminated as soon as the wetting is stopped. When enuresis is viewed as a sign of distress and of sexual conflict, treatment should continue until the child is less anxious about his or her sexual identity and sexual impulses.

Sexual Provacativeness

A rather large group of children are referred to clinicians by schools, courts, and other law-enforcement agencies for sexual provocativeness. These are children who may rape, are exhibitionists or voyeurs, make obscene phone calls, or perform sexually sadistic acts. They are the runaways, the arsonists, and the truants. They are frequently labeled "delinquents," "psychopaths," "sociopaths," or "antisocial characters." Unreliability, untruthfulness, and insincerity are their distinguishing defenses. Often these children demonstrate no remorse or guilt when confronted with the facts of their behavior (Freedman, Kaplan, and Sadock, 1976).

Glover (1960) summarized the major writings on these children, utilizing the label "psychopath." He concluded that the psychopath is

> a constitutionally sensitive person, peculiarly intolerant of frustration; inclined to sexual excess; deeply aggressive and openly negativistic; selfish and egotistical, with an immediately ineffective reality sense; incapable of sustained effort, callous, inconsiderate, unprincipled and lacking in moral sense; incapable of deep attachment; recidivist and refractory to punishment. His psychopathic outbursts are irregular in incidence, stereotyped and on the whole compulsive, but even in quiescent periods his character is disharmonious and often eccentric. At the same time he wears the mask of friendly normality. (p. 128)

Although there is much unanimity among writers that the psychopath is devoid of guilt feelings and has a weak, fragmented superego, a psychosexual perspective on such a child's behavior makes this inference questionable (Strean, 1982).

An early discovery of dynamic psychology which has been mentioned several times is that we can never rely on manifest behavior alone if we are to assess the human being thoroughly (Freud, 1900). One of the dynamics that has been consistently observed in clients who have been assessed as "criminal psychopaths" is their feeling of relief when they are caught and punished. As one example of this, Freud described the "criminal out of a sense of guilt" (Freud, 1916). This is an individual who is so oppressed by a tyrannical superego that he becomes involved in provocative and illegal acts in order to be incarcerated. His punishment dissipates his guilt, which almost always has an unconscious origin.

What has to be considered in the diagnosis and treatment of the psychopathic child is that in most instances he has been deprived of a warm, consistent, and empathetic relationship with a mother, and in many cases he has never had a father (Aichorn, 1935; Gaylin, 1976). When the child who is to become a psychopath feels emotionally neglected and abandoned his initial reaction is usually protest and hostility (Bowlby, 1951). However, he cannot freely discharge his angry feelings because he anticipates retaliation for his aggressive wishes and therefore represses his desires. Inasmuch as the "would-be psychopath" usually experiences his parents as sadistic, rather than oppose them he introjects their punitive voices into his conscience. The more anger he feels, the more he becomes subject to his own punitive, primitive, and sadistic superego.

For the helping professional to be of therapeutic assistance to the psychopathic child, he should be aware that this child is not devoid of guilt, but rather has to squelch strong wishes to hug, kiss, and be given emotional sustenance. Because he feels that his libidinal wishes are wrong and will never be gratified, his antisocial behavior should be regarded as a strong protest against his own severe superego. Many children who brutally attack their siblings or peers are really sexually attracted to them, but because they feel that their sexual wishes are taboo, they fight their own internal restraining voices by hurting the ones they love. In contrast to the child with empathetic parents who have been able to provide him with maturational experiences which have yielded what Schafer (1960) has called "the loving and beloved superego," the psychopathic child has a sadistic superego which constantly condemns him.

Joe, age ten, was referred for psychotherapy because he had physically assaulted other children, sexually molested young girls, stolen goods from stores and sold them at enormously high prices, defied authorities, and seemed to feel unperturbed by his behavior.

In the therapeutic situation, Joe at first denied that he was involved in any antisocial activity. His defense of denial was not challenged, and in his tenth session he pointed out that he had, in fact, participated in some of the illegal acts that he was accused of, but he was merely "protecting myself." First he accused teachers, and then later his peers, of "picking on me." "They are all unfair people," he bellowed. His injustice collecting embraced "unfair" acts on the part of almost every citizen in his community.

In Joe's fortieth session, he was asked by his therapist if his parents ever treated him unfairly. In contrast to his response to teachers, peers, and others, Joe made several idealizing statements about both of his parents. Although he rarely saw his alcoholic father and felt very vulnerable in the company of his neglectful mother, who was a prostitute, he told the therapist that his "biggest wish is to please both of my parents." When the therapist asked Joe how he was progressing in this effort, he described himself as "a failure." He "could not memorize everything in the magazines that my mother leaves me when she goes out, nor can I make everything spick-and-span like she wants it." Joe also mentioned that he could not hit home runs the way his father wanted him to.

As Joe continued in his therapy, he began to realize that he was trying to be an omnipotent giant to please his parents. When he couldn't succeed he "had to lie," and "when lying doesn't work," Joe pointed out, "all hell breaks loose and I want to hurt everybody."

It was not until Joe's third year of treatment that he could acknowledge his strong sexual wishes, which he had to fight. "Yes," he would say tearfully, "I'd love to grab my father or mother and hug them, but that's wrong." "I'd love to put my head on your shoulder, but that's wrong."

The term "psychopath" is rarely used benignly, and usually the child's antisocial characteristics are described in derogatory terms. Terms like "irresponsible," "inability to accept blame," and "incapacity for love" are suggestive of what Erikson (1956) has called "diagnostic name-calling." It would appear that many therapists feel a sense of indignation when confronted with the client's abusive antisocial behavior and that much of their therapeutic pessimism may be attributed to their negative countertransferences. Rather than recognizing that the child's provocative behavior is a defense against primitive sexual yearnings, they subtly condemn the antisocial behavior and label the child a psychopath who is untreatable. This child's initial resistances to treatment must be patiently weathered by the therapist, and in addition the therapist must demonstrate a consistent attitude, throughout the therapy, of "unconditional positive regard" (Rogers, 1951).

Children Who Are Victims of Incest

Incest, as commonly defined, refers to sexual victimization of a child by a parent. The government estimates that at least 10,000 children are sexually abused by relatives in the United States each year (*New York Times*, October 11, 1981). Incest is primarily a male problem that young girls are forced to bear the brunt of. Research is still scanty, but some common patterns of the incestuous family have begun to emerge. The mean age for the first assault is about eight, but sometimes the victims are younger (*Time*, November 23, 1981).

As the dynamics of the incestuous family are being studied (Justice and Justice, 1979; Butler, 1978), what appears to be emerging is an abusive father who tends to be strongly authoritarian and desperately insecure about his own sexuality. He usually cannot sustain a mature relationship with a woman, so he turns to a child, who is much less threatening to him. Often he has strong homosexual wishes and is unconsciously identified with the daughter he sexually victimizes. The mother emerges as a masochistic self-effacing woman, deeply depressed, who does not feel very secure about her feminine identity. Often her self-image is that of a little girl. In some cases, she has strong yearnings to have a close relationship with a father, and she may unconsciously promote her daughter's sexual relationship with her husband.

A few writers (McIntyre, 1981; Butler, 1978) have contended that much of the current theory of incest as well as the approaches to treatment "ignore the impact of a patriarchal society and culture in promoting and encouraging incestuous assault" (McIntyre, 1981, p. 462). These writers feel that clinicians have been improperly educated about the roles of family members, on which basis the mother, instead of the actual offender, is "blamed" for the assault.

In understanding and treating any child's sexual problem, it is essential for the clinician to understand the unresolved conflicts of all the family members and blame no one. Obviously all the members of the family need long and intensive treatment.

When a girl has been a victim of incest, the aftermath is inevitably horrendous for her. She feels guilty for what she perceives as participating in a horrible crime, angry at both parents for not protecting her against assault, and weak for not being able to control her own forbidden sexual impulses. Inevitably, she feels very mistrustful of everyone, becomes very phobic and even paranoid, and has strong feelings of inferiority which shape her poor image of her femininity (Maisch, 1973; Lustig, 1966). When there is sibling sexual experimentation, mother–son sexual exploitation, or homosexual incest between mother and daughter or father and son, similar psychological problems ensue (Lustig, 1966), although there appear to be fewer reports of this form of incest.

As can be expected, children who have been victims of incest are most embarrassed to discuss their sexual experiences and are frequently distrustful of the therapist. They try to defend themselves against their warm feelings toward the therapist, are frequently evasive in their interviews, and are most inhibited in their play.

Rachel, age ten, was referred to a child-guidance clinic after it was discovered that she had been a victim of an incestuous relationship with her father. For over two years she was forced to perform fellatio on her father, submit to cunnilingus, and compelled to have anal intercourse with him. The father was an alcoholic, frequently unemployed, who gambled a great deal and had a strong sadomasochistic, asexual relationship with Rachel's mother. The mother was described as depressed, often physically ill with migraine headaches, loss of appetite, and insomnia.

In the treatment relationship with her male therapist, Rachel was very guarded, said little, and most of the time looked away from her interviewer. She refused to participate in play and would not accept candy or any food from the therapist.

Although the therapist voiced what he felt was Rachel's mistrust of him and her fears of being involved with him, she continued to maintain her strong defense of noninvolvement in the therapy. Statements about her unhappiness at home met with a similar response. Although the therapist recognized that Rachel was very phobic and anxious, had low self-esteem, and was quite paranoid, he constantly monitored his own feelings of discouragement and his wish to give up. Apparently, after about eight months of therapy, Rachel began to eventually realize that the therapist was not going to seduce or attack her and she did begin to silently play checkers with him. Her play revealed her fear of being attacked by the therapist because she cringed each time she was about to be jumped by one of his checkers.

The therapist told Rachel that the reason she was so upset about being jumped was because it reminded her of her father's sexual attacks. Rachel instantly began to cry and eventually discharged a great deal of anger, first toward her father and then toward her mother for "making me feel so messy inside."

While the therapist's interpretation and Rachel's catharsis were helpful to her—she became less phobic and more trusting—she still maintained her cautiousness in therapy. However, her checker playing took on a new theme. Instead of cringing when the therapist jumped her, she began to coyly ask for it and seemed to welcome being beaten. Slowly the therapist introduced the idea of secret pleasure in being jumped, and he told Rachel that although it was difficult to face, she liked the forbidden idea of touching her father and being touched. At first Rachel vehemently denied this, but when the therapist did not force his interpretations down her throat (as the father had done with his penis) Rachel slowly did acknowledge some of her sexual excitement when with her father.

Because both parents were not very cooperative with the therapy, resisting everything from marital counseling to individual therapy or family therapy, Rachel's treatment moved at a particularly slow pace. Although she emerged as a better-integrated girl after several years of treatment, she retained some scars, feeling inhibited with boys at parties and shy with men teachers. After she formally ended therapy, she continued to see her therapist sporadically for check-ups.

-Although one of the reasons that incest may appear like an epidemic is because we now have better reporting methods, nonetheless, "scholars project that one of every 100 adult women in the United States was sexually molested as a girl by her father—an astonishing figure in itself, and one that many experts think is far too low" (*Time*, November 23, 1981, p. 68). It therefore behooves the helping professional to sensitize himself or herself to the unique dynamics and crucial treatment issues that pertain to victims of incest and their families.

Childhood Depression

As the reader is now, no doubt, aware, few of the problems that we have been considering exist in isolation; i.e., the child with problems of sexual identity may also have learning problems, and a youngster with enuresis may also be suffering the consequences of being in a one-parent family. This obvious fact is being noted now because many of the children who have latent or overt sexual problems are also depressed.

When we say that a child is depressed we mean that he looks and feels dejected, is depreciative of himself, is apologetic, feels inferior, and often tells others that he isn't as worthwhile as other children. The depressed child feels helpless and worthless, ingratiates himself with others, and constantly defers to them. Occasionally the depressed child enacts the role of ignoramus or clown to try to ward off his state of misery (Cameron, 1963).

Most writers and clinicians who discuss childhood depression refer to the child's turning aggression against himself rather than discharging it directly. They also speak of the child's overwhelming guilt and punitive superego. However, there has been insufficient attention given to the sexual dimension of childhood depression.

Many a depressed child is yearning for but feels unentitled to oral and narcissistic gratification. He would like to touch and be touched, hug and be hugged, but feels that these wishes are forbidden and becomes guilty when he entertains them. The depressed child also feels guilty about urinary and anal desires, and when he fantasies enjoying himself in a prolonged bowel movement or defying authority by urinating in the woods he feels like a bad child. Very often the depressed child is very guilty about oedipal wishes and fears retalilation because of his incestuous and competitive urges.

The family atmosphere of a depressed child is often a restricted one in which the child has learned that the expression of sexual wishes is taboo. Occasionally, the child who is depressed comes from an overindulged, sexually stimulating atmosphere and is depressed because he cannot get his libidinal wishes gratified by others all of the time—as he does get them constantly gratified by his parents. In any event, the depressed child is one who feels frustrated that his libidinal wishes must be suppressed.

The depressed child, because he has a core of anger and a punitive superego, often fights the therapy and the therapist. This is usually done in a subtle manner because the child cannot feel free to overtly aggress. Unless the therapist eventually confronts the child with his wish to defeat the treatment, the therapy can stagnate.

Paul, age ten, was seen in treatment for failure in school, enuresis, inability to relate to peers, and frequent insomnia. His parents were described as depressed people and the family atmosphere appeared to be morose.

Paul's history revealed that he was weaned at six months and toilet trained at eight months, and expressions of normal sexual curiosity were consistently squelched by his parents. Paul was also threatened with castration for masturbating, and his parents threw away sexy magazines that he would pick up in stores from time to time.

Although Paul's therapist was aware of the boy's passive-aggressive demeanor and his latent wish to oppose therapy, he nonetheless became too therapeutically ambitious and tried too eagerly to get Paul to "have fun," "not feel so guilty for masturbating," and "like yourself more." The more the therapist championed pleasure and the universality of sexual wishes, Paul retreated. While Paul would passively accept the therapist's interpretations as valid, he did not use them to his advantage, unconsciously defeating the therapist.

The therapist became more and more irritated and tried family therapy and other forms of intervention. However, therapy did not succeed because Paul's wish to defeat the treatment was not confronted and the therapist's sense of personal defeat was not adequately dealt with by him.

When therapy is not succeeding, it is always helpful for the practitioner to ask two important questions: "What is the client enjoying about not making progress, i.e. what latent oppositional wishes are at work?" and "What am I doing or not doing to retard the treatment?" While Paul's therapist was correct in formulating a goal to liberate Paul sexually, he did not recognize his client's wish to fight him, was not aware of his own wish to succeed as a therapist, and did not face his counterresistance in coping with Paul's unconscious resentment toward him.

While family therapy can be most helpful for families whose members can communicate with each other and for families who are very symbiotic and can't tolerate individual treatment (Strean, 1982), when a therapist has constant wishes to modify the therapeutic modality, he should begin to question what dysfunctional countertransference issues are at work.

Psychosomatic Problems

Many children are referred to physicians and other helping professionals for bodily complaints. The sensitive practitioner, while not ever ruling out a physical workup for the child, should be sensitive to the fact that many somatic illnesses are disguised expressions of forbidden sexual wishes. While each child has his or her zones of bodily vulnerability, it is important to bear in mind that children (and adults) can and often do somaticize a sexual conflict.

There are numerous ways that children somaticize sexual conflicts. As has already been discussed, enuresis can be an orgastic
equivalent. Often very fast heartbeats or intense breathing can also
serve as orgastic substitutes. The asthmatic child frequently is calling
out for bodily satisfaction and closeness with a parent, and the child
who gets a paralysis in his hands or arms may be unconsciously trying
to stop himself from performing some unacceptable sexual act such
as masturbating. There are numerous other bodily manifestations of
sexual conflict: headaches; stomachaches, ulcers, and other gastrointestinal disorders; allergies such as hay fever; poor appetite, and so
on (Alexander and Ross, 1952).

In the treatment of the child who is suffering from a psychosomatic disorder, the child's sexual wishes that are being bodily expressed should become conscious.

Mabel, age five, was seen in treatment for a head tic. She was a girl who slept in
the parents' bedroom and was an occasional witness of their sexual activity.
She was also overstimulated be her parents, who walked around in the nude
and encouraged her to do the same.

The parents and Mabel were seen in family therapy. As the treatment
moved on, with the parents doing most of the talking, it eventually became
clear that Mabel's head tic became more severe when she witnessed her parents' intense discussions. The therapist eventually recognized that these intense
discussions reminded Mabel of her parents' having sex. Continued confrontation by the therapist of this familial pattern helped the family and the therapist
to recognize that by shaking her head Mabel was trying to negate many of her
oedipal fantasies. As Mabel could face more openly her own sexual wishes and
the parents could diminish some of their own exhibitionism and seductiveness,
the frequency and intensity of Mabel's head tics diminished considerably.

Psychosomatic problems, like many other conflicts of children
that have ben noted in this chapter, have a strong sexual component.
The professional, in helping children face their transference wishes
and fears and resolve some of their resistances to treatment, can sensitize children to their sexual wishes and enable them to enjoy life
much more.

Chapter 5

Sex and Adolescents

EVER SINCE THE ELIZABETHAN AGE, literary portrayals of adolescence have abounded. *Romeo and Juliet* poignantly depicts teenage passion. Shakespeare's Prince Hal is an excellent example of an adolescent responding to a developmental crisis that creates anxieties about sexual identity. In our own century James Joyce, Thomas Mann, Carson McCullers, and many others have continued the literary tradition of describing the sexual conflicts, the turmoil, and the unpredictability of adolescence (Esman, 1975).

Some of the typical characteristics of teenagers everywhere—their jumpiness, their sexual excitement, and their self-doubts (Kiell, 1964; Muensterberger, 1961)—are revealed in the following passage from Salinger's *Catcher in the Rye* (1945).

> I apologized like a madman, because the band was starting a fast one. She started jitterbugging with me—but just very nice and easy, not corny. She was really good. All you had to do was touch her. And when she turned around, her pretty little butt twitched so nice and all. She knocked me out. I mean it. I was about half in love with her by the time we sat down. That's the thing about girls. Every time they do something pretty, even if they're sort of stupid, you fall half in love with them, and then you never know where the hell you are.(p. 95)

Like Holden Caulfield, the young man in *Catcher in the Rye*, the adolescent can go from the height of elation to the depths of despair in a single hour. He can be enthusiastic one day and hopeless the next. Frequently feeling oppressed by parents, the young person, to establish an identity, loudly proclaims, "I am a rebel, therefore I am!" (Blos, 1967; Erikson, 1956).

Prior to Freud's *Three Essays on the Theory of Sexuality* (1905) adolescence was considered to be the beginning of an individual's sex life. However, since Freud discovered infantile sexuality adolescence has been conceptualized as a period of final transformation, i.e., a bridge between diffuse infantile sexuality and genitally centered adult sexuality (A. Freud, 1958). In 1922 the psychoanalyst Ernest Jones, in a paper called "Some Problems of Adolescence," pointed out that "adolescence recapitulates infancy, and that the precise way in which a given person will pass through the necessary stages of development in adolescence is to a very great extent determined by the form of his infantile development. . . . The individual recapitulates and expands in the second decennium of life the development he passed through during the first five years" (pp. 398–399).

Clinical investigators have continued to document that the *Sturm und Drang* of adolescence are to be expected (A. Freud, 1937). It is now most apparent that oedipal and other childish fantasies are revived in intense form during adolescence and that therefore, under the impact of anxiety, the teenager has a desire to regress. The wish to regress, to be a young child again, conflicts with the adolescent's desire to be independent and emancipated from parents. This emotional seesaw that teenagers experience—wanting cuddling, hugging, and dependent gratification versus the wish for autonomy—accounts for their moodiness.

Adolescents tend to show considerable volatility of feeling. There seems to be no measure in the young person's love or hate, interest or boredom; each emotion fills the teenager totally, but not for long. Allied to this intensity of feeling is the adolescent's desire for frequent and immediate gratification; furthermore, he is often unlikely to be aware of the consequences of his actions. At times he suspends his ego functions of judgment and reality testing and fails to show any self-criticism. Frequently regressing to an infantile state of narcissism, the teenager may appear to be indifferent to the needs and wishes of others (Fountain, 1961). Adolescence, therefore, can be described as an "interruption of peaceful growth, and the upholding of a steady equilibrium during the adolescent process is in itself abnormal" (A. Freud, 1958, p. 275).

It is normal for an adolescent to behave for a considerable length of time in an inconsistent and unpredictable manner, to fight his impulses and to accept them; to ward them off successfully and to be overrun by them; to love his parents and to hate them; to revolt against them and to be dependent on them; to be deeply ashamed to acknowledge his mother before others and unexpectedly, to desire heart-to-heart talks with her; to thrive on imitation of and identification with others while searching unceasingly for his own identity; to be more idealistic, artistic, generous, and unselfish than he will ever be again, but also the opposite—self-centered, egoistic, calculating. Such fluctuations between extreme opposites would be deemed highly abnormal at any other time of life. At this time they may signify no more than that an adult structure of personality takes a long time to emerge, that the ego of the individual in question does not cease to experiment and is in no hurry to close down on possibilities. (A. Freud, 1958, pp. 275–276)

A close-to-universal phenomenon that adolescents demonstrate in coping with their sexuality is "bribing the superego" (Alexander and Ross, 1952); that is, they vow not to "go all the way." They pet above the waist but not below, they do not neck on the first date, and they do not have sex until there is an agreement to go steady. These compromises appease the superego and assuage guilt feelings. Some current writers contend that these compromises are not as predominant in the 1980s because of shifts in teenage morality, a phenomenon related to the wider culture's modifications in attitude toward sexuality (Esman, 1979). This issue will be discussed in further detail in the next section of this chapter.

Although the young person's compulsive compromises, volatility, desire for immediate gratification, and periodic regressions may be considered par for the course during adolescence, many young people cannot cope with the *Sturm und Drang* and resort to dysfunctional solutions which bring them to the attention of the helping professional (Dulit, 1975). For a while the teenager may become a rigid celibate and recluse and then follow this modus vivendi by trying extreme forms of sexual promiscuity. A young man may experiment with homosexuality and then become a Don Juan. Often sexual terror can lead to paranoia, depression, or antisocial behavior; occasionally a young person becomes a truant, a runaway, or a delinquent. Sexual anxieties can invade learning experiences and inhibit vocational planning. Young people may try drugs or, in desperation, even suicide. All these problems, which may be viewed in large part as behavioral manifestations of the teenager's anxiety and even terror, will be examined in detail in this chapter.

Adolescent Sexuality and the New Morality

Chapter 1 made mention of a "new sexuality" which appears to represent a significant change in cultural patterns. Evidence of the effect of these changes on adolescents has been well documented in the literature. In 1973 Sorenson reported that in his large national sample 19 percent of girls age thirteen to fifteen agreed with the statement "If you really dig a boy it's all right to have sex with him even if you've only known him for a few hours"; 53 percent of all adolescent boys shared a similar attitude toward girls. Sorenson in this study coined a term, "serial monogamy without marriage"—"a close sexual relationship of uncertain duration between two unmarried adolescents from which either party may depart when he or she desires, often to participate in another such relationship" (Sorenson, 1973, p. 219).

Findings similar to Sorenson's are reported by Schmidt and Sigusch (1972) from West Germany, where the age of first sexual intercourse in comparable adolescent populations declined between 1966 and 1970, particularly among the more educated students. The girls in the 1970 study had a "much greater sexual motivation for their first coitus and correspondingly the first coitus was more often the result of mutual initiative" than had been the case in 1966. Also, they "more often felt happier after the first coitus and less often found it unpleasant, repulsive and/or disgusting" (Schmidt and Sigusch, 1972, p. 41).

In his 1973 survey, Yankelovich (1974) found that "fewer unmarried students (61 percent) personally look forward to getting married than in 1968 (66 percent)" (Yankelovich, 1974, p. 59). Yankelovich also found in his study that in 1969, 43 percent of college students said they would "welcome more acceptance of sexual freedom," while only 22 percent of the noncollege population shared this view. By 1973, 47 percent of the noncollege youth took this position. Similar attitudes were found in regard to questions on abortion, homosexuality, and premarital sexual intercourse.

From these sociological studies, several writers (Esman, 1979; Hunt, 1974; Hendin, 1975) have concluded that a "new morality" has developed that encourages a freer sexuality among adolescents, particularly among girls, and that "serial monogamy" is the most characteristic pattern. It would appear, however, that the decline of traditional restraints on sexuality has given rise to alternative institutions like cults and religious groups which champion a puritanical code of morality and set limits on sexual behavior (Johnson, 1975).

The Hare Krishna cult, for example, limits sexuality to marital relationships for reproduction only and prohibits sexual activity after the age of thirty.

While some commentators contend that there is no evidence that the greater sexual freedom has "interfered in any significant way with the adaptive success of most of this generation's adolescents" (Esman, 1979, p. 27), this conclusion may be somewhat dubious. For example, teenage suicide has reached its highest level and has increased 250 percent in the last twenty years (Jacobs, 1971); the drug culture is now proliferating (Feinstein, Giovacchini, and Miller, 1971) and the dropout phenomenon has intensified (Strean, 1982). In his intensive study of four hundred college students who were nonpatients, Hendin (1975) found that suicidal preoccupation was high, depression was common, the drug problem was pervasive, impotence and frigidity were frequent, homosexuality was popular, and there was much enmity between young men and women. Throughout Hendin's study the typical college student emerged as very frightened to feel. Such a student was particularly threatened by feelings of love, warmth, and the kind of sexuality that fuses tenderness and eroticism. It would appear that just as the "new sexuality" has not liberated adults of the 1980s, it has not freed adolescents of the 1980s to have happier lives.

Adult Reactions to Adolescents

Inasmuch as adolescents are sexually anxious and fluctuate in mood, they inevitably induce intense and perplexed reactions in their parents and other adults. Psychoanalyst Edith Jacobson gives an example of a parent's consternation in weathering the stormy changes of an adolescent girl: "Last summer I was told by the mother of an attractive, lively, intelligent girl of seventeen, "nothing but poetry existed for June. During the winter her only interests were dancing, flirtations, and boys. This summer she has spent sitting alone on the rocks, gazing dreamily at the ocean.' " (Jacobson, 1961, p. 162).

In a poll of teachers, more than 80 percent of them subscribed to the opinion that adolescence was a phase of "great emotional disturbance," and more than half of them believed that the child at this time underwent a complete personality change (Denny, Feldhause, and Condon, 1965).

Many psychotherapists have contended that adolescents should not be seen in treatment because of their volatility, undependability, and proclivity to act out and drop out. Anna Freud (1958) says that treatment of an adolescent "is like running next to an express train." The psychoanalyst Geleerd (1957) likened adolescence to "an active volcanic process with continuous eruptions taking place, preventing the crust from solidifying." Of course, as Anthony (1975) has pointed out, once therapists think they have to deal with a bomb that might explode or a volcano that might erupt or an express train that will outpass them, they will approach the treatment with very mixed feelings.

Although most adults agree that the adolescent is a difficult person to reach and teach and although they offer many valid reasons to account for teenage inaccessibility and undependability, few acknowledge that the teenager is sexually attractive to them. Frequently, the degree of sexual stimulation that is induced in a father by his teenage daughter or in a mother by her teenage son can be so anxiety-provoking that the parent has to try to obliterate his or her sexual feelings by avoiding the attractive daughter or attractive son. Many arguments between teenagers and their parents may be viewed as lovers' quarrels in which both parties are trying to rid themselves of their mutual sexual tension. Particularly is this true of father–son and mother–daughter fracases, in which all of the parties are trying to deny their mutual homosexual attraction. As Bell has correctly stated, "The very individual toward whom the parent was able to show overt signs of love during childhood has now become a sexually stimulating and taboo object. As a result parents must mobilize defenses to handle the anxiety provoked by their own incestuous fantasies" (Bell, 1961, pp. 276–277).

As was suggested earlier, each stage of a child's development reactivates the parent's struggles of that particular period. Not only does a parent (or teacher or therapist) have to cope with the reactivation of his or her own autoerotic, homosexual, and oedipal conflicts, but anxiety may be compounded by the contrast between the restraints of the adult's own adolescence and the permissiveness of 1980s-style morality.

When a parent's sexual impulses are aroused, they may break through into overt sexual behavior between parent and child. A weak incest barrier may crumble at this time and a spate of miscarriages and pregnancies may result. In one survey at an obstetrical hospital, it was calculated that at least one-third of the illegitimate pregnancies were the products of incestuous union, mainly with the father (Anthony, 1975). Newspaper accounts of teachers having sexual relations with teenagers are also quite plentiful.

Just as each parent responds to his or her child's developmental tasks through the lens of his or her unique history, the response to pubertal events varies from family to family. How the family reacts to the development of the young person's secondary sexual characteristics, seminal emissions, and menstrual flow is closely correlated with the extent to which sexuality has heretofore found a comfortable acceptance in the home.

Another factor accounting for the "conflict of the generations," which is not discussed too much in the literature, is the adult's envy of the adolescent's burgeoning sexuality. A mother may unconsciously resent her daughter's cute figure, frivolity, and intense excitement. A father may feel vulnerable as he observes his virile son date girls and achieve other feats which are beyond the father.

While adolescent feelings persisting in the adult can interfere in relationships with the teenager, they can sometimes lead to greater empathy and understanding, as well. Parents with a better recollection of their own adolescent tasks can use their own experiences constructively in dealing with their youngsters. Usually, when parents can identify with the teenager and are empathetic, they respond to the adolescent's problem with "a lighter touch" (Anthony, 1975). They may react with "a felt nostalgia for the youthful exuberance [and] fresh love impulses, and a sneaking adoption of the rebellion" (Miller, 1962).

In working with the parents or teachers of the teenager, it is imperative that the helping professional be able to identify and empathize with them. It is quite easy to feel impatient with a parent or teacher who is punitive about youthful masturbation or condemns adolescent sex play. It is equally difficult, at times, for the professional to identify with the prurient parent or teacher who sexually molests young people. In these situations, the practitioner must bear in mind that the adult who cannot cope with a teenager's sexuality has not resolved his or her own psychosexual tasks and needs empathetic understanding.

There is growing support for the concept that society gets the type of adolescent it expects and deserves. Based on an intensive study of teenagers, Offer and Offer (1975) conclude that the pattern of tumultuous growth, characterized by overt behavior problems in the home, in the school, and in the community, is found to be much less common than has been assumed by both behavioral and social scientists. They further contend that parents and others should be helped to rid themselves of stereotypes of the adolescent such as rebelliousness and sexual discomfort. Whether the Offers are correct or not, there is no doubt that if we expect adolescents to be too difficult to teach, reach, or treat, we will somehow achieve a self-fulfilling prophecy and fail in our dealings with them.

The Adolescent in Treatment

While there is no doubt that some of the skepticism on the part of clinicians in working with adolescents in treatment is based on their own discomforts and stereotypes, there is also no doubt that helping adolescents with sexual and interpersonal problems can be difficult. Adolescents in treatment may change from one moment to the next in attitudes, values, and feelings toward the therapist. They may get frightened of dependency on the therapist and fight hard to quit treatment before being ready to do so. Feelings toward the therapist of a heterosexual or homosexual nature may induce so much anxiety that the adolescent may have to try to provoke fights so as to avoid facing sexual components of the transference. As teenagers fight their own superego mandates, they can project them onto the therapist and experience the professional as an "uptight character." Not infrequently, teenagers project their forbidden id impulses onto the clinician; they may fear that he's "a dirty old man" (or woman) and have to flee treatment lest they be seduced.

What activates so much pessimism and discomfort for the therapist in working with adolescents on sexual conflicts is that teenagers frequently handle their anxieties through rebellion and defiance. When they feel strong oral hunger and a wish for closeness they may say to the therapist, "Who needs you?" On feeling their wishes to please the therapist—to appear well toilet-trained, so to speak—they may announce, "I resent putting out for you." When they feel homosexual stirrings, they may tell the practitioner, "You are not my type." Finally, if the therapist is of the opposite sex, the teenager may defy the therapist by saying, "You never have any effect on me. You can't help me!" All of these provocative and rebellious statements can make the therapist feel impotent.

Adolescent clients can go through long periods of silence and evasion, come late for appointments, and continually threaten to quit treatment. Due to their powerful narcissism, frequent lack of relatedness, and impeded ego functions at times, they have often reminded some clinicians of an adult schizophrenic (Spotnitz, 1961). Indeed, the original Greek term for schizophrenia, *dementia praecox*, means "the disease of adolescence."

It is the adolescent's frequent wish to establish distance between himself and the therapist by engaging in provocative behavior or social withdrawal that particularly reminds the clinician of a schizophrenic client. Often the teenager sees giving material to the practitioner as a humiliating self-revelation, which then causes a perception of the therapist as an intruder who will shake a tenuous balance.

Frequently teenagers do not come for help with their sexual and interpersonal problems on their own accord. This can make the helping process appear as a punishment and they can unconsciously make the therapist an arbitrary and punitive superego figure.

The therapist must try to keep in mind that however difficult it is for adolescents to express themselves, however rebellious and defiant they may be, their main difficulty is feeling quite helpless and wanting to be dependent while at the same time trying to prove their independence (Lorand, 1961).

Countertransference Problems

Many therapists avoid working with teenagers or have difficulty helping them with their psychosexual conflicts because these clients induce considerable anxiety in them. The therapist's discomfort is frequently similar to that of many parents. Some clinicians have to fight their own sexual feelings toward the teenager; if their own homosexual or heterosexual fantasies cause them discomfort, they may defend against them by becoming "a detached professional." This aloofness often antagonizes the adolescent, who understandably becomes aloof also.

When the teenager handles sexual anxiety by antisocial behavior like promiscuity and violence, the therapist can become frightened of the teenager's aggression and start to "set limits." This, too, can provoke the client.

Often therapists who have unresolved problems with their own parents can be too sexually stimulating, overpermissive, and indulgent, and subtly champion certain actions rather than help the young person resolve conflicts. For example, rather than helping the client better understand his or her mixed feelings about masturbation, group sex, or homosexuality, they in effect say, "Go masturbate, go have group sex, go be homosexual!" This creates anxiety and guilt in the teenager, who ends up feeling even more conflicted.

Sometimes the therapist can be in competition with the teenager's parents and join the client in rebellion. Again, this, in the end, exacerbates the teenager's conflicts and interferes with the helping process.

As is also true with many parents, practitioners can unconsciously use their teenage clients to vicariously act out what they couldn't do during their own adolescence: defy authority, have sexual orgies, and so on.

Just as life during adolescence is stormy and stressful, so treating the teenager is often stormy and stressful. The practitioner treating adolescents must be a very mature person who is honest (Dulit, 1975) without being seductive, empathetic without being seduced, and firm without being hostile or defensive.

Despite the adolescent's frequent reluctance to get help with psychosexual conflicts, treatment that bases itself on the client's maturational tasks, respects resistances, permits either closeness or distance as necessary, and offers a relationship that is corrective may succeed. The therapist and the therapeutic situation must provide concomitantly, and in nice balance, a dependable relationship and emotional freedom, security and developmental stimulation, control and an ego ideal (Blos, 1953).

Psychosexual Problems of Adolescents

The remaining part of this chapter will discuss some of the major psychosexual problems brought to the helping professional by the adolescent. Focus will be on the assessment and treatment of these problems.

Rebelliousness

Although many professionals from many disciplines have offered many valid reasons to account for adolescence as a time of rebellion, few have discussed the sexual dimension of adolescent rebellion.

When puberty is attained and sexual urges are intensified, the young person has desires to have physical contact with the opposite sex and, to some extent, with the same sex. What is not always understood is that the desire for physical contact invariably conjures up associations to earlier times when physical intimacy first began—with Mother, Father, grandparents, and others. One of the reasons that teenagers are self-conscious and anxious when they are seen necking or holding hands is because they feel, to some extent, that they are little children again and must fight the feeling of being a "sissy," a "fagot," or some other derogated figure. Very often teenagers are most sadistic toward persons who sexually attract them. To deny dependency feelings, wishes to be nurtured, and uncertainty about being a sexual person, the adolescent often attacks the person who is sexually stimulating in order to dissipate the anxiety provoked.

Many murders are committed because the attacker cannot bear experiencing the anxiety connected with sexual excitement. Some of the adolescent would-be presidential assassins, for example, confessed that they had been very attracted to the personage they had tried to kill. Here we are dealing with the terror connected with homosexual attraction, when the murderer literally does what the lyrics of a popular song suggest: "hurt the one you love." Much of the rebellious and antisocial behavior of teenagers can be viewed as a defense against intolerable homosexual wishes.

Sexual desires toward the opposite sex inevitably stir up infantile oedipal wishes. When an adolescent girl unconsciously perceives her boyfriend as a father figure or an adolescent boy experiences his girl friend as a mother figure, their anxiety and guilt over incestuous wishes can impel them to be very sadistic to their partners. This same phenomenon occurs in some of the hostile attacks on teachers and other parental figures.

Very often teenagers who run away from home or from school are trying to escape sexually stimulating situations which make them feel helpless. Many an adolescent thinks that internal sexual wishes will be tamed by changing the external environment. This hardly ever works, which may account for why many of the runaways eventually return home.

As has already been suggested, sexuality involves some dependence on another person. When the teenager has not resolved problems of "trust versus mistrust" (Erikson, 1950), dependency on a sexual partner may induce suspicion and even paranoia, so that eventually the loved object is made an enemy.

The psychosexual conflict of trust versus mistrust is frequently a powerful etiological factor in teenage delinquency. If we investigate the histories of delinquent adolescents, we frequently find that early trust or confidence has never reliably existed, and that early in life a sadomasochistic bond developed between mother and child. Through the control rather than the mastery of the environment, the child avoids tension and pain, and in order to maintain control of the environment he or she assumes an omnipotent position. The delinquent in an omnipotent state tries to prove that the environment has no power over him or her. This maneuver masks strong dependency wishes and feelings of helplessness (Blos, 1961).

Rebellious adolescents, of course, rebel against the practitioner. They fight the intimacy and dependency inherent in the therapeutic encounter and do not want to attend sessions. The therapist must avoid trying to convince the "rebel" to come for therapy. If the prospective client feels forced into treatment or seduced into it, he or she will fight harder to stay away. Therefore, the therapist, at the beginning, must not appear too eager—only interested. This attitude may help the young person eventually trust the helping person so that later he may work on his sexual problems.

Alex, age fifteen, was picked up by police authorities after he had been found truanting from school. He hated school and all that came with it—"horrible teachers, dumb kids, and dull subjects. Why the heck should I go there? There are better things to do!" he said in his first interview with his male counselor.

Alex very quickly transferred to his counselor many of the qualities of a strict school disciplinarian. "What the heck do I want to do with you? There's nothing wrong with my head, Doc! You work for the school, anyway, and you only want to get me back there. You are a headshrinker and you know it!"

Recognizing that Alex was trying to provoke him, the counselor said, "That would be a lousy way to do my job—forcing you to go to school." Alex responded, "So what the heck do you want to do with me?" The counselor said, "I don't think you want me to do anything with you, and even if I tried, you'd probably stop me." Alex tried to cover up an anxious smile and then said, "You are pretty wacky, aren't you? Are you some kind of fairy?" The counselor responded mildly, "I think you think so!" Alex giggled and exclaimed, "You must have been an interesting jerk in your day." He then speculated that the counselor was a criminal "let loose from a booby hatch" who had "never been caught." He wondered if the counselor had ever gone to college.

Alex went on to say that the conversation was "OK," but he didn't think he'd want to visit the counselor again. Then, after a long silence, he said very quietly that maybe he'd come back in three weeks if he had nothing else to do. Here the counselor asked, with a smile, "Are you sure you don't want to keep rejecting me?" Alex then went on to point out that he had nothing else to do the next week and made an appointment for the following week.

For the next several weeks Alex kept his appointments but used his interviews to "rank the counselor out." He commented in his twelfth session, "You know, I hurt you and hurt you; doesn't it ever bother you?" The counselor—realizing that Alex was projecting onto him his own defense of omnipotence, which was designed to protect him against unacceptable feelings of weakness and dependency—said, "Sometimes I'm quite capable of feeling hurt." Alex, after a long silence, laughed and then became tearful. Slowly he acknowledged some of his own feelings of hurt at times.

Alex then canceled several interviews and resumed "ranking the counselor out." By around the twentieth interview the counselor could say, "Sometimes I think you prefer to fight with me than like me. Liking me might be frightening to you." Although Alex fought the counselor's interpretation, and although he missed several more interviews, when he saw that he couldn't destroy the counselor he eventually could talk about his fears of rejection and some of his secret wishes to be loved. After about a year of counseling he could talk about masturbation and some homosexual fantasies. He also was able to tell the counselor about his strong yearnings for a father (his own father deserted the family when Alex was six).

As the counseling moved on, Alex could see for himself that his provocative and rebellious behavior served as a defense against his anxiety about homosexual wishes and strong desires to be kissed and hugged by parental figures. His treatment continued with many ups and downs, but the more he could feel comfortable with his sexual wishes, the less rebellious he became.

The above vignette illustrates some of the therapeutic principles that can be applied to work with a rebellious teenager. When Alex arrived at the counselor's office, he was ready to meet somebody who was a police officer. Because the counselor did not insist on Alex coming for counseling, Alex did not feel that he had been "arrested" and so he could try the counselor on for size, thus subtly showing his unconscious desire for help. When the counselor did not get trapped into fights, but, on the contrary, could confess that he was capable of feeling hurt, Alex was then able to identify with the counselor and confess some of his own hurts. While the therapist had to constantly monitor his own wishes to argue or be defeated, he weathered the storm and passed the test so that Alex could eventually share his sexual problems and other issues that distressed him.

It is important to emphasize the special attempt of the rebellious adolescent to fight off powerful sexual impulses. That is why he or she frequently fights the therapist, who may activate, just by his or her mere presence, these impulses; particularly this is true of sexual feelings toward the therapist.

The impulse to flee from treatment, as we saw so poignantly in Alex, is present in many adolescent clients, particularly in those who have to defend against strong dependency wishes. When desires to abandon the therapist become manifest in the treatment, it is often helpful to the client if the practitioner can resist trying to convince him or her to remain. If adolescent clients who are defending themselves against dependency feelings are told that they do not have to be in therapy, a power struggle is less apt to occur between therapist and client, since the latter does not have to fight the therapist's control with so much tenacity.

The Unmarried Mother

When an adolescent girl becomes pregnant, it often creates a dilemma not only for the young mother and her child but for the prospective father, threatening both their immediate and long-range interests (Furstenberg, 1976). While unmarried motherhood is viewed as a serious social problem because of its prevalence, most researchers acknowledge that statistics on it are not reliable. Underreporting is due to false information given by many women who have been able to make private medical and adoption arrangements; to uncertain reporting in rural areas, especially when delivery is by someone other than a licensed physician; and to the fact that many states do not record illegitimacy on birth certificates (Perlman, 1964). Estimates by the federal government point out that in the United States there are around 200,000 illegitimate births each year (Furstenberg, 1976).

Although there are many social, economic, educational, and ethnic factors associated with unwed motherhood, in this section we will focus on the psychosexual factors inherent in this problem. With the increased availability of contraception and abortion, it would appear that there would have to be some unique psychodynamic factors that impel a young teenage woman to have a baby and not choose to be married to the father.

Until fairly recently most of the researchers who have focused on the psychosexual factors in unmarried motherhood have looked to the client's conflicted relationship with her own mother. The unmarried mother has been described as being the recipient of fragmented mothering, who therefore has grown up with a narcissistic character structure; i.e., the girl is extremely preoccupied with her own infantile wishes, which she has to discharge impulsively. The baby she conceives has frequently been considered to be a narcissistic extension of herself, and her wish to mother the baby has been viewed as similar to psychologically mothering herself (Bonan, 1963; Judge, 1951; Goldsmith, 1957; Shlakman, 1966).

The treatment of choice for unmarried mothers has been an ongoing relationship with a female counselor. Often deserted by the putative father and having experienced emotional abandonment by her own mother, the client allegedly needs "a motherly person who will serve as a refuge during a time of stress" (Blos, 1961, pp. 27–28). A woman counselor, it has been concluded, can most appropriately serve as a healthy object for identification, making it possible for the client to accept herself as a woman (Lifschutz, Stewart, and Harrison, 1958).

Additional research in the past two decades has enlarged the diagnostic picture and treatment planning for the unmarried mother (Strean, 1970; Guttmacher, 1981). More often than not, the client is not only caught in the web of an ambivalent, cold mother–daughter relationship, but frequently she has been a pawn in a tempestuous marital relationship. More than occasionally, her birth has stimulated much rivalry between her parents, with the mother clinging to her and the father behaving quite seductively. It is frequently the father's seductiveness that has overstimulated her immature ego and aroused powerful sexual fantasies with which she has found it extremely difficult to cope. As a result, it is not uncommon to find in the histories of unmarried mothers strong prudishness, puritanical attitudes, and other forms of defensiveness (Bonan, 1963).

As the power struggle between the girl's parents intensifies and she attempts to deal with her divided loyalties, identifying for a time with her mother and then for a while with her father, the potential unmarried mother gradually finds it more and more difficult to achieve a stable identity for herself. She is never quite certain whether she is male or female, and is almost incessantly flirting with each possibility. As adolescence approaches and the need to prove herself assumes much importance, sexual promiscuity becomes one avenue by which to reassure herself of her tenuous femininity (Blos, 1961).

Quite frequently the girl's parents have separated or divorced, with the father usually being the one who has left the home. His absence usually activates for the client intense oedipal conflicts and incestuous longings, but because of her recognition of her mother's deep anger toward her husband, the young girl has to repress and suppress her attachment to her father. Furthermore, she cannot discuss her distress with her mother because of the latter's bias.

Perhaps being left alone with a mother who the young girl feels has deprived her of a father may account for what has been referred to as a "pathological and ambivalent mother-daughter relationship" (Judge, 1951). Possibly it is the father's withdrawal that may arouse in the client the self-image of being ugly, "deprived and depraved" (Judge, 1951)—"deprived" not only of a mother's love, but of contact with a father; "depraved" not only because of a poor maternal object with whom to identify, but because she has been overwhelmed by sexual fantasies toward her absent father. The psychiatrist Schmideberg (1951) has pointed out that many girls become promiscuous during wartime because their fathers are away.

The absence of the father altogether or the presence of a father who deprives his daughter of the satisfaction of being a girl (and not just a sexual object) seems to be correlated with the highest incidence of unmarried motherhood, namely, among lower-socioeconomic-level black families. The girl during the course of her development has usually had some relationships with older men that have frequently been tantalizing, but the consistent unavailability of a mature father figure is ubiquitous. While the host of economic and social variables inherent in the black constellation should not or cannot be minimized, it is nonetheless a virtual truism that unmarried motherhood is prevalent in circumstances in which the father is unavailable (Strean, 1970).

Although the importance of the father in a girl's psychosexual development has in general been relatively undefined and the effects of paternal deprivation largely unspecified, we are beginning to become sensitized to the uniquely paternal contributions necessary for a girl's development. As Forrest (1966) has pointed out, for a female to be fulfilled as a person and a woman, the father's presence from infancy through childhood, girlhood, and adolescence aids and abets psychological growth.

Experimentation with a treatment approach based on the aforementioned notions that involves help from a male and a female therapist has proven quite successful (Strean, 1970). The opportunity to work with both a man and a woman offers the client the opportune situation of which she has been deprived. A nonseductive male and a mother figure who is genuinely concerned about the client can enhance the latter's self-image, can mobilize previously untapped ego functions, and can frequently enable the client to reflect genuinely on herself and her interaction with her environment.

This triadic relationship continues after the birth of the infant and as long as the client needs it. In addition, if the girl's father or mother, or the baby's father, can be part of the treatment plan, the client will not feel so alone but will be able to enjoy the attention for which she deeply yearns. The rationale for treatment with both a male and a female worker is explained to the client: "We want you to have the opportunity to experience a man and woman working together in your behalf."

Barbara, a young black woman of twenty-one, had five illegitimate pregnancies. Living in a housing project and on welfare, she was frequently drunk and depressed, and managed her home and children with limited care and discipline. The management of the project sent a woman case aide to "see what could be done" before processing an eviction.

The caseworker found Barbara's house extremely untidy, her children poorly cared for, and Barbara in the third month of her sixth pregnancy. The case aide told Barbara that the management of the project had suggested she be seen, but before the worker could finish her opening remarks the client bellowed, "Oh, they want to throw me out because they don't like the way I keep the house!" The worker looked around and said calmly, "I'm sure things are very difficult for you. You must have it very rough." The client spent the next half-hour talking about what a burden her children were to her and how difficult it was to meet their physical needs and make ends meet financially; the only pleasure she got once in a while was "a little sex and a little drink." The worker remarked that she could understand how sex and drinking could be her only pleasures but wondered if there was anything that she, the worker, could do to bring her some pleasure. Barbara pointed to the children's clothes and her poor furniture, and mentioned that she had limited time for herself. The worker immediately responded, "I'll get in touch with a few places and people and see what can be done."

The worker did get in touch with the department of welfare and other agencies in the community in order to supply Barbara with some of the tangibles she requested. Therefore, with some physical needs met—clothes for the children and mother, mattresses and beds, and a volunteer for some baby-sitting—the client began, in her second interview, to talk about her current pregnancy and previous ones as well. She said that she knew "damn well that I don't appeal to men" and that all of her sexual affairs turned out to be one-night stands. When the worker took note of the client's feelings of depreciation vis-à-vis men, and said, "You think that the only reason men would have anything to do with you is to go to bed, don't you?" Barbara tearfully reported how she remembered as a little girl wishing that a boyfriend of her mother's who intermittently visited the house "could be my father." She then spent some time talking about her wish for a father who "would have really cared about me," but said that her mother "just didn't meet up with a good man to live with."

As Barbara continued to talk about her feelings of deprivation in her heterosexual relationships, the worker gradually introduced the subject of a male worker, who was part of the same social service department of the housing project. Barbara did not ask for any explanation of the entrance of the male worker into the situation but seemed to sense the rationale behind the introduction and merely said, "Great!"

In contrast to the manner in which Barbara usually cared for the house, the male worker at his first interview found it to be extremely tidy, and the children and Barbara well groomed. This held true at subsequent visits. While Barbara continued to see the female worker about plans for the baby and dealt with the situation quite responsibly, with the male worker she talked about the possibility of getting a job, which he encouraged. Through his effort, Barbara took a job in the post office; she did excellent work there (enough to receive part of a maternity leave with pay) and talked with both of her case aides about the new "but different" men in her life "who seem to respect me."

While a case situation like Barbara's requires long and intensive effort, the effort appears to meet several of the maturational deficits of the client and helps to enhance her psychosocial development.

Sexualization as a Defense

As the reader is now no doubt aware, helping individuals resolve their psychosexual problems is a complex task. In many problems, such as adolescent rebellion, the sexual conflicts are not immediately visible, and it is only by patiently unraveling the client's history, transference problems, and other variables that we can clearly see the sexual dimensions of the situation. In other conflicts, such as unmarried motherhood, where the unresolved sexual problems are more apparent, we still have to carefully expose the complex gestalt of the client's past, her ego functions, and other variables. This effort is also necessary when we meet a teenager who on first blush seems to feel comfortable with his or her sexuality. Here we are referring to the young person who seems to be able to relate to the opposite sex with ease.

He or she welcomes sexual pleasure, is usually uninhibited in initiating sex, and can be equally free when he or she is not the initiator. Moreover, this client can usually discuss sexuality quite easily with the adult professional.

As has been constantly reiterated, one of the main reasons that the dynamically oriented practitioner cannot rely on behavior alone when assessing a client is because the content of sexual behavior by itself does not reveal very much. Although there are, of course, children, adolescents, and adults who are comfortable with their sexuality, there are many individuals who seem to have a "good" sexual life but are nonetheless in conflict. Later chapters on adult pyschosexuality will discuss some of these individuals.

In this section we will consider the adolescent who utilizes sexuality as a defense. This is the adolescent who may have an active and enjoyable sexual life but cannot easily assert himself or herself. Although sexually active, the teenager may be very passive in school or at work. Furthermore, when this young person is not engaged in sex, he or she may become restless or depressed. Often such a teenager, like the unmarried mother, suffers from separation anxiety and may need the closeness of another person's body to feel alive. This teenager may be the Don Juan who can only like himself if he is "scoring" or the promiscuous girl who can only appreciate herself if she is giving and getting sexual satisfaction.

Of course, these teenagers do not come to the practitioner for assistance with their sexual problems. They are referred because they are not doing well in school or on the job; they may be recluses at home, or perhaps some sensitive adult has noted their subtle and underlying depression.

What the worker with adolescents must be alert to is that sexuality can cover up intolerable feelings of anger, depression, separation anxiety, weak self-image, or weak body-image. When the professional recognizes that the client is utilizing sex compulsively, sexual expression is probably serving as a defense against anxiety. It often takes a while for the practitioner to discover this, because the teenager sees his or her sexual life as something that is "OK" and does not wish to recognize its compulsive nature and defensive purpose.

Charlie, age sixteen, was referred to his school guidance counselor because he did not seem to be able to concentrate in class, was getting poor grades, and often was involved in fantasy. He was described as restless and easily irritated.

He was an only child whose parents had separated when he was eight years old. He had contact with his father on weekends and he described both of his parents as "warm, caring people." Charlie did not have close relationships with any male friends but he did "like to ball with girls."

In his relationship with his male counselor he was very tentative, did not speak very much, and frequently came late for his appointments; at times he "forgot" that he had an appointment.

Since Charlie's counselor took note of the client's resistance to him and wondered what Charlie didn't like about coming to see him, Charlie at first was quite protective of the counselor and told him that he was a "nice guy." Further exploration in subsequent interviews yielded the information that coming to see the guidance counselor was experienced by Charlie as similar to a visit with his father on weekends, and this "wasn't bad."

As Charlie discussed his weekend visits with his father in his sessions, a great deal of ambivalence toward the father emerged. On one hand, he was very angry at his father for not being more available to him, and on the other hand, he enjoyed being "alone together" with his father. As the counselor focused more intensively with Charlie on his feelings toward Father, many sexual fantasies eventually were exposed. Charlie wanted to be rocked, petted, and hugged by his father—in effect, he wanted to be his father's lover. His anger toward Father was really that of a scorned lover.

Charlie slowly began to realize that part of his compulsive interest in sex with girls was a defense against feeling his anger and sexual interest toward Father. With regard to girls he could "find them, feel them, fuck them, and forget them" much the way he unconsciously felt his father was treating him. These same conflicts with Father were later experienced in his transference relationship with his counselor, who, he felt, was also "using me."

As treatment moved on, Charlie also began to realize that he wanted to "hurt my mother" sexually because she "deprived me of a father." Actually, Charlie began to become aware of the fact that he was angry at both of his parents because they deprived him of each other. As he got more in touch with his feelings of anger, depression, and separation anxiety, Charlie's sadistic and compulsive sexual activity with girls lessened, and he started "to like them" and became "more friendly" with them.

Although sexual pleasure may be regarded unquestionably as a constructive form of pleasure and a basic directing force of mental life, it can also serve as a defense and obscure anxieties and terrors that are not always visible to the client or the practitioner (Coen, 1981). This is particularly true among many adolescent clients.

Celibacy

Just as sex can serve defensive functions, the absence of sexual interest can be a protective device. With the advent of puberty and the recrudescence of many infantile sexual wishes, the adolescent may cope with the onslaught of primitive desires by denying their existence. In the 1980s, an "age of sensation" (Hendin, 1975), many teenagers have to work overtime to deny their sexuality because they are burdened by excessive stimulation which arouses considerable guilt.

Growing up always implies some effort at renunciation of sexual impulses. When children are weaned they have to forego some oral pleasures; when they are toilet trained certain anal and urethral desires must be curbed; the family romance also necessitates further impulse control, and latency also has its frustrations. When adolescence arrives with its resurgence of oral, anal, and oedipal wishes, teenagers can feel so overwhelmed and guilty that they pretend that sexuality, as a dimension of life, does not exist.

Celibate teenagers may turn to a rigid religious life in which "desires of the flesh" are repudiated. They may embrace a philosophical perspective which denounces sexual pleasure or become anti-vice crusaders and expose those who "give in" to their sexual desires.

What is sometimes overlooked in working with the adolescent (or adult) who repudiates sexuality is that the very act of crusading against sex involves a preoccupation with it. The teenager who gossips about peers' sexual overactivity has to think about the sexual activity itself while involved in tirades against it. The anti-vice crusader has to gather pornographic material in order to frown upon it, and the religious philosopher has to read and think about sexuality to formulate arguments against it. Celibates, in reality, are "protesting too much." Often the very issue that they damn is one that unconsciously very much interests them, and by denouncing it to others they are renouncing it in themselves. As they protest against rape and other forms of sexual violence, as they are contemptuous of gays, prostitutes, lesbians, fetishists, and others, they are really curbing these proclivities in themselves.

Celibate teenagers who campaign against sexuality usually reveal their anxiety about it when they seek professional help. The practitioner inevitably finds that these teenagers are suffering from neurotic symptoms such as insomnia, nightmares, and anxiety attacks. Often they are in an agitated state trying to subdue intense anger or depression. They may have difficulty with their peers or with adults.

Dorothy, age nineteen, referred herself to a college mental health clinic. Her presenting problem was her inability to cope with her anger at her psychology professor, who seemed "obsessed with sex" and "too influenced by Freudian principles." In an articulate but overly intellectual presentation, she told the social worker that she did not know whether to drop the course or report the professor to the dean's office for "corrupting the innocent minds of college students."

In her first twelve interviews, Dorothy did not let her female social worker get in a word. She turned the sessions into forty-five-minute lectures and blasted professors, students, politicians, and the theater for not having mature attitudes. "They are obsessed with sex and should be eliminated," she stated with much conviction. Although the social worker felt irritated and impotent as she worked with Dorothy, she realized that unconsciously Dorothy was trying to put her in the same powerless, ineffectual position that she, Dorothy, felt in the face of sexuality.

In Dorothy's fifteenth interview she asked the social worker, "What do you think of all my attitudes?" The social worker, sensing that she was being tested, asked Dorothy, "What are you feeling when you ask me that question?" Dorothy, feeling frustrated, told the social worker that she was the same as all those "imperious, arbitrary people in authority who don't like to take responsibility for their own shortcomings." The social worker, feeling that the client's statement was a projection of Dorothy's own self-image, asked Dorothy what responsibilities she thought the worker was abdicating. Dorothy then spent several more interviews lecturing about how "you don't have to face your contemptuous attitudes, your wishes to dominate people, and your unwillingness to be soft and flexible."

After six more months of treatment in which Dorothy kept castigating the worker, with the latter being nondefensive, quiet, and interested, Dorothy finally allowed herself to be a little self-revealing. She haltingly reported, "Sometimes I feel there's no other way to get along other than to argue." When the social worker asked for more associations, Dorothy talked about fears of being submissive, weak, and powerless if she was involved in a relationship. Slowly she began to face the fact that any form of relationship was one in which she felt she was being "used." This was particularly true of a sexual relationship.

While Dorothy superficially faced her weak self-image and stated that "all women are second-class citizens if they have sex," when her competition with men and her envy of their sexuality became an issue in the treatment she prematurely broke treatment off, feeling that she had gotten all she wanted. The therapist tried to show Dorothy that once more she was arranging a power struggle, but her need to weaken the therapist was powerful and she insisted on leaving.

When helping professionals work with adolescents, they have to face the fact that a group of them feel so vulnerable in relation to the therapist that they are often compelled to defeat the therapist by leaving treatment. This "dropout" phenomenon often occurs after the adolescent has realistically been helped. Like Dorothy, dropouts have to repudiate the therapist's strength. Feeling powerless themselves and potential victims of psychological rape, they have to eradicate the therapist before he does so to them.

Transient Homosexuality

In the process of growing up, every child develops sexual feelings indiscriminately, and a certain amount of sexual feeling toward one's own sex remains in everyone. In certain situations where there are no members of the opposite sex, such as in some reformatories, camps, or schools, individuals who have been heterosexual turn toward homosexual relationships. This is what Fenichel (1945) has referred to as "accidental homosexuality," and it tends to prove that latently every individual is capable of a homosexual object choice.

Although the subject of homosexuality will be discussed in more detail in a later chapter, it is important to consider transient homosexuality in adolescence at this time.

When teenagers are confronted with their burgeoning sexuality, they inevitably reexperience strong oedipal wishes. If their competition with parental figures of the same sex creates anxiety and their erotic feelings toward the parent of the opposite sex stir up guilt, one means of coping with their frightening heterosexual wishes is to regress and submit to members of the same sex. When a boy feels in jeopardy from his father or a girl feels that her sexuality threatens her mother, the fear of retaliation and/or loss of love makes homosexuality a safer position.

Often those teenagers who have experienced parents and other adults of the opposite sex as rejecting, react by rejecting their own sexual wishes toward the opposite sex, and instead turn toward members of the same sex and develop what is known as an "adolescent crush." In this type of romance the teenager is also identifying with someone who appears bigger and better than himself or herself, and is using the other person for security and nurturance.

Because the wish to turn toward homosexuality during adolescence is close to a universal phenomenon, a frequent visitor to the practitioner is the adolescent who is terrified that he or she "is going to become a homosexual." This terror often emerges in the army or in institutions which are not coeducational. Often the fearful client can profit from short-term treatment which provides reassurance that the urges in question are typical and not the same as actions.

Eli, age nineteen, referred himself to a mental health consultation service of an army installation. In his initial interview with a male social work officer, he said that he did not think he could stay in the army because "I am a homosexual." Investigation revealed that with the exception of some limited homosexual play at twelve and thirteen years of age, Eli had no homosexual contacts. As a matter of fact, he described a very happy life with girls in high school, and in addition he looked at his relationship with his parents and siblings as satisfying.

As Eli talked some more about his life in his home town, it was very clear that he was homesick, i.e., he missed his girl friend, parents, siblings, and friends a great deal. When the social worker took note of how sad Eli appeared, he began to weep and confessed how much he wished he were back home, but he felt that this was "sissified" and that he must fight his yearnings. When the social worker informed Eli that there wasn't a man on the army post who didn't miss home, Eli visibly relaxed, voicing his anger about being drafted into the army and his strong wish to be back at his old job.

In Eli's second and third interviews, he reported that his obsession with homosexuality had diminished, but he couldn't understand how it got started in the first place. As he talked some more about having to "fight my homesickness and adjust to the army," the social worker was able to explain to him how in fighting his wishes to hug and kiss his parents, his girl friend, and others whom he cared for he was turning to his army buddies for emotional support and then hating himself for wanting to use them for a family. Once more Eli welcomed the social worker's understanding and said he was feeling "less like a queer" because the worker had made it clear that "when you don't have your girl friend, you turn to whoever is around."

While there were certainly many aspects of Eli's preoccupation with homosexuality that were not explored—i.e., his fear of being an adult man, his strong dependency wishes for a mother figure, and his somewhat passive demeanor—he was able after six interviews to function quite well in the army. Follow-up interviews revealed that his therapeutic gains sustained themselves.

One of the reasons that a client like Eli could utilize short-term treatment successfully was because he was a very trusting individual who could very much enjoy his contact with the social worker. A somewhat passive and dependent young man who did not defend himself too much against his passivity and dependency, he could easily depend on the social worker and use him as a source of strength and nurturance, i.e., use him as a good mother and father figure. Finally, Eli had many ego strengths and limited neurotic conflicts. Consequently, he could easily move back into a state of good adaptability because a relatively healthy adaptation was something with which he was consistently comfortable and familiar.

Paranoia

Adolescence is a period of extreme self-consciousness. As the teenager experiences new and at times uncomfortable sexual sensations, as he copes with intense sexual fantasies which he may think are peculiar or even crazy, and as he tries to adapt to a new body image, he often projects his feelings of craziness, vulnerability, and peculiarity onto others and feels that they are "looking at me as if something is wrong with me." Particularly if the teenager is entertaining homosexual fantasies which he thinks are very shameful and should be hidden, he may worry about being found out and then become most suspicious of others who might criticize him at any moment.

It is the forbidden sexual urges which the adolescent feels are punishable that move him toward a paranoid state, a state in which he feels people are out to mock him and exploit him (Meissner, 1978; Anthony, 1981). If he believes his movements, voice, sexual fantasies, or thoughts are subject to disapproval, he will be ready to be pounced upon for whatever *he personally cannot sanction*.

As with any other dysfunctional adaptation during the teenage years, paranoia does not just appear on the scene with the onset of adolescence—it has its roots in the young person's formative years. Often paranoid teenagers are those who as children felt that their dependency wishes were forbidden, and they have been on guard for years lest anybody accuse them of needing somebody too much. Usually such teenagers have felt that play of any kind, particularly masturbation, is taboo, and they have had to be hardworking people lest they be accused of frivolousness. Most often, paranoid adolescents have felt very guilty about any form of pleasure; many of their oral, anal, and phallic-oedipal wishes create anxiety and need to be defended.

What has already been implied is the punitiveness of the paranoid adolescent's superego. He is forever feeling that his impulses, thoughts, and actions are terrible, and he projects his superego sanctions onto others, who, he feels, are always ready to judge him malevolently.

In working therapeutically with this type of teenager, there are usually many difficulties and it is easy for the therapist to fall into one of two traps. Sometimes the reports of paranoid adolescents sound so convincing that it is not difficult to genuinely believe that their environment is indeed a persecutory one. On the other hand, because these clients can be formidable injustice collectors (Bergler, 1969), the practitioner can ascribe all their difficulties to their internal state and ignore their reports regarding their external life. It is important to recognize in work with any client—child, adolescent, or adult—that the environment is always impinging on the client, whose communications are almost always a mixture of everyday fact and internal fantasy (Anthony, 1981). As Anna Freud has said: "The [therapist] who interprets exclusively in terms of the inner world is in danger of missing out on his [client's] reporting activity concerning his—at the time equally important—environmental circumstances" (1965, p. 51).

As was suggested in the early part of this chapter on the treatment of the adolescent, most adolescents tend to be suspicious of the therapist, who is seen as a potential disrupter of a tenuous balance. The paranoid adolescent, sensitive to his inner turmoil, is "fearful that the 'shrink' will confirm his own worst fears and deem him crazy" (Anthony, 1981, p. 746). Consequently the client will frequently try to avoid the therapist, evade introspection, and sabotage the treatment.

Flora, age eighteen, was referred to treatment for academic difficulties in college. She immediately tried to provoke her woman therapist into an argument by pointing out that she was being scapegoated by her peers and professors. The college that she was attending had been, for many years, a men's college, and Flora felt that "everybody is feeling uncomfortable about having women around." As her therapist listened to Flora's complaints she did think that there was some reality to her client's perceptions but concomitantly noted that Flora seemed to delight in just complaining. "They watch me for my every word and are ready to disagree with me," she stated repeatedly and with much conviction. She also asserted, "They think that women are just people to screw and don't have brains."

As Flora's history unfolded, it turned out that she was the only girl in a family in which she had three brothers. Interestingly, while describing the fact that she also felt scapegoated at home, she remarked, "You'd probably say that I'm repeating my past here at college, but that's baloney." Flora ascribed other "stupid" interpretations to the therapist which the latter felt had a great deal of validity. For example, in one interview Flora suggested, "You think my problem is hostility and competition with men but that's your problem working in a male college. You project a lot of your difficulties onto me."

Although the therapist was frequently tempted to point out to Flora her defense of projection, she knew that the client would experience this as an attack and eventually flee from the treatment. Consequently she continued to listen to Flora's accusations, criticisms, and "diagnostic assessments" of the therapist with interest and compassion. After about four months of treatment, Flora reported a dream in which she made the therapist a lesbian with a penis who was trying to seduce her. Flora said the dream "confirmed my doubts about you. You'd rather be a man with a penis because you don't accept your femininity." Again the therapist offered no interpretation of Flora's unconscious homosexual attraction toward her, but listened some more. As Flora saw that the therapist did not criticize, judge, or feel defensive about Flora's proclamations, the treatment situation became less threatening to her. Slowly she could consider some of her own jealousy of boys, her own wish for a penis, and her own devaluation of her vagina.

The more Flora could tolerate her own homosexuality, the less paranoid she became, and the less paranoid she was, the more others responded to her positively.

Paranoid teenagers are very frequent visitors to the helping professional. They can tax the patience of the helping person because they are so self-righteous in their complaints, take no responsibility for themselves, and want others to suffer since they are contemptuous of them. It is important to recognize that like Flora in the above vignette, these clients are tortured by unacceptable wishes, feel powerless and helpless, and often need quiet understanding for long periods of time.

Educational Difficulties

One common adolescent maladjustment is difficulty coping with the educational requirements of school. Here we are referring to teenagers who are inattentive in the classroom, often daydreaming or annoying their peers. Usually they neglect their homework, forgetting to bring home the proper books. Before they sit down to study they usually have many pursuits to take care of first: TV programs to watch, friends to call, or magazines to read.

When parents or teachers confront such teenagers about neglect of schoolwork, they usually become annoyed and blame their difficulties on poor teachers, disagreeable classmates, or unchallenging curricula. Occasionally they want to go to a different school, or get a different program or different teachers. If environmental changes are effected, after a short spurt of activity these young persons return to their former state.

Passage of time rarely improves the difficulty, and rarely do parents' or teachers' admonitions motivate these teenagers to study. What is all too frequently overlooked by parents and teachers of adolescents who are having educational difficulties are their inner conflicts, particularly sexual conflicts.

Many adolescents who have been good students in grammar school inhibit their ambition and motivation when they enter junior high school or high school. As their sexual loves resurge and particularly as their oedipal fantasies are revived, they become frightened of their aggressiveness and assertiveness. In order to succeed in learning, the student must be an active person. When activity conjures up unacceptable hostile fantasies toward the parent of the same sex, the activity is suspended because the teenager feels too guilty to continue it. Many educational problems of teenagers, like learning problems of children, are really sexual problems. Educational success is experienced unconsciously as sexual success, and this sexual success cannot be permitted by teenagers who feel too guilty and shameful about hostile, competitive wishes toward the parent of the same sex and incestuous wishes toward the parent of the opposite sex.

One of the "best" ways that the adolescent can cope with unacceptable sexual and aggressive wishes is to avoid them. By not studying or achieving, the young person is unconsciously saying, "I'm no competitor; I'm a nonthreatening failure." Activity is turned into passivity and the teenager's ambitiousness is repressed (English and Pearson, 1945).

Often a teenager's prior success in school has brought him or her close to the parent of the opposite sex. If a mother has lauded her son for his educational achievements or a father has shown his pleasure when his daughter has succeeded at school, the teenager may stop doing well at school because the closeness creates too much sexual anxiety. To avoid having sexual feelings toward the loving parent of the opposite sex, the teenager can do things which will displease the parent. The same phenomenon can occur with regard to homosexual feelings toward the parent of the same sex.

When sexual wishes are rigorously defended against, this saps the teenager's energy, for the energy that could be used in learning is utilized in warding off dangerous sexual stimulation. Also, as with many younger children, the adolescent can associate curiosity in general with sexual curiosity, and to avoid experiencing the anxiety that sexual curiosity can stir up he or she stops utilizing energy to satisfy the desire to learn.

Teenagers who must squelch assertiveness lest they become destructive come into the therapeutic situation very passively. They usually have "nothing much to talk about," and of course resist learning about themselves in therapy. Consciously, they are not aware of their conflict—they only know that they don't feel motivated for therapy and that they have limited curiosity about themselves or what is around them.

George, age fifteen, had done very well in school until his sophomore year of high school. Formerly an enthusiastic student, he became depressed and argumentative, and once a curious, attentive young man, he turned into a compulsive daydreamer. On being referred to his school guidance counselor because his grades had dropped and his attitude had changed drastically, George seemed superficially compliant and said, "I guess something is going wrong." However, when he was asked what he supposed was going wrong he could not elaborate any further, and he spent much of the interview in silence.

While George cooperated in subsequent interviews in giving his history and describing his family, he remained very detached from the interviewer and very far away from his own feelings. When the guidance counselor suggested that George seemed to feel toward school the same way he did in his interviews with him—disinterested—George mildly protested and said he was interested in "doing what I'm supposed to do." However, he then retreated into silence again and refused to say anything further.

In one interview after many unproductive ones, George began to eye a set of checkers in the counselor's office. When the counselor asked George if he had some interest in playing checkers with him, George first denied it. The counselor said, "I think you'd like to play checkers, but you don't feel comfortable in saying so," and George replied, "I'll play if you want me to play." When the counselor reiterated that George seemed more concerned about pleasing him than deciding to do what he wanted, George said with some irritation, "OK, I'll play checkers!"

In the games George was again lethargic and passive, and he showed a strong fear of winning. When he was anywhere near moving ahead of his counselor, he retreated. It became obvious that he feared competition and was extremely frightened of surpassing his counselor. On having this interpreted to him, George denied the interpretation, but, interestingly, talked about always losing in competitive games with his older brother and father. This was also true in competitive games with peers.

George could eventually reveal to the counselor that he felt more comfortable "being a loser" because he wouldn't antagonize anybody that way. As he voiced more fears of his aggression in sports and in interpersonal relationships away from school, the counselor could eventually show him that he was frightened to succeed in school because he was worried that he might antagonize other people. George could then reveal that his father had never graduated from high school but "only went as far as the tenth grade—the grade I'm in now" and that his brother was "never a good student." He also mentioned in passing that his mother, until this year, had referred to George as "the smart one" compared to his brother and father.

George's oedipal problem was quite apparent. He was frightened of surpassing his father (and his brother) and had to stop achieving in his sophomore year, the year his father dropped out of school. Furthermore, to do well in his courses at school would endear him too much to his mother, and this petrified him.

As George became able to feel safer with his counselor, he eventually faced his wishes to vanquish his father, his brother, and the counselor and to be his "mother's one and only," and he realized that he did not have to be a loser in his courses at school. As he saw that his success did not kill or destroy anyone, he became less fearful of achieving and improved in his work and in his interpersonal relationships.

Educational problems, as mentioned, are very common during the teenage years. Adolescents, unknown to parents, teachers, and others, are often frightened to succeed. Failures are devices that protect them against facing their desires to assert themselves sexually and interpersonally. Sometimes nothing short of psychotherapy can resolve adolescent educational problems.

Masturbatory Conflicts

There have been recurrent swings of the social and psychological pendulum between suppressing and encouraging masturbatory behavior. At one time it was felt among clinicians that neurasthenia resulted from masturbatory activity, and some laypersons still believe that masturbation can cause everything from pimples and warts to schizophrenia and brain damage.

It is now accepted as a truism that the act of masturbation in and of itself can hurt no one. It has even been recognized that masturbation can prepare the adolescent for enjoyable sex relations later, and that inhibition of masturbation can lead to later inhibitions in intellectual pursuits and in work.

Masturbation is of interest to the helping professional when it is linked to other conflicts. For example, there are many teenagers who cannot cope with huge quantities of rage. Fearing a loss of control of their hostile impulses, they can eroticize their aggression—i.e., utilize sex as a defense—and masturbate. Masturbation, when invested with much aggressive energy, may become compulsive because of the insatiability of the aggressive drive (Marcus and Francis, 1975). It is usually when sadistic fantasies accompany masturbation that the adolescent feels "dirty" and guilty.

Also, many of the fantasies that accompany masturbation are derivatives of oedipal wishes. How conflicted and guilty the adolescent is about oedipal conflicts will in many ways determine how conflicted and guilty he or she will feel about masturbation.

Masturbation is also of interest to the clinician when it is an expression of conflicts related to sexual identity. For example, if an adolescent boy suffers from castration anxiety and wonders how much of a male he is, masturbation can provide some reassurance to him that indeed he has a penis. Similarly, if a girl has doubts about her femininity, masturbation can assure her that her vagina is still intact.

Often masturbation can serve to ward off anxiety about unacceptable homosexual wishes. The adolescent, on feeling a dread of his or her homosexual desires, masturbates and has fantasies of having sex with a member of the opposite sex, thus gaining the reassurance of being a heterosexual person.

As with any other behavior, masturbation can be seen as healthy or neurotic. It can prepare the adolescent for later sexual activity but it can also be an expression of identity conflicts, castration anxiety, and anxiety about homosexuality (Harley, 1961). It is when the adolescent is in conflict about his or her masturbation that he or she seeks out the helping professional.

Hazel, age seventeen, was a freshman in college who referred herself to a mental hygiene clinic. After spending a few interviews being vague, evasive, and embarrassed, she finally brought out what made her seek help in the first place.

Since she started college three months ago, she had been masturbating four and five times a day. As a result, she felt she was a "pervert" who was having more gratification making love to herself than with others.

After Hazel made her "confessional," she began to discuss the problems that precipitated her compulsive masturbation. In contrast to being a very popular girl at home, she felt close to no one at college. Her yearning for her hometown boyfriends and girl friends was not finding any outlet in her present circumstances, so she was using masturbation as her only solace. Because she was having very few dates at college, which was in marked contrast to her experience at home, she began to question her physical and personal attractiveness. Masturbation gave her some reassurance that she was a woman with sexual feelings.

As Hazel discussed her conflicts with her male therapist, she was at first direct and warm but then began to retreat and became evasive and inhibited. Exploration eventually revealed that she was inhibiting her sexual fantasies about her male therapist. When the therapist suggested that this seemed to be what she was doing with people on campus—peers and instructors—she acknowledged the truth of this interpretation and began to see that all of her life she had inhibited her sexual wishes. She could only allow them to be a valid dimension of her life if another person initiated the contact. This insight helped her immeasurably. Although there were other characterological conflicts that went unexpressed, she was able to feel much more liberated after just four months of treatment. She dated more and pursued her work with more enthusiasm, and her compulsive masturbation diminished a great deal. Apparently she experienced the therapist as giving her permission to initiate contacts and not wait to be asked.

It is important to again emphasize that the teenager's degree of conflict about masturbation, and the pathology or health the masturbation expresses, can only be derived by an understanding of the client's history, use of ego functions, superego mandates, and reactions to the therapist.

Drug Use

This past decade has witnessed an epidemic of drug use. In one recent survey (DeLuccia, 1981) it was estimated that in one fairly typical state, New Jersey, nine of every ten high school students used alcohol at some time and approximately two-thirds of them used drugs. It is estimated that approximately one out of every twenty teenagers in the United States is a drug addict.

Drugs may be used in a variety of ways—as a transient or recurrent phenomenon; they may be taken in secret or their use may be flaunted (Wieder and Kaplan, 1969). Psychological investigation of the use of drug addiction "begins with the recognition of the fact that not the toxic agent, but the impulse to use it, makes an addict" (Rado, 1933, p. 2).

While many social and psychological factors have been utilized to account for the use of drugs among adolescents (Brill, 1981), limited attention has been given to the sexual dimension.

Very often drugs are a substitute for sex. When sexual wishes are strong but the teenager is afraid of the intimacy and excitement in a relationship, he or she may get "high" on some drug. Very often the tension that precedes taking a drug and the temporary relief that follows can be experienced as a sexual equivalent.

Usually those teenagers who start drugs in adolescence have had a great deal of difficulty in their earlier psychosexual development. Often they are individuals who have been poorly mothered and therefore are quite distrustful. While their sexual appetites are increasing in adolescence, their suspiciousness of people makes them turn to drugs to feed themselves. It is interesting that in the argot of the addict the supplier is often called "Mother" and the supplies have been dubbed "mood food."

Inasmuch as adolescence recapitulates the earlier psychosexual stages, the less psychosexually mature adolescent begins to feel very weak and strong passive wishes come to the fore. Taking drugs is an attempt to surmount unacceptable passive wishes and feelings of vulnerability. While on a high the drug user can feel like a sexual superman or wonderwoman, omnipotently controlling the world (Berthelsdorf, 1976).

What is not sufficiently appreciated in drug use is the sequence of sexual regressions. For example, a young man may be so frightened by incestuous wishes and oedipal competition when he faces young women that he avoids them, sexually regresses, and "goes out with the boys." As his homosexual wishes get stimulated, further anxiety is engendered and he regresses once more and wishes to be a passive child. The passive wishes may scare him so much that he turns to a needle or alcohol, feeding himself in order to avoid people altogether who are exprienced as awesome, engulfing, and unreliable.

Still another component in the use of drugs is defiance. Teenage drug users are those who have not felt appropriately nurtured during their oral, anal, and phallic-oedipal periods. Their participation in something illegal and antisocial gratifies some of their defiant feelings.

Because the drug itself has pathological effects and inasmuch as the habitual drug user is an angry, distrustful person, he or she is usually poorly motivated for treatment.

Ian, age seventeen, was referred to a mental hygiene clinic by the courts in lieu of going to prison for his illegal use of drugs. Although superficially compliant in his intake interview, it was clear that he was keeping away from his male therapist and did not want to invest in the relationship.

He missed his first two interviews, telling his therapist, who called him each time, that he "just forgot." Although the therapist became irritated, he realized that this was what Ian probably wanted him to feel; consequently he tried to be understanding. In the next interview, on being told that there was something he didn't like about coming to the clinic, Ian said, "It was OK." He resisted further exploration and then was absent from three more sessions. The therapist had fantasies of telling Ian that he would have to report him to the court authorities, but he restrained himself and tried his best to understand Ian's resistive behavior rather than punish him.

In the next face-to-face interview the therapist said that he was quite sure Ian didn't like coming to see him but was afraid to tell him that this was so. Ian did respond that he had "nothing against you" but he didn't like to have much to do with people. The therapist thought out loud and suggested, "Maybe people haven't been nice to you." Ian sat in silence for several minutes and then said, "You see, I can't talk to anybody." When the therapist said that Ian didn't want to talk about how people had been unkind to him, Ian said "Maybe" and went back to being silent. As was getting to be a routine, Ian didn't show up for the next two interviews, but the therapist kept calling him and telling him he wanted to see him.

In Ian's next interview, he started off by saying with a little smile, "Don't you ever give up?" The therapist smiled back and said, "I think you sometimes want me to!" Ian remarked, "Well, you work for the court and you have to do your job." The therapist said, "You can't believe that I care about you, can you?" Ian held back some tears but did start talking about his impoverished background. He lived alone with his very depressed mother and he rarely saw his father. He told the therapist how he had "always been a loner because nobody gives a damn about me."

As Ian continued to talk about his life of deprivation and his paranoid view of the world, the therapist quietly listened but was attentive and empathetic. Eventually Ian started to talk about the way drugs gave him a good feeling that no other experience did. "I can't go out with girls or talk very much to the guys," he confided. Girls reminded him of his mother, who "just wants for her-self," and "guys remind me of my old man, who is never around."

Many times Ian tested the therapist by asking him if he "should get off drugs." The therapist never took a stand, but instead wondered about Ian's mixed feelings toward drug use. The more Ian could face his underlying passiv-ity, his unacceptable dependency, and eventually his strong homosexual yearn-ings and incestuous desires, the more his drug intake diminished. However, as Ian eventually himself said of the therapist, "I'm addicted to you now instead of to heroin."

Ian's experience is instructive. Not only does it offer ample evi-dence that there is a strong sexual component in drug use, but, of more importance, it indicates that the best way to help an adolescent give up drugs seems to be through a loving, therapeutic relationship. Helping the adolescent drug addict is frustrating and difficult but not impossible. This may be said of many adolescents who visit clini-cians' offices, who feel extremely threatened by an adult who wants to help them.

Chapter 6

Sex and Marriage

Cultural Considerations

As suggested earlier, one of the most conspicuous features of the twentieth century is rapid social change. Our societal norms are questioned in the media almost daily (Deburger, 1978), and the most notable shift in interpersonal relationships has been in the interaction between men and women. Today more than half of all married women are gainfully employed outside the home. As they move into parts of the economic orbit traditionally restricted to men, contemporary women are actively competing with men and are actively repudiating their formerly subordinate roles.

In the last decade or so, women have begun to assert their rights and demand that men make a new accommodation to them. Anxious over the loss of some of his traditional privileges and threatened by the new competition from women, many a man in contemporary society copes with his fears by feeling and acting hostile toward his wife and often toward women in general.

Many writers conclude that because of the sweeping changes in the institution of the family and the sharp shift of marital roles, marriage is in a state of calamity (Lederer and Jackson, 1968; Paolino and McGrady, 1978). Current trends indicate that the divorce rate is higher than ever before in history and apparently climbing at an unprecedented pace (Prochaska and Prochaska, 1978). The United States is experiencing a divorce epidemic; there are approximately 1.6 divorces for every three marriages (Atkin, 1982), which means that the United States now has the highest rate of divorce in the world (Prochaska and Prochaska, 1978).

Infidelity is also on the rise. When Kinsey (1953) gathered his data on extramarital affairs in the 1950s, he found that about half of all husbands and about a quarter of all wives were unfaithful to their mates at some time during their marriages. Today the estimate for married men is about 60 percent, and for married women it is about 35 percent (Strean, 1980).

Wolfe (1976) has characterized the 1970s as the "me decade" in which individuals seem able to care only about themselves. Contemporary self-help books insist that happiness is to be achieved by self-aggrandizement, that the desires of others are important only to the extent that they contribute to one's own well-being, and that involvement in social or altruistic causes is a waste of time unless it enhances one's success. Many psychotherapists claim that nothing one does or does not do should be considered wrong or immoral unless it gets the person in trouble. In the popular film *An Unmarried Woman*, when the distraught wife tells her therapist that she feels very guilty because she believes she provoked her husband to leave her for another woman, the therapist orders her to "take a rest from guilt!"—opting not to help her patient with the anger and other feelings and fantasies that created her guilt.

In today's society, in which we all want a lot, a married woman is expected and expects herself to be a combination of emotional empathizer, intellectual stimulator, orgastic playmate, and cathartic absorber—plus a strong and independent person. Not only does the wife of the 1980s expect a great deal from herself, she expects as much, if not more, from her husband. He should be a willing and abundant provider of material goods, yet encourage her gainful employment; he should be a sparkling conversationalist, yet respect his wife's need for solitude and privacy; he should help with domestic chores, yet have a stable role as a masculine father; he should be an appetizing sexual partner, yet tolerate his wife's flirtations with other men.

The modern husband is in tremendous conflict because he, too, is often plagued by unrealistic expectations; he must be an accomplished sexual athlete, a source of profound wisdom, and a provider of plenty of money. If his inevitable failure does not lead to obsessive self-berating, he is frequently preoccupied with the fantasy that life could be more fulfilling if his wife were more motherly, tender, supportive, and "feminine"—and at the same time ecstatically erotic, decisive, and brilliant.

Psychiatrists Grunebaum and Christ (1976) have pointed out that to be a best friend, a favored bed-companion, and a "therapist" are difficult tasks, especially "through sickness and health, for richer and poorer, for better or worse." Stability, loyalty, and dependability are qualities which do not easily coexist with stimulation, excitement, and variety.

In the 1980s married people seem to expect their spouses to be embodiments of the omnipotent parental figure who gives all, knows all, and can anticipate needs and wishes before they are verbalized. Yet despite the hunger for parenting by the spouse that most marital partners exhibit, they also want to be admired for their strength, praised for their autonomy, and rewarded for their independence. Given the demands that husbands and wives place on themselves and each other, it is surprising that approximately 50 percent of the marriages in Western society survive.

Much of married life is a paradigm of discontent because of the reduced capacity of men and women to give of themselves and feel protective and loving toward each other (Hendin, 1975). The institution of marriage as it now exists challenges our mature ego functions: high-level judgment, object-related interaction rather than narcissistic joy, frustration tolerance rather than instant pleasure, mature reality testing and deferred gratification, and acceptance of criticism rather than adulation. These are demands that most married individuals resent in an age of "doing one's own thing."

Dr. Reuben Fine (1979b) has pointed out that the happy marriage is more a myth than a reality and "the hate affair" is statistically far more frequent than "the love affair." In the hate affair two people are held together by a bond of hatred which they are unable to break. The roots of the hatred go back to childhood, when the person was brought up in an atmosphere of frustration and antagonism.

On Choosing a Mate

Perhaps one of the reasons that a harmonious marriage is unusual in our society is that there is a lack of understanding of why potential mates select each other. Researchers on marital choice generally agree regarding the influence of such factors as age, socioeconomic status, geographical propinquity, race, and education. If two people are similar in these respects they are more likely to marry (Murstein, 1976). However, the psychological factors involved in choosing a mate are more crucial and more difficult to describe because they are subtle and unconscious. Those writers who have investigated the phenomenon (Eisenstein, 1956; Bolton, 1961; Blanck and Blanck, 1968; Strean, 1980) have noted the strong unconscious determinants in the decision and unanimously concur that marriage is rarely, if ever, a result of free, rational choice. Although unhappy mates usually ascribe their incompatibilities to lack of mutual interests, this is a gloss over their mutual hatreds, mutual anxieties, and mutual competitiveness.

The psychologist Carl Jung believed that the search for a mate was completely unconscious: "You see that girl . . . and instantly you get the seizure; you are caught, and afterward you may discover that it was a mistake" (Evans, 1964). The philosopher George Santayana described the process of falling in love and wanting to marry as "that deep and dumb instinctive affinity" and the sociologist Ralph Linton (1936) described the ecstasy and madness of the person in love as similar to an epileptic fit. The ancient Romans viewed falling in love as a form of madness: *Amare et sapere deis conceditar*—"The ability to keep one's wits when in love is not granted even to the gods."

Mate choice is apparently very much influenced by what was referred to earlier as "the romantic ideal." Few individuals are exempt from being influenced by the childish fantasies that unconsciously shape mate selection and in fact constitute much of the romantic complex.

Freud (1939) likened the romantic lover to the fond parent who projects his own ideal onto his child to substitute for the lost narcissism of his own childhood. He pointed out that what the lover wishes he could have been, he fantasies his beloved as being. The loved one is made into a father or mother figure and becomes the recipient of fantasies that emanate from the lover's childhood.

In the early stage of a romance the lover, having idealized his or her partner, is convinced that this is the best person on earth and that paradise has been discovered. The lover lives only for giving to the beloved; the paradox is that the partner demands little but gets everything, inasmuch as he or she is at the same point—giving all and asking nothing but to bestow love on the other.

Romantic love seems to carry the seeds of its own destruction in that eventually reality begins to assert itself. Lovers who were originally sufficient unto each other are no longer so because they begin to perceive each other in terms of their real characteristics. As the demands of living become a reality, each partner begins to give less, to focus more on his or her own needs, and to expect more of the mate. It is the coincidence of giving less and expecting more that punctures the romantic ideal and sparks many conflicts between spouses (Ables, 1977).

Another important dynamic that disrupts the romantic complex is sex. Because romantic love is idealized, the lovers' sexual desires for their romantic partner often induce guilt and anxiety. Anatole France (1933) in *Penguin Island* pointed out that when the penguins turned into human beings they lost their virtue only when they put on clothes—when they hid the rejected realities of their bodies. So, frequently, does the taboo on sex influence romantic lovers. Rejecting their own bodies, they feel that their love is degraded by their participation in an "animal act." In this regard it is noteworthy that the famous lovers in history, such as Romeo and Juliet, Antony and Cleopatra, Cyrano and Roxanne, all lived apart from each other and had very limited sexual interaction.

Despite all the evidence that the romantic ideal is a false illusion, many people still think that marriage will solve their problems and bring them lifelong bliss (Neubeck, 1969). A remarkable paradox exists in our society. In the very era in which the institution of marriage is in grave difficulty and is even said by some to be dying, it is also more popular than ever. The marriage rate, far from declining, has been climbing ever since 1959 (Hunt, 1977). Although the romantic ideal is elusive and unrealistic, to many people it is obviously worth pursuing.

One of the major reasons that the romantic ideal lingers on is because many marital partners cling to a fantasy that there is an omnipotent, omniscient, perfect parent available somewhere. Not only does this fantasy eventually create tremendous disappointment, but it contributes to many of the sexual problems in marriage.

Sexual problems in marriage, the major focus of this chapter, have as their major cause the unconscious wish that the marital partner be a parent. When a wife wants her husband to be a mother or father or both, she then has to cope with anxiety involving incestuous wishes, homosexual desires, and symbiotic cravings. In addition, she will tend to make her husband a superego who punishes and an authority who controls. The same syndrome occurs, of course, when a husband unconsciously makes his wife a maternal and/or paternal figure.

Marital Interaction and Marital Incompatibility

In understanding mate selection, marital interaction, and marital incompatibility, the complementarity, or "fit," of the two individuals is of enormous importance (Lutz, 1964). Marriage counselors of many persuasions have for some time noted the complementarity of the sadist and the masochist, the dependent alcoholic and the nurturing spouse, and the deceiver married to the naive individual who enjoys, albeit unconsciously, being deceived. Pathology often is a binding factor when it provides for complementarity in the marital interaction.

Clinicians have also been able to determine that regardless of how much a spouse complains about a partner's sadism, competitiveness, or insensitive or inadequate sexual performance, unconsciously the person is attracted to it and receives vicarious gratification from identifying with the spouse as he or she rants and raves or is sexually deficient. While the overt behavior of marital partners may differ, the mates often share similar unconscious fantasies. In the film *The Days of Wine and Roses*, although the wife was very upset by the behavior of her alcoholic husband, it turned out that she was addicted to chocolate bars. Like her husband, she had strong oral cravings which were difficult to control, but of equal importance, she derived unconscious gratification from watching her husband get inebriated.

As clinicians listen to marital arguments, they learn that spouses unconsciously share very similar values despite the fact that they overtly disagree with each other. The author recalls a client who became furious every time she became aware of her husband's watching sadistic porno films. She criticized her husband's sadism, interest in barbarism, and lack of decency. One day in her anger she exclaimed, "Somebody like you should be mangled, torn limb from limb, and deposited in the gutter."

It becomes reasonably clear that husbands and wives receive vicarious gratification from the behavior of their mates, which they consciously condemn when only one member of the dyad is in treatment. Although one member of a couple may urge the other to enter therapy to resolve sexual inhibitions, sexual fears, or some other interpersonal problem, when the partner in treatment improves, the one not in treatment frequently becomes very threatened and then tries to get the mate to stop seeing the therapist.

Abe, a married man of thirty-eight, was in treatment because his wife insisted that he be helped with his problem of premature ejaculation. Feeling intimidated by his wife, Rena, and consciously eager to please her, Abe tried to please his woman therapist and worked cooperatively with her.

After several months of treatment, Abe became more potent with Rena and was able to sustain his erections for longer periods of time. After one mutually enjoyable sexual experience, Rena turned to Abe and said, "Your therapist can hold your hand but she'll never turn you into a good lover!"

Rena was clearly threatened by Abe's gains. Despite the fact that she had urged him to get help, when she saw that he was becoming more potent she had to try to undermine it. This is what many parents also do after their children progress in treatment.

Husbands and wives unconsciously are sensitized to their mutual fears, wishes, defenses, and history, all of which provide for an equilibrium in their marriages. Marriage counselors have utilized the concept "neurotic choice of mate," which describes a marriage in which displeasure exceeds pleasure. According to Eidelberg (1956): "Whenever a neurotic choice is made, the patient, instead of choosing a person with whom he could be happy, has selected an object he needs in order to avoid recognizing what he is afraid of. The defense mechanisms used to achieve this aim lead to various pathological formations" (p. 58).

As has already been suggested, the individual seeking help for marital conflict usually describes himself or herself as a victim of the spouse's problems. Like individuals suffering from phobias, compulsions, psychosomatic problems, or recurrent nightmares, who do not realize how they are unconsciously arranging for a good part of their plights, an unhappy husband or wife who feels exploited, is impotent, or is frigid rarely recognizes his or her own contribution to the marital woes.

Marriage counselors, sex therapists, and other helping professionals have concluded that a chronic marital complaint is usually an unconscious wish (Strean, 1980). The husband who perpetually complains that his wife is cold, sexually inaccessible, and castrating needs such a wife to protect him against experiencing his own forbidden sexual desires. Similarly, a wife who continually complains that her husband is a poor sexual partner and incapable of romance needs such a husband; if he were an interested and romantic sexual partner, she would be flooded with anxiety. If helping professionals can truly perceive that chronic marital complaints are similar to recurrent nightmares—consciously upsetting but unconsciously arranged—they will be more able to assist the troubled married client resolve his or her sexual and interpersonal problems in the marriage.

That a spouse's derogatory remarks about the marital partner are expressions of unconscious wishes becomes apparent when we observe how the spouse conducts himself or herself in the treatment relationship with the therapist. Almost always the client will experience the practitioner in the same way that the marital partner is experienced. For example, the man who feels that he is a victim of a demanding wife will eventually feel that his therapist is too demanding of him; the wife who says that her husband is sexually disinterested will sooner or later feel sexually unappreciated by her therapist; the spouse who thinks his or her partner is oversexed will at some point in the treatment label the therapist the same way.

The therapist is experienced in the same way as the spouse because that is the way the client unconsciously wants it to be. As the client begins to see that he has a cold therapist and a cold wife, he begins to wonder if indeed he is writing his own script. It should be stressed, however, that the client will not gain this insight if the therapist takes sides in the marital conflicts. Only if the practitioner sees his or her task as one of helping clients understand their wishes, defenses, superego mandates, and ways of distorting reality will it be possible to help them see how they are recapitulating their marriages in their therapeutic relationships.

Beverly, a married woman of forty, was in treatment for marital counseling. Although she had many sexual and interpersonal problems of her own, she utilized most of her sessions with her male counselor to complain about her husband, Mort. Her major complaint about Mort was that he suffered from premature ejaculation, which, Beverly felt, was the main reason their sexual life was not enjoyable.

In her relationship with her counselor, Beverly was very distant and frequently critical. She often complained that the treatment sessions were "long and drawn out" and that she would "like to get this whole thing over with quickly." As the counselor reflected on Beverly's complaints about himself and about the treatment, it became clear that these complaints sounded very similar to her dissatisfactions with Mort. The counselor became even more convinced of the similarity between Beverly's marital transference and her treatment transference when he noted that she would seek out interpretations from him on issues which, if the counselor were to have given them, would have made them "premature" interventions.

Beverly's case illustrates that when a person complains that the spouse is emotionally or sexually inhibited (and the spouse very well may be), the complainant unconsciously wants it to be that way. Just as Beverly was afraid to get too close to her husband, she was also afraid to get too close to her therapist. However, she constantly complained about the inadequacies of both.

As the case vignettes in this chapter will reveal, virtually all chronic marital complaints are symptoms of internal conflicts which the client had long before he or she got married. The vignettes will also demonstrate that if the practitioner does not give advice or take sides in the marriage, but helps the clients to understand themselves better, marital complaints become complaints about the therapist. If these complaints are seen by the therapist, and eventually by the clients, to be unconscious wishes, marital relationships generally improve.

Psychosexual Problems in Marriage

Only happy people can have happy marriages. A marriage never made an unhappy person happy, nor has it ever made a sexually conflicted person sexually free. It will be seen in the ensuing discussion of the sexual difficulties of married people that in each case maturational conflicts have not been resolved. While full maturation is an ideal that no person achieves, it can be said that the more severe a person's marital difficulties, the more severe are his or her maturational difficulties. Although there are many therapeutic modalities that can be utilized in helping married people cope better with their sexual problems, this chapter will focus primarily on situations in which one-to-one long-term treatment was the treatment modality utilized.

Disturbances of Potency

For the man, the average duration of intercourse is from one to five minutes from the act of insertion until the completion of orgasm. In most instances, ejaculation is achieved after some thirty to fifty thrusts, lasting about three to four minutes. However, there are wide individual variations; some men can perform active coitus from ten to twenty minutes before ejaculation. Ejaculation which takes place in less than one minute should be considered premature (Eisenstein, 1956).

Impotence takes many forms. It may be partial or vary in frequency. It may manifest itself in *ejaculatio praecox* (premature ejaculation) or *ejaculatio retardata* (late ejaculation), in which erection is maintained within the vagina for half an hour or more without ejaculation being achieved. In complete impotence, there is inability to attain or maintain an erection during an attempt at intercourse. Finally, a less noted form of impotence is one in which the man can sustain an erection and ejaculate at the appropriate time but receive no pleasure from his ejaculation; in effect, he has no orgasm.

There are many unconscious motives that combine or stand alone to create sufficient anxiety in a man to cause one or more forms of impotence. Perhaps the most common etiological source of impotence is based on the persistence of an unconscious sensual attachment to the mother. Because the man unconsciously makes his wife a mother, he "castrates" himself and becomes impotent before he is castrated for his incestuous act. The client believes that sexual activity is dangerous, and the defensive forces that demand avoidance of the sexual act are sustained and assured by interference with the physical reflexes (Fenichel, 1945).

In addition to conflicts at the oedipal level, impotence may be activated by problems at other levels of development. For example, many men with a latent homosexual disposition who have strong unconscious wishes to be the wife will "turn off" their erection and try to simulate a situation in which they do not have a penis but unconsciously ascribe the role of man to their wives. In addition, unresolved anal problems can contribute to impotence. Some men unconsciously equate ejaculation with soiling or urinating, and therefore have to restrain themselves sexually, lest they dirty the one they love. It should be noted that when an individual refers to sex as "dirty," he usually has anal fantasies about sex which create anxiety. In other instances, the client becomes impotent to defend himself against aggressive and sadistic fantasies having to do with stabbing or piercing. Finally, when a man has problems on the trust–mistrust level he will not feel relaxed with his wife, and his grudging and nongiving attitudes toward women will contribute to his impotence (Glover, 1949; Eisenstein, 1956).

Impotence, unless due to a chemical, hormonal, or some other physical anomaly, evolves from one or more unresolved maturational problems. While physical problems should be ruled out first, successful treatment will involve helping the client face forbidden infantile wishes such as incestuous desires, oedipal competition, homosexual submission, anal sadism, or oral dependency. Often the impotent husband can have problems on all psychosexual levels of development.

Mel, age thirty-three, came to treatment because of sexual impotence. He had been married to Bessie for over a year, and with the exception of one or two successful performances he was impotent virtually all the time. Prior to the marriage, Mel had been able to be potent with Bessie and with other women sexual partners. "It's only since I got married that I'm in trouble," Mel lamented.

In their interpersonal relationship, Mel was quite submissive to Bessie. She made the major decisions and Mel consulted her about everything from his business affairs to his wardrobe. He acknowledged in his early interviews with his male therapist that he felt quite intimidated by his wife, who sometimes reminded him of his "tyrannical mother."

Mel's mother, in addition to being described as tyrannical and prone to many temper tantrums, was also quite seductive with Mel. She would frequently ask him, when he was a young boy, to zip and unzip her clothes, and "to hug me and show me how much you love me." Mel's father was described as authoritarian, strict, and distant. Unexpectedly, when Mel was thirteen, his father died, and Mel became "the man of the house" and "took care" of his mother and younger sister.

In the treatment situation, initially Mel was very cooperative with his therapist and was glad to find a father figure with whom he could share his woes. The "honeymoon stage" of treatment strengthened Mel, and some of his sexual potency was restored. "As long as I have you, I feel stronger and more erect," he told his therapist.

As the treatment went on and Mel looked more deeply at his relationship with Bessie, he got in touch with his deep incestuous wishes and his oedipal conflicts. He was in the throes of much discomfort while discussing these issues and his impotence returned. He told the therapist that he found it very difficult to discuss his sexual life with him. He said in one interview, "It is as if I'm talking about screwing my mother and telling my father all about it. It's disgusting."

When it became clear that Mel was making his therapist his father, he talked more about his relationship with his father. There had been much love and hate in their interaction, and Mel gradually was able to realize that he had wanted to kill his father at times and that after the father died he always wondered just how much his wishes had to do with it.

Still later in treatment Mel was able to talk about his wish to destroy the therapist. When his hostile and competitive expressions were not criticized or refuted, Mel's sexual anxiety was reduced and his potency was increased.

One of Mel's fantasies about his mother that emerged near the end of his treatment was that she took his father away from him. He had strong sadistic fantasies toward her, which, when discharged and better understood, also contributed to more joy in sex with Bessie.

Impotence evolves if the unconscious meaning of the sexual act causes the man anxiety or guilt. Treatment should be aimed at freeing the man's childish fantasies so that his sexual energy is not sapped by defenses and anxiety. As in the case of Mel described above, impotence can be an overdetermined symptom. The man can suffer from anxiety and guilt over incestuous desires and oedipal competition as well as sadism and distrust.

Frigidity, or Anorgasmia

The first wave of sexual liberation was having its major effect on women born in the 1920s and 1930s, and by 1938, Terman, in his study *Psychological Factors in Marital Happiness*, found that two-thirds of the wives he interviewed had orgasms "usually or all the time," while only one-third had them "sometimes to never" (Terman, 1938). By the 1940s Kinsey found that a majority of wives at all social and educational levels were having orgasm "most of the time" (Kinsey et al., 1948). Hunt (1974), in his study *Sexual Behavior in the 1970s*, reported that his statistics demonstrated that more married women were having orgasms than at Kinsey's time.

Due to the continued waves of sexual liberation, with the result that most of contemporary society now encourages married women to enjoy themselves sexually, those married women of the 1980s who do not receive sufficient pleasure with their husbands feel very deprived. Because they feel they have a legitimate right to fulfilling sexual lives, they actively seek out mental health practitioners and other helping professionals to enhance themselves sexually. The most common sexual problem brought to the practitioner by married women is frigidity, or anorgasmia.

By frigidity, or anorgasmia, we are referring to the inability of the woman to have sexual pleasure, and more often than not this inability exists in relation to any marital partner. Some researchers still hold to a rather narrow definition of frigidity, contending that it should refer to the woman's inability to attain a climax from coitus.

A woman may on one occasion suffer from near-total frigidity and on another have an almost complete orgasm. Some women experience relatively strong excitement in anticipation of sexual intercourse but lose their desire during the act. There are others whose lack of vaginal pleasure is manifest even in the absence of lubricating glandular secretions in the vagina during sexual stimulation. In the most intense degrees of frigidity, fear produces painful intercourse in which the vaginal sphicter muscle closes so tightly that it is difficult if not impossible for the penis to enter the vagina. In all types of frigidity, strong sexual excitement may be felt, particularly in the clitoris, but pleasurable vaginal sensation ends before the involuntary contractions of the vagina, characteristic of true orgasm, can be achieved (Eisenstein, 1956).

As is true regarding impotence, there are many causes of frigidity, and an anorgasmic woman can suffer from one or many of them. One of the most common sources of difficulty is the unconscious comparison of the husband with the father. When a husband is unconsciously made an incestuous object, the woman must hold herself back sexually; otherwise she will feel excessive anxiety and guilt. Often, when a married woman makes her husband a father figure, she is in active competition with her mother; therefore, sexual excitement and orgasm are unconsciously equated with destroying her mother. To avoid feeling destructive, the client inhibits her excitement.

When a married woman has intense oedipal guilt, she may regress and unconsciously turn her husband into a mother figure. The activation of homosexual desires can create anxiety, and again, she must squelch her sexual excitement and orgasm.

Frigidity may also have unconscious anal and oral significance. Fear of losing control during orgasm may be the equivalent of losing urinary or sphincter control. As mentioned in Chapter 2, in cases where the husband is made a parental figure, sex may also be equated with symbiosis and fear of engulfment and therefore is dreaded.

A final and common source of frigidity is the woman's rejection of her vagina. In what has been termed our patriarchal culture, many women tend to depreciate their own genitals and unconsciously or even consciously idealize the penis. However, when something like a penis is idealized, there is usually unconscious resentment toward it. Consequently, frigidity may be an expression of anxiety connected with repressed sadistic impulses, such as revenge upon the penis and the man, or with masochistic wishes of being genitally injured.

Generally speaking, frigidity cannot be altered appreciably by changing partners or manipulating the environment. In some cases, when a woman unconsciously makes her husband an incestuous father she can become orgasmic with an extramarital partner. However, should the lover become a husband, she will be anorgasmic with him, too. Frigidity, like most psychosexual problems, usually needs intensive psychotherapy to resolve it.

Faye, age thirty-two, had been married for four years but had never been able to have an orgasm. Although she felt her husband was "a potent man" he never "turned me on." She told her male therapist that Max, her husband, was "a pleasant fellow" who was "considerate and attentive" but "unable to satisfy" her.

Although Faye had never been orgastic prior to marriage, she presented herself as "a sexual woman" who had "not married a sexual man." Behind her polite demeanor was a thinly veiled air of contempt as she discussed her marriage.

Faye described her father, a physician, as a handsome, seductive man who was not home very much during her childhood. She said sadly, "Although he was humorous and loving, I never had enough of him." An only child, Faye described her mother as "a woman with a temper who was very strict with me."

Although Faye dated a lot as a teenager and was quite popular, she never had any close relationships with men. This pattern continued throughout college and in her later years. Although she derived much satisfaction from her work as a professional nurse, she often felt depressed and was unable to account for her depressions.

In her therapy Faye was able to resolve her sexual anxieties chiefly by exploring her relationship with her therapist. When the therapist noted her maintenance of a distance from him and her frequent sarcasm toward him, slowly Faye brought out a lot of hostility toward the therapist and then toward all men—particularly her father—for their "standoffish" posture. Eventually she could bring out secret yearnings to be closer to the therapist and her father and could also begin to sense her own fears. As her fears were explored, she learned that she had intense wishes to dominate her father and all men and then "gobble them up."

In her later stages of therapeutic work, Faye had fantasies of eating up the therapist's penis so "I can gloat over you the way you do over me." As Faye discharged a great deal of sadism toward the therapist, without his retaliation, she could begin to examine her depreciation of her own vagina and her penis envy. Concomitant with her discharge and examination of her sadism and envy, she began to enjoy sex with Max much more and eventually did become orgastic with him. At first her orgasms were clitoral orgasms, but as she began to view her vagina less as a castrated penis and more as an organ to be valued in its own right, she had vaginal orgasms.

The last phase of her treatment was an examination of her relationship with her mother, whom she devalued, afterward identifying with the devalued image. As her fight with her mother diminished and her revenge toward her father and the therapist subsided, Faye was able to end treatment and have a fulfilling sexual life with Max.

As we saw with impotence, frigidity has many possible etiological sources and all can exist in the same woman: oedipal wishes, incestuous desires, penis envy, and fears of dependence. As the client becomes able to unearth these conflicts and "live" them in a benign and understanding therapeutic relationship, the frigidity is no longer needed as a protection.

The Celibate Spouse

As suggested in the earlier part of this chapter, a marital dyad is a system. Two role partners unconsciously participate to maintain an equilibrium, albeit at times a neurotic equilibrium. This is particularly obvious when a spouse wishes to maintain an asexual marriage—he or she needs a partner to help do so. While both partners in an asexual marriage often ascribe blame to the other for their empty existence, each is participating in maintaining the situation.

When marital partners participate in an asexual marriage they often are not aware of their sexual fears. Frequently they arrange schedules whereby one partner is sleeping during the day and up at night while the other partner does the opposite. This "lark-owl" marriage is not perceived accurately—the partners often attribute their opposing sleep routines to biological factors that set the pattern of energy and fatigue in the individual (Brozan, 1982). Some asexual marital partners arrange to work in different cities and believe that their lack of sexual intimacy is solely because of their work requirements—not wanting to realize that they have mutually arranged their lives so that they are away from each other most of the time.

What often puzzles the observer of the type of marriage we are considering is that the partners frequently are overtly compatible and there seems to be an absence of tension in the relationship. This absence of overt tension is because there is no sex life. Both partners are usually people who must isolate their sensual desires from their tender feelings. To have sex with the one they love is seen as disruptive because they unconsciously perceive sex as something dirty; consequently, they do not wish to contaminate the beloved. In effect, they maintain an adolescent platonic relationship.

One of the reasons that the asexual husband contends that he will be "messing" his wife by having sex with her is because the wife is unconsciously viewed as a parental figure. By participating in sex with a parental figure, the man experiences himself as a degraded "mother-fucker."

Similar to the impotent husband or frigid wife, asexual marital partners not only have unacceptable incestuous wishes and unresolved oedipal conflicts, but frequently they are repressing rage. As children they may have had superficially pleasant relationships with their parents and family members (as in their current marriages), but there was also a lack of emotionally gratifying experiences, which subtly induced intense aggression in them. However, these people have had to control their anger, and their plight manifests itself in their abhorrence of intimacy. Obviously, one cannot easily "make love" when one hates. The celibate spouse also may have problems on the trust–mistrust level and become suspicious of anyone who tries to draw near. This dynamic, of course, interferes with the possibility of sexual fulfillment.

Celibate spouses rarely seek treatment. Just as they fear the closeness and intimacy of a sexually satisfying marriage, they shun therapists and counselors in whom they would confide and with whom they would be emotionally intimate. When they do seek out or are referred to a counselor or therapist, it is usually not because of discomfort about their sex lives, but for some other reason.

Erik, age thirty-nine, was referred to a mental health clinic by a physician because he had migraine headaches, insomnia, and shortness of breath. A hardworking accountant, he was away from his wife and children most of the week and "rested and recuperated" on weekends.

Erik described his relationship with his wife and two children as "friendly and well organized." It was clear from the beginning of his contact with the therapist that Erik shunned emotional intimacy and feared spontaneity in himself and others. He described the atmosphere in the home with his parents as also "friendly and well organized."

No mention of sex was made by Erik until the tenth interview, when his therapist asked him about it. Blushing and anxious, he said, "We have no time for frivolity." When the worker tried to pursue his resistance to having sex, Erik changed the subject, and started to miss sessions. Eventually, he quit the treatment altogether.

Many clients who are in treatment wish to hide the fact that they are sexually abstinent. The therapist has to wait until a comfortable working relationship is established before exploring this because the client feels very vulnerable in a discussion about his sexual anxiety. Just as the client wishes to avoid sex in his daily life, he wishes to avoid discussion of it with the therapist. Consequently, the therapist has to respect the client's resistance and wait until he manifests some readiness to open the area up for exploration.

The Sadomasochistic Spouse

As discussed earlier, a task every child has to cope with is toilet training. Many children, unfortunately, are not trained sensitively or with understanding, and as adults they continue to respond to what they perceive as controls, restraints, and responsibilities with rage and revenge. Many a marital quarrel is reminiscent of the power struggles between parent and child over toilet training.

While marital power struggles or sadomasochistic orgies among husbands and wives are far from foreign subjects to marital counselors, practitioners are not always aware of the sexual conflicts inherent in these struggles. The members of a marital dyad who are constantly feuding frequently experience themselves unconsciously as humiliated children who at any moment will be overpowered by a parent who insists on the child urinating or defecating *for* the parent. Very frequently sex is experienced as "doing one's duty" for the mate, as if one were on the potty and being forced to "put out."

Although most people marry because they consciously want to give and receive love, there are probably more sadomasochistic marriages than there are mature, loving ones. The prizewinning play *Who's Afraid of Virginia Woolf]* depicts a couple who fought with each other for over twenty years. Perhaps one reason for the play's popularity was that many of the men and women who saw it could identify with the sadism and masochism of Albee's characters.

When giving love is perceived as an obligation and a duty in which one has to subordinate his or her own wishes, this form of self-sacrifice inevitably induces powerful anger (A. Freud, 1937). After a while the masochistic husband or wife, resenting the inferior status which has been unconsciously self-created as well as imposed by the marital partner, switches roles with the spouse who has been dominant and begins to hurt that spouse. Because giving and receiving love, for such a couple, is always a oneupmanship affair, the couple derive their sexual satisfaction in getting beaten or beating. This explains the so-called good sex life among battling marital partners. Either they fight strenuously before sex or fight afterward. But the sex should not be viewed as isolated from the squabble. These partners are like boxers who embrace before or after a fight and are attracted to each other because each has "a worthy opponent."

Because sadomasochistic spouses have never fully resolved their toilet-training problems, they are not able to differentiate emotionally the sexual functions from the eliminative. Consequently, they also tend to see sex as something "dirty." When they are in the masochistic position they can feel that a "dirty trick" is being played upon them, and in the sadistic position they can feel that it is they who are playing the dirty tricks. One of the reasons a fight can easily break out after sex is that one partner feels angry at being humiliated, while the other feels guilty for having done the humiliating.

The anal power struggle of sadomasochistic marital partners tends to be taken into their day-to-day interpersonal life. They argue about children, money, friends, in-laws, etc. However, if they are to be helped to resolve their problems, the therapist has to help them get in touch with their *wishes* to battle and their need to see much of life, particularly sex, as an anal matter.

Florence, age thirty-two, came into treatment because she needed help in divorcing her husband, Eli. She pointed out at her first appointment that although her mind was made up, she felt that the impact of the divorce on Eli would "destroy him." She described her six-year marriage as very unsatisfying and full of feuds. Florence was nonorgastic, but she felt confident that sex would be very different with someone else.

Florence, an only child, said that her mother had constantly controlled and dominated her, insisting that Florence report all of her thoughts and activities to her. Florence's toilet training was very harsh and premature—she was trained at seven months. At a year and a half she developed severe constipation and had to have several operations. Constipation remained a recurrent symptom in adulthood. Father was described by Florence as an extremely passive man who "took a lot of mother's shit," and there was always tension between her parents.

Florence was very resistive to treatment. Rather early on, she told her therapist that he made her feel like a little girl, always having to report to him. Obviously casting the therapist in the role of her exacting mother, she resented talking to him and eventually said, "I feel I'm on a pot and you're always inspecting my products."

When Florence made many bids to leave treatment and the therapist pointed out that he seemed to appear like her husband, whom she wanted to divorce, Florence again became quite defiant and said, "Neither of you lets me be my own boss."

Inasmuch as Florence's accusations were not refuted, she began to feel more accepted by the therapist. Slowly she confessed that she frequently felt weak, helpless, and hopeless. She also told the therapist that she didn't think he would accept her unless she was in an inferior status. When this conviction was explored, Florence was eventually able to see how she was keeping herself a little girl. "It's either that I'm a little girl or a tyrant and neither are comfortable," she insightfully brought out in the middle of her therapy.

Dreams and fantasies of defecating on her husband, mother, and therapist were very much part of her therapy. As Florence eventually came to see that she was engaging in a futile battle with her mother of the past, she fought less with Eli. As happens in many sadomasochistic marital dyads, Eli became anxious when he was treated more humanely by his wife, but did seek therapy for himself. As Florence and Eli both got in touch with the extent to which they were unconsciously making their relationship a bathroom fight, they could move toward a smoother sexual and interpersonal relationship.

Sadomasochistic spouses can be trying and difficult clients. They see battling as a way of life, and overtly and covertly try to fight with the therapist. The therapist must stay out of the battle in the sense that he should not argue with such clients but should instead help them feel and explore their own needs to participate in oneupmanship fracases. If the therapist does this, the clients may eventually grasp their own desires for the bathroom fights that get them into trouble with spouses and other people.

It should be mentioned that a sadomasochistic battle can mask other sexual problems besides anal conflicts. For example, when marital partners have questions about their own sexual identities, one means of coping with their uncertainities and insecurities is by demeaning the spouse. A husband who has strong but unacceptable wishes to be a woman can cope with his anxiety by being derogatory and demeaning of his wife. Usually this man has selected as a wife one who has doubts about her own sexual identity. Consequently, each time he demeans her she is very apt to cope with her anxiety by demeaning him. The couple trade insults regarding who is the least libidinal, least attractive, and least engaging. Of course, these arguments resolve nothing, but they do give each member of the dyad some unconscious sadomasochistic gratification. When these people enter treatment, they also try to engage the therapist in a battle, and the cautionary notes prescribed in the above paragraph are, once again, applicable.

The Spouse with Oral Problems

An enjoyable marriage that endures requires an acceptance of mutual dependency by both partners. Many married people cannot tolerate their own dependent wishes or their spouse's dependency on them because they have a great deal of unresolved conflict from the oral, or trust–mistrust, period of life (Erikson, 1950; Fraiberg, 1977). Some of these people were so frustrated during the first year of life that they still feel enormous rage, which is often directed at their marital partner, whom they experience as withholding and frustrating. Often the individual who was left hungry at the breast develops "a paranoid orientation to living" (Klein, 1957) and is distrustful of virtually everyone. The spouse, of course, is never trusted for too long.

When distrust is a major issue between spouses (and usually a distrustful man marries a distrustful woman) sex becomes fraught with difficulty. The bodily closeness and emotional intimacy inherent in a good sexual relationship is very much feared. As one suspicious husband said to his therapist in discussing his wife, "If she smiles, I think she wants to manipulate me into bed." At a later session he said, "Love and sex are like poisons. If I take them in, I'm a sucker."

Distrustful couples either avoid sex as much as possible or become alienated and hostile afterward, and for days at a time. Although they work hard to keep a distance from their mates, they often justify their rejecting behavior by accusing their partners of being ungiving and unloving.

Another feature of the oral period is the symbiotic relationship between mother and infant (Mahler, 1968). While a symbiosis should, of course, be outgrown, many married individuals hold onto the wish for one and cling to their mates. The symbiotic mate always wants to know all about his loved one and permits the spouse no privacy. He becomes furious if the mate has loving feelings for others or interests apart from him.

In most cases people at the same level of maturation find each other and marry. Although it is the couple themselves who most often deny the degree of their similarity, most people in their social orbits recognize otherwise. Symbiotic spouses usually project their own strong dependency wishes onto their mates and then feel that they are going to be devoured at any moment. Feeling that they are going to be eaten up, these spouses often have to avoid sex, or approach it in a halfhearted, frightened manner, lest they be smothered.

Still another important feature of the oral stage of development is that the child eventually realizes that one cannot always be "His Majesty." Narcissism becomes punctured as the child is confronted with weaning and other frustrations. At this point the child transfers to the parents the power he thought he possessed and ascribes omnipotent and omniscient qualities to them. One finds people in their thirties, forties, or even fifties who have strong resentment toward their parents for not having met their needs. The reason these feelings do not abate is because the individual maintains the conviction that Mother and Father could have given more love if they wanted to do so.

Although individuals find considerable difficulty in abandoning the yearning for an omnipotent parent, persevering in this belief leads to disappointment in marriage, feelings of weakness, and sexual dissatisfaction. If one believes that the marital partner is omnipotent then one feels very small in relation to such an immense figure. After a while the individual who ascribes such qualities to a partner becomes resentful because he feels overpowered by the partner's superiority. In such a state, sex can be very distasteful. The client feels used, abused, demeaned, and most unequal in the sexual interaction.

George, age thirty-five, sought therapy because he was very unhappy in his marriage. Sex was infrequent and George never felt "turned on." Rather, he felt like a servant, taking care of his master.

As George discussed his marriage in further detail, it became clear that he was transferring to his wife, Hilda, all the qualities of a gigantic mother. "When I'm away from her and think about her, I think of her as twice my size. I'm shocked when I come home and see that she's really shorter than I am." George remarked.

George's father died early in the boy's life, and being an only child, his relationship with his mother became extremely important to him. "I guess I always felt that Mother knows best," George lamented, adding "Hilda is the same way. I guess I've made her my mother."

As George talked more about how he was making himself a little boy with Hilda, he could begin to sense why sex was so unfulfilling. "I guess anybody who feels like a midget with a giant isn't going to get a 'hard-on' so easily," said George insightfully. He was also able to see that he expected to be castrated when he had sex with Hilda, "because I do feel like a mother-fucker."

In his transference relationship with his woman therapist, he tried to make her an omnipotent mother by asking for advice, needing answers to "important" questions, and often making himself a vulnerable boy with her. When the therapist frustrated his symbiotic yearnings for a merger with her by not answering his questions, but encouraged him instead to seek his own answers and look at his own motives for asking them, George initially became very angry and blasted the therapist for her "indifferent, callous, and unempathetic attitude." When his perceptions of the therapist were not refuted, he tried several times and in several ways to engage her in arguments. In response to the therapist's pointing out to George his wish to fight with her, he started to recall memories of his mother when she disappointed him "by not having all the answers all of the time." As he began to sense that he was still clinging to the belief that an omnipotent women was available, George began to reevaluate his current relationships. Slowly he tried bringing the therapist "down to size," and when this didn't seem like "the end of the world," he was able, a little later, to begin to see Hilda as she was. Perceiving women less as giants, he could eventually feel more sexual with them. Slowly he became more potent with Hilda and their sexual life became more fulfilling.

There are many married individuals with trust problems who seek out helping professionals. Most of them report unhappy sexual lives, but are not able to see that their own suspiciousness and distortion of relationships are causing their sexual frustration and emotional deprivation. Treatment is very slow with these clients because they need a lot of time before they can trust the therapist.

The Extramarital Affair

Many therapists and social scientists, if not most, agree with Margaret Mead (1967) that monogamous heterosexual love is probably one of the most difficult, complex, and demanding of human relationships. As suggested earlier, marriage challenges our more mature ego functions—high-level judgment, object-related interaction, frustration tolerance, mature reality testing, acceptance of criticism. These are demands that most married individuals resent in an age of sexual freedom and "doing your own thing." Consequently, many people seek escape from marriage. Perhaps because the requirements of the institution of marriage are so difficult for so many people to cope with, there are many socially acceptable escape routes. One can seek escape by being a workaholic or by compulsively engaging in hobbies, organizational activities, or travel.

An increasingly common and acceptable means of escaping the difficulties of marriage is the extramarital affair. As mentioned at the beginning of the chapter, the percentage of married people engaged in prolonged affairs keeps rising, with the current rate about 60 percent for married men and 35 percent for married women (Strean 1980).

In an extramarital affair, the individual has two part-time marriages, both of which are important to him or her. To those involved in "open marriages" (O'Neill and O'Neill, 1972), one intimate, monogamous relationship feels frightening, demanding, frustrating, or boring. However, many individuals, for complicated psychological and social reasons, cannot leave their marriages. The extramarital arrangement helps the person feel less demoralized, and the yacht, hotel, or motel seems like a pleasant oasis in a desert.

Yet people involved extramaritally rarely marry their lovers or divorce their spouses (Ziskin and Ziskin, 1973; Block, 1978; Bartusis, 1978; Strean, 1980). Therefore it would seem that there are a unique cluster of men and women in our society who want to preserve their marriages but at the same time experience the need to engage in extramarital relationships.

One of the rationales utilized by advocates of the extramarital affair is that after a while any two people in a marriage grow apathetic. While it is true that coping with the vicissitudes of marriage is not easy for anyone in the 1980s, it is also true that neurotic people grow tired of each other because they are unable to maintain a fusion of tender and sensual feelings for one person for a long period of time. These individuals avoid confronting their inhibitions and anxieties by trying to prove that a marital relationship fosters boredom whereas an affair creates stimulation and excitement. They are not aware of the fact that much of the excitement they feel in an affair is not sexual excitement but evolves from the defiant fantasies that they are gratifying by spiting their spouses, whom they experience unconsciously as parental figures.

Any therapist who has worked with men and women in prolonged extramarital affairs comes to recognize that these are basically unhappy people who need two part-time relationships; a single, mutually loving relationship frightens them, although they are the last to recognize it. They choose the route of an affair and tell themselves that they need greater sexual enjoyment. What they don't want to confront is that they cannot enjoy sex in marriage.

When psychosocial tasks are resolved, one can enjoy a monogamous marriage and cope with its frustrations, but when these tasks are not mastered, there is a neurotic choice of mate, the marital relationship induces anxiety, and the individual will seek to escape from it in one way or another (Strean, 1980).

Many people involved in affairs are symbiotic spouses. As has already been suggested, a person involved in a symbiotic relationship inevitably begins to feel like a very small child who is being smothered by the parental figure. One means of ridding oneself of the smothering feeling and the anxiety that strong dependency feelings generate is to have an extramarital lover. The individual who is having an affair does not have to feel too attached to either his spouse or his lover. As he moves from one to the other, he can convince himself that he is quite an independent human being who does not have to attach himself to any one person. However, should either the spouse or lover threaten a breakup of the relationship he becomes quite desperate, because *he is really* a very needy person. Furthermore, should one of the partners insist on more exclusiveness, such as when the extramarital partner discusses marriage, the client can get into a state of emotional chaos because he has to worry about getting into a symbiosis all over again.

As discussed earlier in this chapter, an individual who has problems on the trust–mistrust level is going to be suspicious of the spouse and feel controlled. Overburdened by what he or she perceives as a gigantic parental figure, the client may wish to defy the marital partner; an extramarital affair may be one means of doing so. As mentioned in Chapter 2, according to the psychoanalyst Melanie Klein (1957), when a child experiences the mother as sometimes cruel and unloving, he or she is likely to have a dual image of "the good mother" and "the bad mother." The "bad mother" may become the wife or husband and the lover may become "the good mother."

According to Spotnitz and Freeman: "If the mother has been cruel and unloving, her son is likely to reject monogamy when he grows up. If she was the 'bad' mother one moment, the 'good' mother the next, he may refuse to settle for one woman, for his childish fantasy is that two women took care of him, one 'bad,' the other 'good,' and he will seek to find another two, then another two" (1964, p. 31). What Spotnitz and Freeman have said of the boy is also true for the girl, because all love relationships for both sexes recapitulate the early mother-infant interaction to some extent.

A task of childhood that has to be resolved before one can have a healthy and mature marital relationship is an acceptance of the fact that one's parents are not omnipotent. When a child clings to the belief that a perfect parent exists, as an adult he is inclined to believe that the perfect mate exists—and he is going to look for her. Inasmuch as the spouse always punctures the wish for a perfect mate, the omnipotent partner is sought elsewhere, and often in an extramarital affair.

Earlier in this chapter we referred to sadomasochistic spouses; they are prime candidates for an extramarital affair. Feeling picked on, they initially feel justified in seeking a lover who will treat them properly. Usually the lover they choose encourages them to voice their complaints about their spouse, and this they enjoy. The idea of going behind mother's or father's back and doing something secret and forbidden makes it appealing to have sex in some hideaway motel or hotel. But the sadistic gratification of the extramarital affair does not sustain itself indefinitely. Guilty over their rebellious activity and uncomfortable about not facing their aggression directly, sadomasochistic spouses either begin to feel depressed about the affair or arrange unconsciously to get caught.

Perhaps the most common reason for an affair is an unresolved oedipal conflict. When the spouse is ascribed the role of parent, sex takes on incestuous connotations and has to be avoided. Many men experience their wives as "virgin mothers," who must be avoided sexually, and experience their mistresses as "whores," who excite them sexually. While these men rationalize their sexual inhibitions, dissatisfactions, and frequent impotence with their wives by finding fault with them, they unconsciously feel that they are little boys with big mothers. The same may be said for the many women who unconsciously turn their husbands into fathers and must avoid them sexually and seek out another partner.

When men and women with oedipal conflicts are involved in an affair, the thing they fear the most is that their lovers will want to marry them. This they cannot tolerate, for sex can only be exciting to them if it is away from home. Even if they live with their partners for only a few days, their incestuous wishes become activated and the bliss of the affair deteriorates.

Harry, age thirty-five, sought treatment for several reasons. He was dissatisfied with his poor job performance as a stockbroker, was insomniac, was depressed on frequent occasions, had difficulty in most relationships (he would get involved in power struggles), and had several psychosomatic complaints.

Fairly early in his treatment with a male therapist, Harry complained about his wife. He described her as warm, pleasant, kind, good to their two children, but unexciting. He felt that his marriage was like "having a noose tied around my neck" and he had to break out of it. He blamed his sexual impotence with his wife on her "unexcited" behavior in bed. He found her statements of love to him "abominable" because "she sounds like my mother, who wants to envelop me." To prove that his impotence was his wife's problem, Harry boasted of his big erections and sustained potency with an unmarried girl friend who was "exciting," "stimulating," and "never controls me."

During the course of treatment Harry reported that he had decided to take his girl friend away on a vacation to a motel. However, part of the deal was that the girl friend would cook and assume other traditional chores of a wife. While the first few days of the vacation were blissful, Harry, to his surprise and humiliation, became impotent with his mistress. As he later said in treatment, "As soon as a broad becomes like a wife I make her into a controlling mother. She even begins to smell like my mother and I want to run."

Harry needed intensive treatment to resolve his problems. He had to face his strong incestuous wishes, his powerful competition with his father, and some of his latent homosexual urges toward older men. In his transference relationship with his therapist, he perceived the latter as his father and alternated between opposing him and submitting to him. As he faced his own childish wishes, he became less frightened of his wife and less needy of a mistress.

It is quite clear in Harry's case that because he had a strong incestuous attachment to his mother (and unconsciously wanted to have sex with her) he had to split a woman in two, i.e., into the virginal mother and the whore (Freud, 1910; Eidelberg, 1956). As long as he did not have a living, day-to-day relationship with the woman, he was safe. Living with a woman and then making her into a mother figure stimulated a feeling in him of being controlled and attached by a "noose."

The following case with a similar theme is that of a woman client.

Isadora, age forty, also came into treatment for several reasons. She had difficulty getting along with an aged mother and wondered how much time she should give her; she felt insecure on her job as a librarian; she often got involved in sadomasochistic quarrels with her co-workers or friends; and she had a lot of resentment toward her husband, who acted "like a know-it-all," "considers me beneath him," and "screws like a naive boy."

During her treatment, as Isadora began to voice her resentment toward her husband for being a "bossy know-it-all," she moved into an affair with a married man. In contrast to her husband, her lover was not a "know-it-all" but a "man of the world." Although most of their sex was pregenital (fellatio and cunnilingus), her paramour was described as "a great lover." In further comparing her lover with her husband, Isadora brought out that her lover's cool detachment "turns me on" whereas her husband's lovemaking "makes me sick."

When Isadora and her lover went on a camping trip for several days, the relationship "cooled." The couple engaged in *Who's Afraid of Virginia Woolf-*-type dialogues and had all kinds of oneupmanship arguments; the love and bliss which previously characterized their relationship broke down. Isadora ambivalently declared after returning from the sojourn with her lover, "When I was with him over time, everything lost its glamour. We fought and never got anything settled."

Isadora, like Harry, needed her marriage. Like young children, they wanted the ministrations of parental figures, but, of course, could not tolerate sexual expression directed toward or received from their spouses. Sexuality was experienced as overwhelming, controlling, and debilitating—much as a child would experience sex if he or she participated in it with an adult parent.

The extramarital affair, although considered a "life-style" by many and culturally acceptable in most societies, is also an expression of a conflicted marriage and a conflicted person. The unfaithful spouse is one who usually experiences the marital partner as a superego who must be defied, an incestuous object who must be avoided, a symbiotic partner who must be shunned, or a homosexual mate who must be castigated. Marital infidelity has, more frequently than one believes, a neurotic origin; it is not necessarily a sign of liberty and potency, but frequently it is the opposite (Fenichel, 1945).

Preference for Masturbation

The sexual life of many married people may be described as "masturbatory intercourse" (Eisenstein, 1956). Intercourse is avoided by these people on one pretext or another; however, these pretexts merely rationalize unresolved guilt over sexual activity. Husbands who avoid intercourse with their wives and masturbate instead, rationalize their activity by saying that they do not want to hurt their wives, they are tired, their wives don't "turn them on," etc. Wives who prefer masturbation to sexual intercourse offer similar rationalizations.

Many husbands and wives who go through the motions of sexual intercourse actually achieve more pleasure from being masturbated before, during, or after intercourse. These people usually feel vulnerable with and hostile toward the opposite sex. The men unconsciously perceive the vagina as something hurtful and women experience the penis similarly. This difficulty, like all the sexual difficulties that have been discussed in this chapter, is a function of unresolved childhood conflicts, and the individuals suffering from them need a therapeutic experience. Drugs or advice on the techniques of coitus, as prescribed in marriage manuals, offer little to remedy such disorders. Only a well planned and sensitive therapeutic approach can effectively modify disturbed psychosexual attitudes.

Chapter 7

Sex and the Single Person

ALTHOUGH THERE ARE many people in our society who continue to regard marriage as a viable institution for self-fulfillment, and although there are millions of individuals who see marriage as the most
expedient method for sustained sexual satisfaction, the 1970s and
1980s have witnessed several alternatives to marriage. Many contemporary scholars, therapists, and popular writers are contending that
marriage is passé and are championing the virtues of the "single"
life. According to one well-known social scientist, Margaret Adams
(1976), to be single is to be "blessed." Another scholar, the psychologist Dr. Gabrielle Brown (1980), has pointed out that "the new celibacy" has many advantages over marriage, and she has attempted to
document why more men and women are abstaining from sex—and
are enjoying it. The popular journalist Shere Hite (1976) has averred
that marriage is an outmoded institution and that masturbation and/
or lesbianism may be more stimulating and enhancing for women.
Hunt and Hunt (1977) have pointed to the self-discovery that can
emerge from a divorce, and Libby (1978), the social psychologist, has
contended that remaining single is a "creative" act.

At the same time, several forms of interpersonal relationships that
have been considered deviant and/or a manifestation of neurotic suffering are being championed as legitimate life-styles. The male homo-

sexual is now "a gay" person; the commune which consists of married and unmarried people practicing group sex is "the new surrogate extended family"; swinging is "co-marital sex"; and living together without being married is "cohabitation." We are living in an era in which we have "androgynous" marriages (Lyness, 1978), "contract" marriages (Ryder, 1978), and "open" marriages (O'Neill and O'Neill, 1972). An interesting phenomenon that has evolved during the last decade or two is the increasing number of purposefully unattached men and women who are annexing motherhood or fatherhood to their single status (Drabble, 1966). One of the outcomes of the massive social changes discussed earlier, is that single men and single women are becoming an accepted feature of society's fabric and in this role are receiving both respect and support (Adams, 1976).

Buttressing the notion that the traditional man–woman marital relationship is being questioned is the attempt to categorize the many different groups that fall under the rubric of one alternative life-style. Bullough (1978) has noted the organization of such groups as the gay academics, gay librarians, gay militants, gay students, gay artists, and gay churches and synagogues. Burk (1978) has referred to healthy and unhealthy homosexuals and identified "the gay identity process" in which a man or woman learns to accept and enjoy his or her homosexuality. Similarly, Brown (1980) has categorized various forms of celibacy, e.g., secular celibacy, religious celibacy, modern celibacy, and many other types.

The number of adults between twenty-five and thirty-four who have never been married increased by 50 percent between 1960 and 1975 (U.S. Bureau of Census, 1974), and about half of those aged eighteen to thirty-nine are unmarried (U.S. Bureau of the Census, 1974). Census figures do not allow for a precise delineation of living arrangements, but the high divorce rate, the rise in the average age of first marriage, and the longer period between divorce and remarriage (when remarriage occurs) provide a clear demographic basis for speculation about the dissolution of couples and the emergence of singlehood as a life-style. It is also important to take into account separated and widowed people when discussing singlehood as a sexual life-style. It may be significant, for example, that widowhood is increasing more for women than for men because men are older when they marry than are women, and women tend to live longer (Libby, 1978).

Many groups have been providing social and ideological support for singlehood as a positive option to marriage. Among these groups are the women's liberation movement, the human potential movement, Planned Parenthood, and the National Organization for Non-

Parents (Adams, 1976; Libby, 1978). Government has endorsed the legitimacy of singlehood by reducing discrimination against single individuals in the tax structure (Dullea, 1975).

Single people, however, have received limited attention in the research. In the studies that have been undertaken, the methodology has been weak in that questionnaires and self-reports have been utilized rather than a set of in-depth comprehensive interviews. However, the research does shed some light on how single people experience themselves. Fishel and Allon (1973) carried out an extensive study of singles bars by utilizing participant observation and open-ended interviews with one hundred people in eight singles bars in New York City. The researchers concluded that singles bars were full of those seeking companionship as an answer to their self-estrangement and isolation from others. The picture was one of disillusionment with self and others, dissatisfaction with the prescribed role-playing in the singles bar, and a sense of boredom which those interviewed hoped to replace by stimulation and intimacy with others.

A study by Starr and Carns (1973) of seventy single people in their middle to late twenties revealed that most of them felt isolated, alienated, and somewhat depressed. Many of them complained that singles bars, neighborhood apartment living complexes, and parties did not offer much in the way of companionship or intimacy.

Several studies have compared singlehood and marriage in terms of relative adjustment and happiness. Knupfer, Clark, and Room (1966) found that single men were more antisocial and maladjusted than married men. In agreement with Knupfer et al., Jessie Bernard (1972) summarized four studies and also concluded that single men were less happy than married men.

James Lynch, in his book *The Broken Heart* (1977), has discussed the medical consequences of loneliness in America, and his conclusions tend to replicate those from the studies just mentioned. Lynch has pointed out that "unconnected humans"—the divorced, the widowed, the single—die sooner than married people, and that among unmarried Americans heart disease is almost double the rate for the married. In the first months after bereavement, the risk of death among the widowed may be ten times as high for the married. The author also noted that both human and animal infants, deprived of both parents and reared in emotionally barren institutionalized settings, fail to thrive—and may be vulnerable, later, to early death. He has also been able to document that sudden and adverse life changes are frequently followed by a sudden onset of illness.

In our "age of narcissism" and "age of sensation," in which people want what they want when they want it, it should not surprise us that more and more individuals shun the responsibilities of marriage and seek sexual and other pleasures through alternative life-styles. The helping professional, however, must recognize that the popularity of a particular life-style such as group sex, celibacy, or homosexuality does not automatically suggest that the individuals participating in the particular modus vivendi are happy, healthy, or mature. On the contrary, I believe that this book has already documented the thesis that when psychosocial tasks are resolved, one can reasonably enjoy a monogamous marriage and cope relatively well with its frustrations, but that when these tasks are not mastered, marriage will be feared because it induces anxiety, and the individual will seek escapes from it in one way or another.

Although the clinician working with people on their sexual and interpersonal problems focuses sharply on his or her clients' internal life, as has already been suggested, the single client's social orbit should never be overlooked in assessing and treating emotional problems. For example, many divorced and widowed women in middle age, after twenty years of marriage, find it difficult to meet suitable men partly because there simply aren't enough of them. Demographic data have changed considerably in the last few decades, and there are now, in the 1980s, many more widows than widowers (Libby, 1978). While social factors are always pertinent in examining any client's plight, the clinician should also be aware of the fact that many clients use realistic social factors to rationalize their internal problems and avoid confronting them.

This chapter will demonstrate that many of the individuals who shun marriage fear it because they have not resolved sexual problems that evolved from their childhood experiences. This, of course, is not meant to imply that all married people are healthier and happier than all single people. The case vignettes in chapter 6 demonstrated otherwise. Rather, the contention is that the single person who insists on remaining single is often avoiding facing unresolved psychosexual problems, and that if the person faces them marriage will not appear so ominous.

Sexual Deviancy: Issues of Civil Rights and Mental Health

In examining some of the psychosexual problems of single people (from which many married individuals also suffer), such as homosexuality, exhibitionism, voyeurism, and Don Juanism, we have to avoid stigmatizing these people and stereotyping them. It is well known that individuals like the homosexual, transsexual, and fetishist can easily lose jobs and other privileges simply because of their sexually deviant status. All too frequently, a psychiatrist or other mental hygienist has participated in discharging the "deviant" from his or her job by labeling the person "emotionally disturbed."

While it is quite clear that homosexuality, bisexuality, or celibacy are usually indicative of maturational lags and emotional conflicts, there is no direct correlation between maturational retardation and poor job performance. In considering the diagnosis and disposition of an individual labeled sexually deviant, the practitioner recognizes that there is a huge range of possible behavior within one given diagnostic category. For example, a person who chooses members of his or her own sex as exclusive sexual partners may be aggressive or passive, very egocentric or quite altruistic, impulsive or controlled, intelligent or unintelligent. The same may be said for celibates, voyeurs, and others.

Because the labels "sexual dysfunction," "perversion," or even "gay" do not fully describe but tend to stereotype an individual, they offer little predictive power in fully determining psychosexual functioning. In dealing with the concept of sexual deviancy, two issues must be clearly separated: the individual's civil rights and the individual's mental health. To ensure an individual's civil rights, the form his or her sexual practices take should not be an issue in the job the person is provided or the house the person rents. Furthermore, the helping practitioner's job is not an administrative or legal one. He or she should not assist legal or administrative officers in determining whether, say, a transsexual or celibate client is capable of assuming a job or is guilty or innocent in court. The role of the clinician in helping people who have sexual deviations should be limited to the consultation room, where the clinician helps them better understand their motives, anxieties, and interpersonal stresses. If practitioners deviate from this role, they contaminate the treatment process and prevent clients from trusting them.

Some Psychosexual Problems of Single People

One of the ever-present dynamics that clinicians observe in many single people is their unresolved emotional tie to their parents. For many single people the idea of having a sustained sexual and emotional relationship with another person, as exists in marriage, unconsciously means that they are obliterating their parents. The frightening prospect of experiencing oneself as a powerful and devastating killer keeps the person tied to his or her own parents and very frightened of having a marital partner. Often these clients can have an enjoyable sexual and interpersonal life with many different friends of the opposite sex, but should the prospect of marriage become an issue, they become impotent or frigid and find many rationalizations to sustain their single lives.

Frequently, although not always, the single person has formed a strong symbiotic relationship with one or both parents, and this symbiosis, of course, has been an unconscious mutual arrangement. When anybody is tied up in a symbiosis, separation unconsciously connotes death. Often the single person who is symbiotically attached will actually be told by a parent—subtly or not so subtly—"If you leave me, I'll die." This latent or overt threat becomes internalized and the client must resist marriage. If the symbiotic single client does not hear threats from parents when he or she considers marriage, the person may take the initiative in discussing negative aspects of a prospective spouse's character with the parents so that they will advise not getting married.

Alice, age thirty-two, sought treatment because she was unable to sustain a relationship with a man. Although she always had "good times" on dates, whenever the idea of a commitment was introduced she had severe anxiety attacks, became belligerent toward the man, and could not participate in sex.

An only child, Alice was extremely close to both of her parents. They shared everything with each other and Alice had never slept away from home until she was thirteen years old, when she went to camp. On describing to her therapist her departure from home to go away to camp, she recalled with tears that "it seemed either that I was going off to Siberia or I *was getting married* and they were losing me."

An attractive and bright young woman, Alice was an excellent student in high school and was well liked by both peers and teachers. The same was true in college, where she excelled. The college she attended was in the same town where her parents lived, and Alice commuted daily, "never thinking of going to school out of town."

Alice was twenty-three when she had her first sexual experience. She said it was the first time she had done anything without informing her parents, and she had "felt like a traitor." Even though her male partner was very likable and understanding, she had to break up with him soon afterward because she felt "dirty and corrupt."

As Alice got older and found that she was resisting sexual experiences with men, she discussed the issue with her parents. After they gave her "some permission" to have sex, she was a little freer, but "not completely free."

An interesting development occurred in Alice's transference relationship with her male therapist which helped her to get in touch with her fear of marriage. She continually wanted to change the day and hour of her weekly appointment with the therapist. When this pattern was explored with her, she eventually remarked, "A weekly appointment would be like making a commitment to you and I'll be damned if I'll do that. It's like getting married, and that's the last thing I want to do with you."

As Alice explored her fear of committing herself to a relationship with her therapist, she got in touch with fantasies of maiming and eventually destroying both of her parents. These fantasies would be followed by much guilt accompanied by a desire to quit treatment. Slowly she learned that she was in a power struggle with her parents and that she unconsciously wished to destroy them. As she became emotionally convinced of her wish to defy her parents by marrying, she felt much freer. She then could feel closer to the therapist and began to date a man on a consistent basis. When she learned that she could enjoy sex without wanting to destroy her parents, she got much more satisfaction from it.

While a symbiotic attachment to parents is one of the prime reasons that keep many people single, other unresolved maturational problems can contribute as well. Many people unconsciously equate marriage with a victory over the parent of the same sex, i.e., an oedipal victory, and have to give up "the prize" as soon as they have won it. This is one of the reasons why many engagements are broken and marriages are not consummated. Furthermore, it is one of the main reasons why the individual's sexual interest toward the future marital partner can decline as the date of the marriage gets nearer.

Although men and women have many rationalizations to explain their single status, in most cases they are unable to separate from a symbiotic attachment from their parents or have other unresolved maturational problems of which they are unaware. However, it is these unresolved maturational problems which interfere with their ability to have a sustained sexual and emotional relationship with a marital partner.

Widowhood

Many men and women who are widowed fail to resume a sexual life after the loss of the spouse. Again, many rationalizations are offered to support their celibate modus vivendi, but the reasons for their celibacy are usually found in the dynamics of their internal psychic lives.

In a historical analysis of widows in America and England during the eighteenth, nineteenth, and part of the twentieth century, Fox and Quitt (1980) point out that widows had to face a society that felt threatened by the seductive image of a sexually experienced but unmarried woman. It was felt that the sinful, or "Eve," part of a woman's nature would emerge if she continued alone in her widowhood (Pearson, 1980). Therefore, it was often expected that widows would remarry. In England and America, where the male death rate was high and where there was a severe shortage of women, many, in fact, did remarry quite soon after their husband's death. Puritan widows were advised to remarry shortly so as not to idolize their departed spouses, while Quakers were expected to wait for upwards of a year (Fox and Quitt, 1980).

Although our forbears did not prescribe a life of celibacy if one's spouse died, many widows and widowers of the 1980s feel an obligation to the desceased to "be faithful" and not have sex with anyone. What clinicians have learned about these men and women is that they cannot permit themselves to have sex and/or remarry after the death of a spouse because of their punitive superegos. Like children who bring the image of a restrictive parent with them wherever they go, many widows and widowers do the same thing with their deceased spouses. Said a widower in his fifties, "I can't even consider remarriage. My wife is always watching me, and if I have a date with a woman I feel I'm two-timing my wife."

The dead spouse as the superego who always watches and punishes is the theme of Neil Simon's play *Chapter Two*. The protagonist, although very much in love with his second wife, is so tormented by guilt for defying the image of his dead wife that he has to shorten his honeymoon, leave his second wife, and "return" to his deceased wife.

The interference of allegiance to the dead spouse with the widower's remarriage is also the theme of Noel Coward's *Blithe Spirit* and of the famous Thurber cartoon in which the first wife is perched on top of a bookcase in order to maintain her constant presence.

When a widow or widower is too guilt-ridden to move on to another sexual relationship, we have to ask, "Why does he (she) make the deceased spouse such a punitive superego?" What clinicians have been able to determine is that there is usually a great deal of unconscious hostility toward the deceased when the widow or widower cannot permit himself or herself sexual pleasure. Having secretly wished that the departed would drop dead, widows and widowers then magically reason that their wishes have killed their spouses. They then are tormented with guilt, need punishment, and keep their departed spouses alive, hovering over their everyday activities and stopping them from having any sexual gratification (Kübler-Ross, 1969; Freud, 1917).

Ben, age fifty-two, sought treatment because he had been in a continual depression ever since his wife, Elsie, died three years ago. Although many of his friends and relatives wanted to help him get remarried, or at least have some dates, Ben refused their offers and continued to brood and mourn.

Although Ben described his life with Elsie as "beautiful" and his sex life with her as "ecstatic," he had been unable to permit himself any sexual fantasies about any women since Elsie died.

After spending several months with his female therapist telling her what a wonderful woman Elsie was and how much he missed her, Ben began to have warm feelings toward the therapist. He demonstrated his warmth by bringing her flowers on one occasion and chocolates on another. However, when his therapist took note of Ben's seductions and suggested that perhaps he was looking at their interviews as "dates," Ben became very self-conscious, frightened, and evasive. With help from his therapist, Ben went on to point out that he liked her very much and in fact did have a fantasy of taking her out to dinner and to the theater, and then maybe to his apartment. However, Ben pointed out sadly, "Elsie is watching us and forbidding me to do anything much with you."

Ben reacted with surprise when his therapist asked him, "How come you want Elsie to watch us?" He did not realize that he was arranging this, but thought that Elsie was somehow just imposing her image on him whenever he was thinking of having sexual pleasure. Slowly he was able to see what he was arranging, as he indicated when he said, "I guess I'm like a guilty child who wants my mother to punish me for transgressing. Gee, I make Elsie my mother!"

A significant change took place in Ben's sexual and interpersonal life when he was able to get in touch with his murderous wishes toward Elsie. When he began to realize how much of a symbiosis he had had with her, "owing her my body and soul," he could then begin to recall his many fantasies of being single and "on my own" instead of being trapped. The more Ben could acknowledge his resentment of Elsie (and not be punished or condemned for it), the more he could feel warmer with the therapist. As he had less of a need to punish himself for his wish for Elsie to die, he could allow himself more sexual pleasure with other women, and eventually he did remarry.

Many widows and widowers like Ben in the above case illustration are so guilt-ridden that they cannot permit themselves any sexual satisfaction at all. Some move toward new partners but their guilt traps them and they either deaden their sexual appetites or stop the new relationship altogether. This can also happen with some divorced spouses.

Divorce

Less than a generation ago divorce was considered a tragedy and a disgrace. Few divorced people discussed their feelings about it and virtually no researcher or journalist wrote about it. Recently divorce has become so common and so widely discussed that in the past fifteen years more than five hundred books and articles on the subject have been published. By 1976 there was one divorce for every two marriages—an all-time high (Hunt and Hunt, 1977).

As divorce becomes commonplace, more people are viewing marital failure in relatively sophisticated and complicated terms of multiple, interrelated causes with contributions on both sides (Krantzler, 1975). There are now no-fault divorces or equal-fault divorces.

Although the divorce experience often propels formerly married persons into a life of casual and egalitarian sex in which there is an openness about sexual behavior (Hunt and Hunt, 1977), many such people become sexually abstinent and sexually crippled and live a life of loneliness and depression. Their reaction to their divorces is psychologically similar to that of some widows and widowers, who unconsciously believe that they have killed their spouses and need to punish themselves and not permit themselves any sexual or interpersonal pleasure.

Many divorced people have been involved in sadomasochistic relationships with their spouses, with oneupmanship fracases that continue after their divorces. Their deep yearning to fight keeps them in contact with each other, and arguments about alimony, visitation rights, and old injustices sustain their battles. Obviously, such sadomasochistic spouses are very attached to the marital partner, and although legally divorced, are still emotionally married. When one of them becomes involved with another sexual partner, the unconscious aim is frequently to defy the divorced mate rather than to give and to receive sexual pleasure. Usually, when sex is utilized to gratify revengeful wishes there is limited if any pleasure attached to the sex, because the person is involved in an angry fight and unconsciously can arrange for his or her just punishment by becoming impotent or frigid.

When men and women divorce, they do not divorce themselves from their neuroses. Consequently, many depressed husbands and wives who have been convinced that the sources of their sexual and interpersonal unhappiness are their uncompromising, insensitive spouses are shocked to find themselves feeling vulnerable, weak, and full of self-doubt with new sexual partners. Feeling uncomfortable at the dawning realization that maybe they contributed to the sexual and interpersonal incompatibility in their marriages, they can move toward celibacy and defend themselves against recognizing their own sexual anxieties and psychological immaturities.

One of the factors that sparks many a divorce is the "romantic ideal." Though elusive and in many ways unrealistic, to many people it is still worth pursuing. Many a person who divorces several times is still unconsciously trying to find a Garden of Eden. Consequently, in comparison to the Paradise that the romantic seeks, his or her partner's sexual and emotional responses are unstimulating and unfulfilling.

When Carol, age thirty, sought out treatment she had been married three times. She brought out during her initial consultation with her female therapist that she was "a romantic and I'm still trying to find a romantic man." She would fall "happily in love," believing that she was with "the perfect man," but after a few months the marriage "seemed bland and our activities got mundane." Then she would initiate a divorce.

After a few months of therapy Carol began to "tire of treatment" and wanted to quit. As with her marriages, when her strong, infantile yearnings were not gratified she wished to run. When her therapist attempted to show her that she was arranging the same thing in her therapeutic relationship that she did in her marriages, she fled treatment in indignation.

Although divorce is a very popular institution in our society, the clinician should constantly bear in mind that a happy marriage consists of two relatively happy people. Stories about a "normal" woman who becomes the victim of a neurotic man, or vice versa, tend to be distortions of the truth. While there are many divorced people who are more mature than their married counterparts, nonetheless clinical experience demonstrates that two neurotic individuals look for and find each other with uncanny regularity (Bergler, 1963).

Homosexuality

Our liberated sexual climate of the 1980s has permitted clinicians, social scientists, writers, and the community at large to discuss homosexuality openly, dispassionately, and more sympathetically than was
true in the past. The gay liberation movement has in many ways won
for its constituents legal and social equality with heterosexuals and
has helped to temper medical opinion and legal penalties concerning
homosexuality (Hunt, 1974). Yet, according to most sexual researchers, the incidence of overt homosexuality has not increased. As Arno
Karlen pointed out in 1971 in his comprehensive research, *Sexuality
and Homosexuality*, no recent study has even hinted at an increase in
homosexuality since Kinsey's time (1948). This point was reaffirmed
by Morton Hunt in his study, *Sexual Behavior in the 1970s* (1974),
and in the book *On Sexuality* by Karasu and Socarides (1979).

While the incidence of homosexuality has not changed, the study
of it by professionals has been very much intensified (Bieber, 1962;
Hite, 1976; Hooker, 1957; Socarides, 1978; Weinberg and Williams,
1974; Fine, 1981). In this freer scientific atmosphere clincians are reporting consistently that virtually all human beings have some unconscious desire to be a member of the opposite sex. Anybody engaged in
intensive therapy has noted that boys and men have wishes to have
breasts, babies, and the rest, and girls and women often fantasy that
the life of a male would be better.

Practitioners and researchers have also found that those who repudiate homosexuality the most vigorously are often trying to deny
their own homosexual fantasies. The late Senator Joseph McCarthy
was an outspoken and punitive opponent of the rights of homosexuals, yet it has been alleged that he found his own intense homosexual
desires quite intolerable (Wertham, 1966). Practitioners who have
worked in institutions like the army or prisons where homosexual
urges are stimulated have often discovered that the administrative
personnel of these facilities are most condemnatory of homosexuality
in any form. It is now a virtual axiom of dynamic psychotherapy that
individuals strenuously repudiate in others what they cannot tolerate
in themselves.

For clinicians to understand their gay and lesbian clients in depth,
they should also recognize that exclusive homosexuality is rarely
found among people who have had consistently gratifying love experiences with their parents. Over and over again, homosexual clients

attest to the fact that a total denial of the opposite sex comes out of a background of severe childhood frustration. When a homosexual pair is examined closely, one sees an enormous amount of vulnerability, uncertainty, and hatred in both partners. In many cases, the two are acting out a fantasied mother-child relationship (Socarides, 1978).

Two theories are quite prominent in the study of homosexuality. One is the psychoanalytic perspective that states that men and women become homosexual because they are frightened and sexually frustrated, and have had unfulfilling interpersonal relationships in childhood. The other perspective is sociological, and it maintains that homosexuality is simply a socially deviant form of sexual expression. What is important for helping professionals to realize is that no social scientist subscribing to the social deviance theory has offered any explanation of why one person becomes homosexual whereas another does not. Investigators such as Weinberg and Williams (1974), Hooker (1957), and Hite (1976) simply regard homosexuality as a naturally occurring variation.

Although many dynamically oriented clinicians (Bieber, 1962; Socarides, 1978; Fine, 1981) have consistently demonstrated the profound psychic conflicts in homosexual patients, their results have been questioned because they have supposedly worked from a skewed sample—clients in treatment. While it is true that people in psychotherapy are usually *more* mature than people who do not have the courage to confront themselves and face their immaturities and irrationalities, the similarities between the two groups are probably much greater than the differences. As Harry Stack Sullivan is supposed to have said, ''We are all human more or less.''

Many lay and professional groups erroneously assume that if a person is in distress about his or her conflicts and seeks out therapy, this is less mature than the person who wishes to ignore psychic conflicts. Distress about a problem is healthier than lack of distress. Homosexuals who repudiate their need for psychotherapy are frequently using much repression and/or denial.

It should also be recognized that in the course of intensive treatment of any client, reports are received from the person in treatment on hundreds of other people. Thus the clinician has a very wide sample, though unsystematized, of homosexual and nonhomosexual people. As a method of research, the course of dynamically oriented treatment reveals far more about the personality characteristics of homosexuals (and heterosexuals, for that matter) than do superficial questionnaire studies—the methodology utilized in most studies of homosexuality.

Fine (1981) has been able to demonstrate that no sexually permissive society ever has led to a wide incidence of overt exclusive homosexuality. Wherever it has been investigated, an exlusive homosexual orientation has been found to result from deep-seated heterosexual frustration. Fine notes: "This commonsense notion has been amply confirmed by analytic theory and analytic experience." He goes on to comment:

> What is there to say, then, about the currently widespread belief that homosexuality is just a "normal" deviation, of no more significance than wearing a hat or not wearing one, which also varies with the times? Two comments: It is, first, totally devoid of objective foundation. Second, it has become part of a profound political battle. Within psychiatry it is the battle against a humanistic-psychoanalysis led by the reactionary organic psychiatrists. Within a number of the professions it is a battle led by militant homosexuals who are out to assert their power. . . . Within the culture it is a battle against a healthy resolution of life in terms of the analytic ideal. (p. 301).

As mentioned earlier, in working with the problems of homosexual clients we should differentiate between their civil rights and their mental health. All clients, regardless of their sexual preferences and neurotic problems, have legal, civil, and moral rights which should always be respected. However, practitioners should also keep in mind that when an *exclusive* attachment to the person of the same sex is carefully examined, it will always turn out to have strong elements of hatred and revenge mixed up with it. Clinicians, in helping to reduce the oppression that homosexual groups endure, should also try, as part of this legitimate aim, to help gays and lesbians get into psychotherapy. Anybody who, after rejecting the idea of the other sex, then behaves in the manner of that sex is suffering and needs sensitive understanding.

In any discussion of homosexuality it is important to remind ourselves that what is termed "masculine" or "feminine" depends in many ways on social and cultural factors as well as biological ones. The roles of "woman" and "man" are based on a host of factors: economic arrangements, ethnic values, family arrangements, traditional mores, and so on. Yet we still have to answer the question, "When members of both sexes are available to the client, why does he or she choose members of the same sex for sexual gratification?"

In male homosexuality, one of the prime etiological factors appears to be castration anxiety. The male, usually because of strong incestuous wishes toward the mother and intense competitive and murderous fantasies toward the father, submits to the father and becomes a lover to a father figure; he would rather submit to father than oppose him. To the male homosexual, the sight of being without a penis is so terrifying that he avoids it by rejecting any sexual relationship with a partner who doesn't have one. The homosexual man is so determined to affirm the existence of a penis that he refuses to do without it in his sexual partner. The recognition of the fact that there are human beings without a penis leads to the conclusion that one might become such a being (Fenichel, 1945).

Frequently male homosexuals have an exaggerated love for their mothers, and homosexuality can express itself not only as submitting to Father but also as mothering oneself. The homosexual gives to his partner in the manner that his mother would tend to him. He can choose as love objects young men or boys who, for him, are similar to himself, and he can love them with the tenderness that he has desired from his mother (Socarides, 1978).

Another etiological factor in homosexuality is a question of identification. Children tend to identify themselves more with the parent from whom they have experienced the most impressive frustrations. Consequently, those men who are more inclined to become homosexual have had a weak father or no father at all and have been frustrated in crucial things by the mother (Josselyn, 1948). However, it is also important to note that boys who have had no mother and have been brought up by a father can also become homosexual because the enjoyment of passive pleasures at the hands of a man, instead of a woman, creates a disposition toward homosexuality (Fenichel, 1945).

In female homosexuality, the etiological factors frequently emanate from oedipal conflicts and penis envy. Many women clients who are homosexual report that they have been severely disappointed with their fathers. Unable to have him and his penis, they unconsciously become him and assume an active sexual relationship with women. This inverted oedipal situation can ward off Mother's disapproval and possible abandonment. The female homosexual tends to regress to an early mother-daughter relationship, and many of the activities of homosexual women consist of the mutual playing of "mother and child" (Socarides, 1978).

For female homosexuals the sight of a penis frequently creates a fear of an impending violation; even more frequently, it mobilizes thoughts and emotions about the difference in appearance between the male and female. The lesbian, in effect, is unconsciously saying to the man (her father), "I hate you for what you have and the pleasures you can have with your penis. I will have nothing to do with it. I will relate only to women sexually—they understand me in a way you don't. We have much more in common."

While almost all heterosexual clients develop some homosexual transference feelings in treatment, overt homosexuals usually do not for a long time. They rationalize their lack of sexual interest in therapists of the same sex by saying "You're not my type," but basically they are afraid of exploring their homosexual transference reactions because they appear to them incestuous activities which are taboo (Fine, 1971). Consequently, it takes a long time for the homosexual man or woman to feel safe enough to examine his or her motives for leading a homosexual life. Nonetheless, Socarides (1978) and Bieber (1962) have reported that over half of their homosexual patients moved to the point of having full heterosexual lives.

Usually most homosexual clients enter therapy, *not* to be treated for their homosexuality, but for depression over a lost lover, psychosomatic complaints, or some other symptoms. While they often have an unconscious wish to become heterosexual, this possibility should not be suggested by the therapist; otherwise the client will feel threatened and will leave treatment. The client must be met where he or she is, and the therapist, as with any other client, should not impose any agenda. Usually homosexual clients test therapists repeatedly to see if they will try to manipulate them into heterosexuality. The therapist, by genuinely conveying the message that empathetic understanding rather than removal of symptoms is the prime goal, meets the client where he or she is, and the client then feels safer with this attitude.

Donald, age thirty, who practiced homosexuality exclusively, sought psychotherapy not for his homosexuality, but for depression, loneliness, and many psychosomatic complaints. He became emotionally involved quite early in the treatment because he "liked the idea of just talking about whatever comes to my mind." The sheer ventilation of aggression toward his parents, complaints about the therapist for being too professional, and "the attention I get sometimes" reduced his sense of loneliness and depression as well as his psychosomatic complaints within a few months of twice-a-week therapy.

When Donald started to feel closer to his male therapist, he began to feel uncomfortable and came late to sessions, canceled several, and threatened to quit the therapy altogether. In the process of investigating what was bothering him about the therapist, Donald embarrassedly reported a dream in which he was sucking the therapist's penis but was spitting out the sperm because "it was too distasteful." Exploration of Donald's feeling of distaste led him to fantasies and memories of having sex with his older brother. He looked at his brother as one who would "give me the strength I never had."

Donald's brother was a substitute "for the father I never had." (Donald's father was described as a cold, distant man; he had died when Donald was ten years old.) As Donald brought out his sadness and his yearnings for a father, he started to feel much better and became closer to the therapist. He then began to talk about his relationship with his mother. It was a mutually seductive relationship with a lot of "biting, hugging, and feeling each other." In telling his therapist about his sexual feelings toward his mother, Donald became more and more "shocked" that the therapist did not "mock" him or "criticize" him. This experience intensified the positive transference and Donald began to identify more and more with the therapist. He experimented a little with women and then became very frightened and returned to men. Further exploration of his incestuous fears and oedipal competition—particularly the recognition that he felt he had killed his father—helped Donald move to more sustained sexual relationships with women.

Biologically, homosexuality is a stage in development. It arises in early childhood toward the parent of the same sex and often toward siblings of the same sex. Later it manifests itself in preadolescence toward same-sexed peers. All of these are stages which many individuals outgrow, but on which the neurotic fixates (Fine, 1971). If homosexuality is viewed, no more and no less, as a halt in growth which can be helped through an understanding therapeutic relationship, many of the mysteries and taboos about it can be modified.

Perversions

Like the more generic term "sexual deviant," "perversion" has frequently had pejorative connotations, and as a result "perverts" and those who regard them as such have not received the understanding and empathy they deserve. Utilizing a psychosexual perspective, all perversions are sexual substitutes. The fetishist, transsexual, exhibitionist, or sadist are people who are frightened of adult sexuality and must regress to sexual behavior that was appropriate when they were children. Perverts feel forced to "like" something even if it is against their will. While guilt feelings may oppose their impulses, they feel compelled to give in to their wishes in the hope of achieving some positive pleasure (Fenichel, 1945).

Perversions have been practiced for centuries in many different cultures (DeMause, 1981). At certain periods some of them, such as sadism and masochism, were even esteemed (Tannahill, 1980). Since the aims of perverse sexuality are the same as those of infantile sexuality, the possibility for every human being to become perverse under certain circumstances—e.g., imprisonment, extreme solitude—is rooted in the fact that he or she was once a child. As we have already learned, virtually all clients are defending themselves against infantile wishes; the difference between the pervert and others is that the former acts on infantile wishes instead of defending against them. As Fenichel stated it: "The simple formula presents itself: persons who react to sexual frustrations with a regression to infantile sexuality are perverts; persons who react with other defenses or who employ other defenses after the regression are neurotics" (1945, p. 325).

If we look at perversions as a form of behavior in which adult sexuality is supplanted by infantile sexuality because something is repulsive to the client about adult sexuality, the specific perversion tells us under which circumstances the client feels comfortable in expressing his sexuality. The fetishist, for example, fearing intercourse, regresses to that time of life when touching, feeling, and holding were major sources of gratification. He may be compared to the small child who loves to touch and play with a cotton blanket and is not capable of achieving more sexual gratification than that. In transvestitism, the client is like the child who is frightened to acknowledge the differences between the sexes. For example, the male transvestite unconsciously insists that the woman possesses a penis and thus overcomes his castration anxiety by identifying with a phallic woman. In exhibitionism, the client is unsure of his or her sexuality, and much like the child who repetitively plays house and insists on enacting a specific sexual role, the exhibitionist repetitively indicates, "See, I do have a penis!" or "See, I do have breasts!" The exhibitionist's act is equivalent to a child "showing off," as if he or she were averring, "I'll show you what I really wish I could be sure of all the time."

If the practitioner keeps in mind that the client engaged in perversions is a child who is terrified of being an adult, he or she can respond with empathy and understanding rather than with horror, anger, or disgust. He or she begins to appreciate that the voyeur can only watch rather than act and that the coprophiliac (one who gets sexual satisfaction out of excretory functions) can only play with feces or urine because sexual intercourse is too overwhelming. The therapist sees that sadists are frightened of their passivity and masochists cannot cope with their violent wishes.

Usually when a client suffering with perversions is referred for help or actively seeks it out, he is most uncomfortable in talking about his perversions. The practitioner must respect the client's resistances and not pressure him to face them. Only after the client feels that he will be accepted, no matter what he talks about or doesn't talk about, will he be able to reveal his discomfort about his infantile acts. Often the therapist's attitude of genuine acceptance in the face of the client's strong resistance can help the client feel less "bad" and less infantile. It is also important for the therapist to convey to the client the attitude that "You are frightened of adult sexuality—let's see why" rather than combing the whys and wherefores of the perversion. Slowly the client can identify with the worker's attitude that he, the client, is trying to compensate for what he fears and deny what terrifies him.

Eric, age thirty, sought help for vocational problems because he could not keep a job. While he did talk about his fear of male authorities, he was very vague about his life and spoke very tentatively to his female therapist. While he stated with much earnestness in his first consultation interview that he very much needed and wanted treatment, he subsequently canceled interviews and came late to many.

When the therapist said to Eric that she wasn't helping him feel comfortable with her—he was avoiding her—Eric became very embarrassed and tongue-tied and said that he found it very difficult to say what was on his mind. Again, the therapist said that something in her behavior must inhibit him and asked, "What can I do to make it safer for you here?" He answered, "You've got to promise not to punish me if I tell you the truth." When the therapist pointed out that she was there to help and understand, not to punish and criticize, Eric told her that he did not believe her. When the therapist related to Eric's distrust and asked what she had done so far that made Eric distrustful of her, Eric finally said, "I'll tell you, I'm an exhibitionist."

Eric then proceeded to relate to the therapist many details of his compulsive need to exhibit his penis to women workers. He knew "it wasn't the right thing to do" but could not help himself. Inasmuch as the therapist learned that Eric's exhibitionism was confined to his work place, she could tell him that there was something about the work situation that made him uncomfortable and that the exhibitionism was utilized to ease discomfort and receive reassurance.

Slowly Eric was able to work first on his fears of male authorities and then on his strong yearning to be close to a father figure. It became quite clear that to defend against his homosexual desires and his wish to be "Daddy's little girl," Eric was compulsively saying, "See, I'm not a girl! I'm a man, I have a penis."

The more Eric could safely talk to his therapist about his wish to be a little girl, the less he needed to defend himself through exhibitionism.

As was observed in the above vignette of Eric, it took the client a long time to talk about his difficulties. Since the therapist made it very safe for him by not criticizing Eric for his resistances and even considered the possibility that she was doing something to inhibit him, Eric could eventually tell his story. It should also be noted that the therapist concentrated *on what the client feared*, i.e., his homosexuality, rather than pursuing his exhibitionism. This is a very important principle in helping people with their psychosexual problems. The masochist should be helped to talk about *his fear* of sadism rather than his masochism per se; the voyeur should look at *his fear* of activity; the woman who wants to be a man should look at *her fear* of and disgust with her vagina, while the man who wants to be a woman should be helped to explore *his fear* of using his penis.

What clinicians have recently recognized about perversions is that the individuals having them have experienced very frustrating childhoods and are full of hatred. Frequently, they are revengeful people and are trying to convert childhood traumas into adult triumphs. Dr. Robert Stoller (1975) has cogently summarized several of the issues relating to perversions: "We no longer need to define a perversion according to the anatomy used, the object chosen, the society's stated morality, or the number of people who do it. All we need to know is what it means to the person doing it; while this may be difficult for us to uncover, there is still no priori reason to reject this technique for defining perversion" (p. 4).

Promiscuity

As has been noted several times, the 1980s have witnessed a conversion of many psychosexual difficulties into life-styles. Like homosexuality, promiscuity has been perceived as merely a socially defined deviancy without concomitant psychological conflicts. Kinsey's findings (1948) have prompted many people to reason that because promiscuous desires are found in almost all human beings and are not statistically aberrant, and because we also know that those who deny having such wishes are protecting themselves from anxiety, it would seem appropriate to encourage people to enjoy their bodies freely as long as they do not victimize others. Unfortunately, this argument leaves out the promiscuous person's motives, anxieties, and fears. Just as those who speak out against promiscuity are far from saints— they are probably trying to stop themselves from engaging in promiscuous acts—those who are promiscuous are not sinners, but people in psychological distress.

What clinicians have been able to conclude from their work with promiscuous, or hypersexual, clients is that they are usually *not* enjoying themselves sexually. Deprived of real sexual satisfaction, they attempt through compulsive sexuality to attain some gratification; however, their attempts are in vain. Although hypersexual clients give the impression of being sexually vigorous and often boast of their feats, they are, quite frequently, orgastically impotent. In many instances, their compulsive need for sex is a desperate attempt to prove that they are sexual. Sometimes these clients are trying unsuccessfully to find the perfect mother or father, and they go from partner to partner, always being disappointed. They are similar to people who must compulsively achieve in order to deny their strong feelings of inferiority (Fenichel, 1945).

The Don Juan and his female counterpart are more interested in seduction than loving. Frequently they boast about how they've "scored" or "made a killing." In most cases these people shun intimacy and concentrate on overcoming their partner's resistance. Frequently, when their partners are interested in them, these clients "turn off." They are more interested in power than in eroticism (Stoller, 1975).

Promiscuous clients usually report negative sexual experiences in adolescence such as sexual abuse, molestation, or some other form of forced sex (Vitaliano, James, and Boyer, 1981). They have frequently had improverished lives as far as the issue of giving and receiving spontaneous love is concerned (Ostow, 1974).

Inasmuch as these people form superficial relationships, they of course find it difficult to sustain a therapeutic alliance; they are prone to leave treatment. It requires much patience and sensitivity on the therapist's part to help the client stay in the treatment relationship.

Freda, age thirty-five, sought treatment for psychosomatic ailments. She was suffering from asthma, migraine headaches, insomnia, and gastrointestinal problems. An excellent teacher, she was very successful with her high school students and loved their praise and admiration.

She told her male therapist in her first interview how handsome, sensitive, and helpful he was as he listened to her story without saying more than a few words. After four interviews in which she described incidents involving her "controlling but nonfeeling" mother and her "weak, passive" father, she said that she had never felt better in her life and attributed all of her gains to her work with her "perfect" therapist.

When Freda's therapist was not seduced by the client's laudatory remarks, Freda became depressed and angry and told him that he had initially seemed to be a responsive fellow but now appeared like a "cold fish." She threatened to leave treatment because she needed "somebody more human." When the therapist suggested to Freda that she was angry and upset with him because he wasn't being charmed enough, she became furious and stomped out of the office saying she would never return. On her not showing up for her next interview, the therapist called her to come back and talk things out.

Freda quickly responded to the therapist's invitation, and, after apologizing for her anger, went on the say in a subsequent interview, "I knew I could get you to call me if I made a sufficient fuss." She further went on to say that she had always considered herself a winner and "nobody is going to puncture that idea."

As treatment went on Freda made several more attempts to tease the therapist, to manipulate him, and to get him to feel guilty for not spending more time with her and for not being more of a friend. When the therapist interpreted to Freda that apparently she would only be able to like herself if she got him into bed, Freda again stomped out of the office and vowed *never* to return to treatment.

Freda could not be persuaded to return to treatment for some time; however, the therapist persisted in calling her until she did come back. On returning to treatment, Freda seemed more subdued and began to reflect on the fact that she never could conceive of a relationship in which she "couldn't make a triumph." She started to describe a long series of one-night stands with men in which she felt like a "successful aggressor" and secretly enjoyed weakening the men.

As her aggression was examined, Freda could begin to see how she used sex as a retaliatory device against her parents. Her strong revenge covered up a lot of powerful dependency wishes. Although she found it very difficult to face these wishes, particularly her dependency on the therapist, as she voiced her desires to be a little girl and reflected on her deprived childhood, her promiscuity declined and she slowly moved into more mature sexual relationships.

What is frequently overlooked by clinicians in working with promiscuous clients are the latter's deep feelings of pain and uncertainity, and their yearning to be given parental affection. Inasmuch as these clients are very frightened of their passivity, their promiscuity is utilized to defend against it. Through promiscuity they feel in control and able to dominate. However, when treatment is successful their strong hunger emerges.

Grace, age twenty-two, was a prostitute and came into treatment for depression and a host of psychosomatic complaints. While she resisted the treatment for some time and was quite contemptuous of her female therapist for most of it, a dramatic shift in her attitude toward the therapy and the therapist was provoked by an incident on her job. One day, one of the men who frequented the brothel where she worked, and consistently sought out her services, brought her flowers. Grace, instead of utilizing her "rough and tough" demeanor, found herself hugging the man, thanking him profusely, and weeping for days.

This experience, which was not only activated by the gift of the flowers but also by what was transpiring in her treatment, got Grace in tune with deep dependency needs which she had been denying and repressing for years. As she voiced them for several more months in her treatment, she began to reconsider her job as a prostitute. She said in one interview, "Depending on somebody isn't so bad. I have been laughing at those guys for needing me. They should be understood better."

The Single Person Who Is Physically Handicapped

A group of people who have been insufficiently considered by helping professionals are the physically handicapped. Especially overlooked are the sexual lives of these people, particularly those who are single (Harrison, 1979).

Although researchers have recognized for some time that physically handicapped people often feel psychologically vulnerable, weak in their self-esteem and body image, insufficient attention has been given to how they can be helped to enjoy more satisfying sexual lives.

Physical obstacles which can result from various handicaps and interfere with sexual functioning have been described in the literature (Harrison, 1979; Gregory, 1974; Heslinga, Schellen, and Verkuyl, 1974). Such obstacles might include problems with erection and ejaculation for men and lubrication for women. More important perhaps are the problems connected with finding positions "which are comfortable and adaptable to sexual intimacy while attending to sensory and motor conditions, spasticity, and urine and bowel incontinence'' (Harrision, 1979, p. 91).

The sexual problems of the physically handicapped are often difficult to fathom. Sometimes it is virtually impossible to know how much a neurological disorder is contributing to the sexual dysfunctioning and how much of the sexual dysfunction is in response to the angry feelings, helplessness, and self-consciousness that have been induced by the physical handicap. Furthermore, sexual inhibitions may arise from the sheer fact that the person feels uncomfortable having sex in a wheelchair or with a catheter tube. All these issues can contribute to a fear of sexual failure and can intensify performance anxiety.

Not all physically handicapped people handle their sexual anxieties by withdrawal. Some overcompensate by trying to have sex as much as possible so that they can reassure themselves that they are still sexually adequate.

In working on the psychosexual problems of physically handicapped clients, it is imperative for the helping professional not to stereotype these clients. Like all clients they have unique histories, unique self-images, and unique attitudes toward intimacy and sexuality. Some of them may be more capable of having a fuller sexual life than they think they can, and in other cases the opposite may be true. What is crucial is that each physically handicapped client be individualized by the helper.

Gochros and Gochros (1977), in their discussion of the "sexually elite" versus the "sexually oppressed," have described the equating of sexuality with intercourse and have pointed out that this perspective restricts the variety of sexual expressions which the handicapped might be capable of achieving.

The helping professional who works with the physically handicapped on their sexual problems has to be extremely flexible. With some of these clients, the job will be to acknowledge their needs and encourage them to have some kind of sexual life, while with others it will be helping them to accept certain, or maybe severe, limitations in their sexual lives. This, of course, requires of the helping professional a thorough understanding of the physical and psychological problems associated with physical handicaps.

Harry was a thirty-year-old veteran of the Vietnam War who was being seen by a social worker at a Veterans Administration Rehabilitation Office. Although Harry was paralyzed in both his arms, his attitude toward physical therapy, further education, and an eventual job was quite positive. He was making steps in all these areas in his consultations with the social worker.

When the social worker realized that Harry had not made any mention of his sexual life, she decided, after about six months of weekly contacts, to bring the sexual dimension of his life into the interviews. Harry's initial response was very interesting. He thought that it was impossible, given his physical handicaps, to ever have a sexual life again, and he didn't know whether to thank the worker or damn her for bringing up something that up to now had been, in his mind, impossible to achieve.

The social worker, armed with her understanding of Harry's physical limitations, told him that he was quite capable of having sexual intercourse but seemed to fear it. Harry then spent many interviews talking about his physical unattractiveness, his strong feeling of impotence, and his "need to be asexual." Like many clients with physical handicaps, he viewed his disability as a punishment. Exploration of this revealed that Harry suffered much guilt from having masturbated (which involves the use of hands and arms) and felt that he had "got what he deserved."

As Harry was able to talk to his social worker about his "sexual misdeeds" and was not punished for them, his guilt diminished and his self-esteem increased. He was then able to feel closer to the worker and entertain some sexual fantasies toward her. As he saw that his female social worker did not reject him, he slowly could move toward other women.

When sexuality is combined with the subject of physical disability, the modal response has been one of denial and repression. Much more attention needs to be devoted to the sexual needs and problems of physically handicapped people, particularly the unmarried, whose support systems are often feeble. The same may be said for all unattached individuals in our society who frequently feel unfulfilled, both sexually and emotionally.

Chapter 8

Sex and the Aged

STATISTICAL LIFE EXPECTANCY has risen with enormous swiftness. In Greek times it was twenty-nine years, by 1900 it had moved to forty-four years, and by the early 1950s it was sixty-two years. In our current era life expectancy is around seventy years (Meerloo, 1969; Wiedeman, 1975). There are now approximately 30 million people in the United States above the age of sixty, and their aging and sexuality are being viewed in drastically different ways than they were perceived just a few decades ago (Waltzman and Karasu, 1979).

Formerly a castoff, the aged person is now treated with much more respect. Instead of being considered a sexual celibate, the senior citizen is increasingly admonished that he or she is entitled to an active sex life. In lieu of the stereotypical picture of the older person as one who resorts to sex as a regressive device or a perversion, more practitioners and writers are regarding the sexual life of aged people as an important and healthy, if not essential, component of their modus vivendi. Researchers are investigating the biological, psychological, and sexual aspects of aging, and practitioners are increasingly devoting themselves to helping older people increase their sexual satisfaction. Woody Allen, the comedian, has been quoted as saying, "I think sex should be confined to one's life-time!" (Murphy, 1979, p. 72).

Many professionals have moved to the point where senescence is being regarded as a developmental phase comparable to latency or adolescence. This view tends to favor a more objective approach and prevents both the overidealization and the pessimism so common in earlier discussions of aging. While it is true that psychosexual functioning in other maturational phases deals with expanding potentialities for development, the senescent person must consider certain diminishing abilities and lessened opportunities (Jackel, 1975).

In this chapter, we will consider some of the cultural influences that impose themselves on aged persons, review some of the research on their psychosexual lives, and discuss some of the actual biological and psychosexual changes that do occur in all aged people. This will assist us in examining some of the diagnostic and therapeutic issues that are important in clinical work with the aged.

Cultural Issues

For countless decades, when sex manifested itself in the older person he or she was immediately considered peculiar, and this distorted image was reaffirmed by professionals. For example, the sexologist Dr. Krafft-Ebing suggested in 1892 that when the older person expresses himself sexually, "a presumption of pathological conditions suggests itself at once" (Krafft-Ebing, 1892, p. 37). He went on to warn against "the dire consequences" of these sexual urges by pointing out that the "first objects for the attempts of these senile subjects are children," and he further stated that the older person is prone to have sex with "geese, chickens, etc. as well as horrible perverse sexual acts with adults" (Krafft-Ebing, 1892, p. 38). This well-known sexologist attributed the "perverse" behavior of the senior citizen to the fact that with increasing age, the person's "brain atrophies."

Misconceptions about sexual expression in the aged did not stop with Krafft-Ebing, and they tend to persist even in the 1980s. The notion of aging persons as polymorphous perverse seems to have its roots in the infantile sexual life of their junior counterparts. Younger people tend to project onto older people their own unacceptable childish wishes. Hence they tend to avoid older people in the same way they wish to avoid facing their own intolerable childish fantasies related to exhibitionism, voyeurism, intercourse with animals, uncontrolled masturbation, and intense lust in all forms.

The senior citizen tends to incorporate such distortions. Like any scapegoated minority, older people unconsciously view themselves as

the majority does. Just as many blacks, women, and Jews tend to regard themselves on an unconscious level (and sometimes consciously)
as second-class citizens, the senior citizen is prone to see herself or
himself as a "has-been," an "old fogey," or a "derelict."

The aged are frequently concentrated in segregated living situations that isolate them from the mainstream of society. Retirement
often induces a loss of status, a loss of purpose, and a loss of income
(Waltzman and Karasu, 1979). As Jackel (1975) has stated:

> Loss is the key word in senescence. The old [person] loses family and
> friends, economic independence, status [and] familiar surroundings.
> . . . The effect is a constriction in his world, with a need to find substi-
> tutes, a task that might well strain the adaptive abilities of a younger
> person. . . . Most important is the fact that these losses deprive the se-
> nescent [person] of the opportunity to satisfy the basic human needs to
> love and be loved, to have people to care for, and to be needed. (p. 436)

In order to minimize the guilt associated with the isolation of the
elderly, they are frequently relegated to areas of low visibility: "old-
aged homes," "retirement communities," or "nursing homes." Isolation and rejection of the old tend to produce in them feelings of
sadness and anger, thereby making them unpleasant to deal with and
easier to abandon. This increasing isolation of the old from the young
tends to reinforce the negative stereotypes of the old and ignores their
strengths (Waltzman and Karasu, 1979).

When society develops an unwitting resignation to the idea that
the aged person is on the way to further and further deterioration, it
is often easy for those who are responsible for helping them—family,
government, and professionals—to overlook the fact that there are
older people who have full command of their mental, sexual, and
physical abilities.

The psychiatrist Joost Meerloo (1969) has discussed the hostile attitude toward the aged which is "concealed by a thin veneer of esteem
and love." This can make for unrealistic solutions to the older person's problems, such as prescribing a mental hospital when psychotherapy could stave off institutionalization.

Although it has been indicated that there is increased tolerance
and understanding of the older person, our cultural view that sex, intimacy, and emotional spontaneity are for young romantics often
blurs the possibility for the older person to be considered a candidate
for sexual counseling.

On referring Mr. and Mrs. Aaron, a couple in their early seventies, to a family
agency, Dr. Smith told the intake worker: "They still think they are lovebirds

able to have a romance. See what you can do to help them accept the fact that the best thing they can do is hold hands." When the intake worker suggested to Dr. Smith that he sounded pessimistic about the Aarons' capacity to have an intimate sex life, he replied, "You, too, are dominated by the unrealistic romantic complex."

As suggested earlier, the romantic complex is a fiction, which, if believed, can even cripple the marriage and sex life of newlyweds. However, if people, young or old, cannot sustain a day-to-day passionate romance, it does not follow that they are on their last legs and doomed to a life of celibacy. As Dr. Gerald Murphy (1979) has suggested:

> Many of the attitudes regarding sexuality are shaped by a "Romeo and Juliet" image. Sex is for the young and the beautiful! The effect of such attitudes and beliefs on people's sexual lives is devastating. Not only are the sexual needs of older people denied and their sexual activity regarded with some embarrassment—if not downright disgust—but so are the sexual needs and behavior of so many others; the physically handicapped and the mentally retarded; not to mention the millions of physically less gifted people in society who would never pass a screen test for either a Romeo or Juliet part in *Love Story*. The notion of romantic love says: "Sex is for very special people!" (pp. 81-82).

In sum, our senior citizens are still victims of longstanding myths and prejudices which they, themselves, often internalize. They too frequently feel that sex should be terminated when they retire from work and therefore can experience guilt, shame, and anxiety when they have sexual thoughts and sexual drives. As has been discussed in earlier chapters, the work one does frequently has a sexual meaning; it can represent one's value in the eyes of others, particularly in the eyes of one's sexual partner. When individuals feel that they are not of value to the work world, they can mistakenly conclude that they have no sexual value. It is to be hoped that this and other lingering myths about aging will be deflated as researchers and clinicians continue to explore aging as a developmental phase which includes a sexual dimension.

A Review of Research on the Sexual Behavior of the Aged

Until Kinsey's studies (1948, 1953) there was a paucity of research on the sexual behavior of older people. Although Kinsey was able to investigate the sex lives of only 106 men and 56 women over sixty years old, he did find that at age sixty only one out of five men was no longer capable of sexual intercourse. He therefore invalidated the hypothesis of the psychoanalyst Theodor Reik (1949): "When a boy is six, he thinks his penis is to urinate with; when he's sixty, he knows it!"

Kinsey did find that by age eighty the proportion of men who did not have sexual intercourse rose to three out of four. While Kinsey did not consider the reasons for this change of proportion—i.e., was it biological, psychological, or both?—he did point out that the rate of decrease in the frequency of sexual outlets was no more rapid in old age than was the relative decline in the years between thirty and sixty.

Observations on women by Kinsey showed a gradual decline in frequency of sexual intercourse between ages twenty and sixty. With regard to single women, their decline was stronger than in married women, and the same was true with regard to single men as compared to married men.

Masters and Johnson (1966) obtained detailed psychosexual histories of a group of 212 men and 152 women over the age of fifty. Of these 133 men and 54 women were over sixty. The researchers reported that the human male's sexual responsiveness diminishes as he ages, and that in comparison to males aged forty-one to sixty, those over sixty have diminished levels of sexual tension, reduced intensity during sexual expression, and decreased coital activity, masturbation, and nocturnal emissions. Masters and Johnson stated that among the most important factors in the maintenance of effective sexuality for the aging male is consistency of active sexual expression. High levels of sexual activity during the formative years and middle age tend to ensure sexuality in old age.

In their examination of women, Masters and Johnson concluded that the older woman's fate is similar to the older man's; i.e., regular sexual expression either by coitus or masturbation is necessary for the maintenance of sexual capacity. They also reported that many women become more interested in sex after menopause because of their diminished fear of pregnancy.

Although Masters and Johnson, like Kinsey, did not offer reasons for sexual decline in old age, they did report that for both older men and women, the major factor relating to good sexual adjustment was earlier satisfactory sexual relationships. For those who had a previous history of unsatisfactory sexual experiences, withdrawal from sex was the modal response.

Christenson and Gagnon (1965) studied a group of 241 women who were age fifty or over. For those married women who were fifty, sexual intercourse with their husbands was the predominant sexual activity, with over 80 percent of them reporting that they had coitus at least once a week. By age sixty, participation had dropped to 70 percent, and by age sixty-five to 50 percent. Masturbation did not drop as much in this particular group of women, varying from 30 percent at age fifty to 25 percent at age sixty-five. For women no longer married, the percentage changed from 37 percent having coitus at age fifty to 12 percent at age sixty to none at ages sixty-five and seventy.

In 1973 Christenson and Johnson reported on some sexual patterns in a group of 71 older women who had never married. Eighty percent of these women were between the ages of fifty and sixty-nine, with the remainder over the age of sixty. About a third of the subjects reported that they had never experienced any overt sexual activity beyond simple petting, and even during the petting episodes erotic arousal had been minimal. These women said that they had never experienced orgasm from any source, including masturbation. The remaining two-thirds reported an active sexual life at varying levels, including 79 percent masturbation to orgasm, 62 percent intercourse, and 52 percent orgasmic sex dreams; eight subjects described extensive homosexual contact.

Although it is difficult to state with assurance what generalizations can be drawn from the research just reviewed, some trends seem to suggest themselves. In most people, sexual activity decreases with age, but the relative decrease may not be sharper than in younger years. While there appears to be a sharp decline in sexual activity and sexual interest around the mid-seventies, it is difficult to know how much the decline is caused by physical disability, unavailability of partners, an internalization of cultural stereotypes, other psychological factors, or a combination of all these variables. Factors which appear to have a strong correlation with continued sexuality are high levels of sexual activity in the formative and middle years as well as a history of satisfactory sexual relationships.

The Aging Process

Few people agree on just what constitutes aging and just when it begins. Furthermore, aging cannot be defined without considering the social context in which it is being examined. For example, an athlete may be on the way out at age thirty, whereas a businessman, businesswoman, or professional of the same age may be just beginning a career.

There is a great variation in time of onset and rate of progress of physical changes from one person to another, and in addition, individual parts of the body may age at differing rates. Balding, graying, deafness, or loss of teeth are well-known examples, and the heart, blood vessels, joints, and musculature can show similar variations (Jackel, 1975).

The interplay between nature and nurture affects the aging process, and there is great variation among people in how they psychologically cope with aging (Linn, 1975). Some people are inflexible in their thinking and attitudes at forty, while others are still flexible at eighty. The chronological age at which a person begins to feel old is also variable and is not always directly related to physical aging. The death of a spouse, relative, or friend may activate such a feeling. Also, the occurrence of an illness may produce an awareness of aging leading to a depression (Jackel, 1975). The depression can sap one's physical energy, which can then accelerate the aging process further. As we know, depression usually interferes with one's sexual desires, and then the depressed person can point to physical changes and lack of sexual desire as proof that he or she is at death's door (Levin, 1963).

Although there are great variations in the processes of physical aging, at one point or another there are typical changes in which the five major senses are all affected. Vision is altered by the loss of lens elasticity, and consequently bifocals are commonplace among the aged. Deterioration is progressive in variable degrees in the auditory sphere and involves high and low pitches unequally. The older person also has less sensitivity to pain than the younger person, and the senses of taste and smell also deteriorate (Jackel, 1975; Zinberg and Kaufman, 1963). Other physical changes are wrinkling of the skin, deterioration of the skeletal muscles, and, throughout the entire body, a decrease in homeostatic function which makes it difficult to "bounce back" to a previous level of functioning after an illness.

The psychological impact of these physical changes is extensive and varies with the specific meaning of the particular loss to each individual. For a man or woman whose self-esteem has centered on physical appearance, facial wrinkling may be experienced as a serious narcissistic injury. Or, if the person took pride in physical strength, its decline can induce feelings of vulnerability, depression, and loss of self-esteem.

When physical changes lead to a loss of income, this can become quite traumatic; when they interfere with pleasure previously derived from eating, reading, or music, the feeling of deprivation can be quite severe. Then the aging person can reason that all pleasure is supposed to be discarded and all sexual activity should be renounced.

> Many of these physical changes, by making reality testing more difficult, lend support to psychopathology latently present in the mature years. A disturbed sense of taste can encourage suspicions of being poisoned. A young person who suspects people of talking about him or laughing at him can, by approaching and listening, convince himself that it is only a fantasy. The older person, with some deafness, has less opportunity to correct such distortions. Uncorrected, these fantasies increase anxiety and further isolation. (Jackel, 1975, p. 434)

In considering the aging process, it is important to keep in mind that the older person is very prone to all kinds of physical illnesses. When he or she has to devote much energy to physically taking care of himself or herself, energy is taken away from relationships. Significant others often feel rejected or irritated and then isolate the older person. This, in turn, induces depression, lack of spontaneity, and a concomitant decline in sexual interest.

The Impact of Physical Changes on Sexuality

Although the decline and deterioration of life functions have a strong organic base, clinicians and others have frequently learned that there is often a close relationship between the decline in bodily functions, which, of course, include sexual functions, and psychoscial factors. Some older people with chronic illness, even with brain disease, may still find their highest mental functions available; in others, we may find early mental involution, i.e., depression, without yet knowing the corresponding bodily changes (Meerloo, 1969).

What seems crucial in assessing and treating our older clients for their sexual disturbances is that physical changes are par for the course but these changes produce considerable anxiety if their significance is misunderstood. As has already been suggested, physical changes do not mean that sexual capacity is lost. However, many older clients are convinced of this and as a result "lose" their sexual capacities. As Waltzman and Karasu have stated: "At no time do physiological changes mean the end of sexuality" (1979, p. 129). These authors go on to point out that any view of the etiology of sexual dysfunction, particularly in the elderly, must encompass the concept of multiple causality, with contributions in varying degrees from "biopsychosocial" factors.

As was mentioned in a previous section of this chapter, knowledge of the effects of aging on sexuality is still shrouded in ignorance for many of the elderly. For example, since menopausal changes in women sometimes lead to pain on intercourse, many assume that these changes mean the end of all sexuality. Men, in their late middle age, aware of losing their accustomed quick erective potential and unaware that it is normal, become anxious, and then their anxiety induces impotence.

What so many clinicians have found in their work with the elderly is that declining physical capacities and slower erotic responsiveness have meant to them that they are "has-beens." Many of them then repudiate sexuality and become very depressed, bored, and apathetic. Very often the helping professional has to educate the senior citizen to the fact that physiological changes do not mean the end of life. Older men need to be told that just as they cannot run as fast as they could when they were twenty years old, they should not expect to achieve an erection as quickly or an ejaculation as rapidly. Similarly, the older woman needs to be informed that she should not necessarily be alarmed if she is not excited in two minutes.

Mr. and Mrs. Berman, a couple in their late seventies, had stopped having sexual relations altogether. Exploration by the social worker revealed that both of them "gave up" when Mr. Berman "did not have a quick erection" and Mrs. Berman "did not get excited quickly." When the social worker told both of the Bermans that they were expecting too much of themselves and advised them to take their time, many things happened which pleased them. By taking their time they were able to enjoy themselves sexually. Of equal importance, perhaps, as a result of having sex relations they felt closer to each other and both of them became less irritable and depressed in general.

When older persons accept the fact that they can achieve sexual gratification but not as quickly as they were previously accustomed to doing, the fear of failure declines. As many sex therapists have pointed out, fear of failure leads to failure, and failure induces further anxiety that one will fail again (Kaplan, 1974).

All too often the aging process, which involves some decline in bodily functions, is utilized by aged clients, by some of their therapists, and by other professionals to rationalize away real psychological inhibitions toward sexuality. Most of the elderly living in the 1980s grew up in an era in which they were trained to view sexuality as at best occasionally pleasurable and at worst depraved. It is therefore quite difficult for many of our senior citizens to discard learned patterns which have been reinforced by family and society. When sex is not completely accepted as a necessary dimension of life, the end of procreation, illness, disability, or age itself will be used as legitimate reasons for the cessation of all sexual activity.

Psychosexual Problems in the Aged

For countless centuries and until very recently, the diagnosis and treatment of the aged was very much influenced by strong counter-transference attitudes which tended to deny them sexual pleasure. Most texts that dealt with the sexual problems of the aged focused almost exclusively on psychotic forms of sexual expression and paid little heed to the typical sexual problems of all aged people. As late as 1969, the psychiatrist and psychoanalyst Joost Meerloo, while pointing out that "if ever there is a time when sexual advice and information are needed, it is when people reach old age," went on to say:

> Organic changes in sexual organs cause changed feelings which make the old-aged [person] more infantilized in his sexual needs. In senile paranoia we encounter illusions of rape and incubus. Symbolic fertilization fantasies are expressed. Infantile scoptophilia is reversed so that the paranoiac woman believes that people are peeping at her. Eventually, the hallucinations assume a special form: the patient feels he is being beaten, pinched or flirted with. (pp. 330–331)

Not only have the psychotic expressions of sexuality been emphasized in the literature, but a great deal of the prescribed treatment has been the use of medication. This may also be considered a counter-transference reaction. Usually when the helping professional is frightened to face the sexual wishes, sexual fears, sexual conflicts, and sexual transference reactions of the client, he can dismiss himself from the interpersonal relationship of client and therapist and instead prescribe medication (Fine, 1981).

Inasmuch as medication of all types is so frequently recommended to aged clients to help them with their sexual problems, the results obtained bear brief review. The use of hormones, vitamins, or drugs has long been advocated. However, there are few well-controlled double-blind studies validating the use of these substances and specifying their precise indications (Waltzman and Karasu, 1979). For example, some of the claims for the use of systemic procaine have been improvement in sexual interest and capacity. Yet, in a review, Ostfeld et al. (1977) surveyed the use of systemic procaine in sexual dysfunctions in older men and women and concluded that the work in the field consisted of preliminary observations which did not reach the point of controlled clinical trials and that "the data are inadequate to support any conclusions."

Attempts to stimulate sexual interest and potency using testosterone formulations have not met with uniform improvement, although in some cases there has been a positive placebo effect (Stearns, 1974). However, the efficacy of replacement estrogens seems to be quite helpful. Estrogen-replacement therapy can improve the physiological problems of postmenopausal women during intercourse, and maintenance estrogen seems to reverse many of the degenerative changes occurring in the organs of the genital tract (Easley, 1974).

Although most of the research on medical treatment of sexual problems of the elderly reports very limited results, very often, when the practitioner utilizes medical treatment and achieves positive results, it is *not* necessarily the medicine that eased the sexual problem. For example, certain types of urological treatment have been utilized to help elderly men with problems of potency. But the principle treatment method connected with this approach consisted of "sympathetic listening to the patient's problems" and "reinforcing his self-esteem by emphasizing the positive features of his history" (Finkle and Finkle, 1975).

It would appear that the most helpful way to assist elderly men or women with sexual problems is to provide them with the type of therapeutic relationship that has been discussed throughout this text. If the elderly are experiencing loss of confidence, loss of self-esteem, loss of sexual capacity, and loss of key relationships, what they seem to be desperately in need of is a human relationship in which they are genuinely listened to, and in which they can feel safe enough to discuss their hurts, angers, losses, and sexual conflicts. Furthermore, because the elderly are so often shunned and isolated, it would also appear that they would benefit the most from long-term therapy. Yet there are many transference and countertransference problems that emerge in the treatment of the elderly which need to be addressed.

Transference and Countertransference

Although it is always helpful for a client to have a physical examination to rule out organic factors, virtually all the sexual problems that the elderly client brings to the practitioner have a strong psychological base. Sexual problems of the married and the single at any age are not particularly different from those problems that the elderly bring to the helping professional: impotency, frigidity, chronic masturbation, and so on. Furthermore, other problems of aged clients such as depression and loss of self-esteem are often manifestations of their sexual conflicts. The conspicuous feature of human sexuality is that it is governed less by hormonal influence, statistics, changing roles, and other factors, no matter how important these factors might be, than by unconscious (and conscious) psychological events occurring at the level of the cerebral cortex (Karasu and Socarides, 1979; Shainess, 1979). Therefore, it is the practitioner's task to become sensitized to the elderly person's psychological conflicts, which create many of his or her sexual problems.

Not only has psychotherapy for the aged person been neglected because of the prejudices that have been discussed throughout this chapter, but there are certain unique problems that transpire in the elderly client–therapist relationship that interfere with successful treatment. Many elderly clients tend to make the practitioner their son or daughter and have difficulty presenting their problems to the practitioner. As one senior citizen said, "It is not easy to be a seventy-five-year-old man discussing masturbation with my twenty-five-year-old daughter." By the same token, it is not difficult for the practitioner to feel embarrassed while having a discussion on sexual intercourse, foreplay, or masturbation with somebody who is experienced as a mother or father figure.

When older people are involved in marital counseling or sexual therapy with young practitioners, unresolved hatred may appear. The senior citizen who feels abandoned and rejected by his or her own children may subtly and unconsciously view the therapist as a neglectful child and not wish to have too much to do with the therapist. This may create a *folie à deux* in which each party feels rejected by the other, and all kinds of therapeutic impasses may result.

Not infrequently clinicians can experience older clients as the parents who did not tend to them with enough love and care. Therefore, they cannot spontaneously give to these clients because their unconscious resentments inhibit them.

As we know, to receive therapeutic help involves some dependency on the practitioner. Many older people who are physically declining and have lost some self-esteem do feel more needy. However, cultural conditioning often creates in them a wish to fight and deny their dependency wishes. Hence they wish to repudiate the clinician's efforts to help. Feeling rejected, the practitioner can reject the client.

One of the common defenses of older people is to reminisce (Cameron, 1963). The older client can frequently utilize counseling sessions by continually talking about "the good old days." While some clinicians may enjoy hearing stories about events that took place long before they were born, others may feel vulnerable and inadequate when they are constantly deluged with material that is unfamiliar. Feeling vulnerable and inadequate, the practitioner may cope with the anxiety by subtly pressuring the client to "get down to business."

Related to the above theme is the older client's desire to avoid talking about current reality. Feeling pained by feelings of sexual inadequacy, depressed by declining physical capacities, and lonely because of an isolated existence, the client may talk about everything but current problems. The practitioner may then become impatient in the face of what appears like the client's uncooperativeness, and begin to feel and act critically toward the client.

Often the older client is preoccupied with death (Freedman, Kaplan, and Sadock, 1976). If the interviewer has not come to terms with his feelings about his own death or the death of family members, the client's concerns can create anxiety for him and he may offer false reassurance or subtly block full discussion of the topic.

Although there are potential problems in helping an older client that evolve from negative transference and negative countertransference issues, other therapeutic stalemates can occur when there are unrecognized positive transference and positive countertransference feelings.

Sometimes the clinician can be drawn into a relationship in which the older client feels that he has found the perfect son or daughter. Elated by the client's flattery, the clinician can avoid discussing conflictful issues such as sex, marriage, or depression. In such a relationship, the practitioner can foster a dependent relationship with the client, overlook his strengths, and block his growth.

When aged people rightfully consider themselves members of a group that is discriminated against, it can be easy to join these clients in attacks against the majority and overlook the way in which their preoccupation with realistic discrimination can serve as a defense against looking at other aspects of their psychosexual functioning. In work with any disadvantaged group it is important for the clinician to be equally aware of the client's social reality and psychic reality (Siporin, 1981).

It is always helpful for the treatment if the practitioner has positive feelings toward the client; therapy cannot suceed without them.

However, if these positive feelings are not monitored by the practitioner, the client's aggression can be blocked and his conflicts concerning sex, love, and other issues can be overlooked.

In proceeding now to discuss some cases of older clients who present problems in their psychosexual functioning, we shall concentrate on examining some of the aforementioned transference and countertransference issues.

The Aged Client in Treatment

As has been said several times, the sexual dimension of the older client's life can be neglected by the client and significant others. Frequently the client does not see sexual abstinence as a problem, and it often is necessary for the practitioner to bring the sexual dimension of the client's life into the treatment.

Mr. Crane, age seventy-one, was in treatment at a family agency. He had been recently widowed and felt very depressed and lonely. Although he had been retired from business for over five years, he had been feeling so depressed since his wife died a year ago that he was seriously thinking of going back to work.

As his female social worker encouraged Mr. Crane to talk about his wife, his release of pleasant memories that involved her and his discussion of old hurts and angers that emanated from his marital relationship eased his depression. It was obvious that the social worker filled a void in his life and Mr. Crane rather quickly moved from a discussion of the past to the present. He began to feel a desire to join groups and sought out old and new friends.

In Mr. Crane's interviews with his social worker, he began to appear like a young teenager who was learning about certain facets of life that had not been experienced heretofore. Although he started to talk about playing bridge with some women and dancing with others, Mr. Crane made no mention of sexual feelings toward them. He focused all of his discussions on his activities, with no references to any specific woman. Furthermore, although animated in his sessions with the social worker, he made no references to her either.

The social worker began to realize that Mr. Crane had a strong resistance to talking about his warm and sexual feelings toward women, including herself, and inferred that there was probably a sexual inhibition operating in his day-to-day life. When the worker said to Mr. Crane in one session, "You are having a good time with women, but you never talk about your sexual feelings toward them," Mr. Crane flushed in embarrassment and went into a long silence. On the social worker's acknowledging that her comment made him uncomfortable, Mr. Crane said, "I'd prefer not to talk about it." The social worker told Mr.

Crane that she would respect his wish, but wondered out loud why this was a topic that he preferred to avoid.

Mr. Crane spent several sessions talking about his belief that after the age of sixty-five all men and women stopped having sex. That was certainly what happened with him and his wife. To the social worker's question about how Mr. Crane got to form his conviction, he could give no answer. He just thought "that is the way it goes."

In later interviews Mr. Crane did talk about the fact that he had never had a particularly active sexual life with his wife, and as the Cranes got older frequency of sexual relations declined quite rapidly. It turned out that Mr. Crane had experienced his wife as a mother figure. Sex, therefore, was more or less taboo for him because it had incestuous connotations.

As Mr. Crane became able to share with the social worker some of his childish feelings toward his wife and to better understand how he avoided her sexually because of his own anxiety, he started to talk about specific women friends more spontaneously. He shared with the social worker incidents at his Golden Age Club when he hugged some women and held hands with them.

When it appeared that Mr. Crane was somewhat more comfortable talking about sexual matters, the social worker then introduced the subject of transference. She asked Mr. Crane why he avoided her and never seemed interested in her. Mr. Crane laughed and said, "I tell everybody what a pretty girl you are and how nice you are to me!" Here the worker commented, "It's easier to tell others about me than to tell me about me." Again Mr. Crane laughed, and he said, "I'm old enough to be your father!" On the worker's saying "If I'm your daughter, you shouldn't notice me?" Mr. Crane became very self-conscious and frightened, commenting, "You're right, a father shouldn't look at his daughter that way!"

Thanks to the worker's sensitive handling of the subject, Mr. Crane was able to focus on how he had fought very hard *not* to feel sexual toward either of his two daughters during most of their lives. Slowly he began to understand his sexual inhibition toward the social worker: she was a daughter from whom he had to keep a distance.

As Mr. Crane further examined his feelings toward his wife, toward his daughters, and toward the social worker, he could better appreciate how incestuous fantasies had created so much anxiety in him that he had been forced to curtail both his sexual life in the past and his current sexual life. Eventually, he was able to look at some of the sexual fantasies that he had about his mother and sisters.

Because Mr. Crane was able to feel increasingly safer with the social worker, he was able in time to feel freer sexually with women. Like an adolescent he began to take one step at a time until he eventually had successful intercourse with a woman who later became the second Mrs. Crane.

The above case illustration is very instructive because it pinpoints several issues in working with the aged on their psychosexual problems. First, an inactive sex life just doesn't happen in senescence. Those senior citizens like Mr. Crane who have a limited sexual life during their middle years are more prone to avoid sex altogether when they reach their late sixties or early seventies. Secondly, many elderly clients have strong convictions that sexual abstinence is a fact of life in the older years, and they need help in exploring the sources of their distorted beliefs. Thirdly, when the clinician strongly believes that an examination of the older client's internal life will enhance the client's sexual enjoyment, the client slowly identifies with this stance and can explore facets of his or her life which have been repressed until now. Finally, the case of Mr. Crane demonstrates that if the older client has a sensitive and empathetic therapist who believes in the client's capacity to grow, the client can indeed grow and can achieve a more satisfying psychosexual life.

Although many older clients resist a discussion of sex and the sexual part of transference, occasionally the opposite can occur. While it is quite possible for some clients, regardless of their age, to experience the therapist as an object who they would really like to sexually seduce, the potential for the lonely, unattached, older person can be a little stronger in some cases. Although it is sometimes tempting for a therapist to hug, kiss, or have physical contact with a client, it is hardly ever helpful to any therapy. What usually occurs when client and therapist have sexual contact is that the client wants more and more, and since he has been gratified once by the therapist, he feels it is his rightful due to have encores! Sooner or later the therapist cannot gratify the client's desires, which do become insatiable, and then the client, feeling teased and unsatisfied, can go into a depression or become suicidal.

In addition to the above considerations, it is important to remember that clients at most stages of development tend to see the practitioner as a family member: father, mother, or sibling. Consequently, sex with a therapist creates a great deal of anxiety and is rarely pleasant for the client because it conjures up forbidden incestuous feelings. In virtually every situation, the client ends up feeling disillusioned and betrayed (Freeman and Roy, 1976).

When the client wants sexual contact with the therapist, the therapist has to steer a course that avoids being either a seductive teaser or a punitive superego. It is necessary to convey to the client that the latter's feelings are very human, but they have to be understood rather than acted out.

Mrs. Drew, a widow of sixty-nine, was being seen at a mental health clinic for problems of depression, loneliness, suicidal fantasies, and psychosomatic complaints. After about six sessions with her male therapist, she felt she was on "a honeymoon," reported that all of her symptoms had vanished, and extolled the therapist for his "miraculous cure." On a few occasions, while praising the therapist she tried to reach for his hand, and at the end of one session she asked the therapist to kiss her. When the therapist said that this "might be enjoyable but let's find out what you are feeling that makes you want to be kissed," Mrs. Drew left the session in a huff and told the therapist he was "an uptight Freudian."

At her next appointment, Mrs. Drew castigated the therapist for being unempathetic, cold, and rigid and told him it wouldn't hurt him if he kissed her. She mentioned that she was an isolated person who needed physical contact and that the therapist did not understand this. She threatened to leave treatment and cried bitterly. When the therapist said that he realized that Mrs. Drew felt very hurt and rejected, the client pointed out, "That just proves you hate me and don't care about me. Since you know that I feel hurt and you go on being aloof, you just want to hurt me."

Recognizing that the client was trying to make him feel guilty and also trying to manipulate him, the therapist told Mrs. Drew that he seemed to appear like a cold parent who should be ashamed of himself. To this statement, Mrs. Drew made no answer for a long time, and then she had associations to her father, who was never available to her. She talked about strong yearnings toward him that were never gratified and pointed out that her relationship with her husband had been quite similar. "Everything ends in rejection," Mrs. Drew lamented.

As the therapist listened carefully to Mrs. Drew's associations, it became clearer that unconsciously she was provoking another rejection. When this notion was shared with her, Mrs. Drew responded in a way that conveyed to the therapist that she was feeling understood. She began to talk about how she "deserved rejection for my dirty wishes" and "never realized that before."

Many of the clients who are sexually provocative with their therapists are unconsciously seeking rejection. In the above vignette it is clear that although Mrs. Drew was a very sexually stimulated woman, she also had much disdain for her sexual wishes and was guilty about them. Consequently, when sexually excited, she provoked rejection in order to punish herself.

Practitoners who have counseled the elderly have reported that many of them prematurely end the treatment relationship (Posner, 1961; Lampe, 1961; Granick and Patterson, 1971). While many reasons have been offered to explain this phenomenon—e.g., the client's fear of dependency, the client's fear of rejection, the clinician's lack of empathy and sensitivity—what has not been given sufficient attention is the aged client's reluctance to face his or her warm, sexual feelings toward the helper. As has been constantly reiterated throughout this text, sexual feelings exist in every human organism and are always part of every client's transference relationship to the helper. When aged clients feel that their amorous wishes toward the practitioner are inappropriate and when such wishes induce discomfort, the clients may absent themselves from interviews or try to quit the treatment altogether.

Mr. Frank, age sixty-eight, was being seen for vocational guidance by a young female counselor. Forced to retire from his job as a mechanic at age sixty-five, Mr. Frank was becoming increasingly bored, irritable, and depressed. He had "time on my hands" and he was getting his wife "very nervous just hanging around the house." Consequently, he wanted to see if he could get some fulltime or part-time employment.

In his initial interviews with his counselor, he emerged as a very cooperative, affable man, who related warmly and talked about himself and his life circumstances with ease. He eagerly came to all his interviews and enthusiastically discussed job possibilities, explored job opportunities that the counselor arranged for him, and dutifully reported his reactions to her. After an interview in which Mr. Frank praised the counselor for her kindness and interest, he failed to show up for his next appointment—without notifying the counselor. When the counselor tried several times to reach him by phone, she was told that Mr. Frank was not home. On leaving word for Mr. Frank to call her back, her requests were ignored. Letters to Mr. Frank were also disregarded.

One evening when the counselor knew Mr. Frank would be home, she was able to reach him by phone. After much persuasion, and with a guarantee that there would only be one interview if that's what he wanted, the client reluctantly agreed to an appointment.

After voicing a series of rationalizations—e.g., he had decided not to work because his wife was getting used to him at home; he and his wife were planning to have several vacations—Mr. Frank attempted to leave the office. Noting his tremendous discomfort and realizing that he was referring to his wife a lot, the counselor said to Mr. Frank, "There's something about being with me that disturbs you. What is it?" Mr. Frank, flushing with embarrassment, said, "You are a nice lady," and again attempted to get up and leave the office. Here the counselor said, "I think that because you feel I'm nice, you have to go. You are frightened of liking me!"

After a few more defensive remarks, Mr. Frank was able to acknowledge that the image of the counselor had been preoccupying him day and night, and that he "formed an obsession" over her. He went on to say, "I can't let this go on. It'll wreck my marriage." Here the counselor explained that if Mr. Frank didn't fight his loving and sexual feelings as much as he was doing and talked about them instead, he would not be so obsessed and so much in pain.

With some reluctance and with some embarrassment, Mr. Frank went on to confess that he thought of the counselor all the time and frequently fantasied being married to her. Then he quickly asked, "Isn't that awful? An old guy like me thinking of living with a young chick like you?" The counselor said, "Awful? I think it's one of the most natural things in the world to think of living with me and marrying me after having some pleasurable discussions with me."

As the counselor became a more benign superego to Mr. Frank, in the non-punitive atmosphere of her office he could begin to examine his sexual anxieties. He realized that now that he had more time on his hands he was thinking of all his sexual "secrets" and was feeling guilty about them. It reminded him of when he had been a young boy hanging around his house waiting to see his mother take a bath and/or get undressed.

As Mr. Frank "received permission" from the counselor to express his sexualized transference to her, he could feel more relaxed with his sexual feelings in his day-to-day life and learn that his sexual anxieties in the present evolved from childhood experiences. He also realized that he had distorted the meaning of these events so that every time he felt warm and sexual feelings toward a woman, he felt guilty because he was making the woman the mother of his childhood past.

Very often, when an elderly person has lost a partner and/or feels that his sexual capacities are waning, he stops having sexual intercourse and replaces intercourse with masturbation. Masturbation or any other sexual activity other than intercourse, such as voyeurism, exhibitionism, or fetishism, can fill the client with enormous shame and guilt. He tends to feel very perverse rather than recognizing that he is merely stopping his sexual activity at some stage of foreplay rather than consummating the sexual act.

What activates the guilt in the client is the punishment he feels he deserves for what seems like an expression of childish sexuality. As we have learned in previous chapters, sexual problems almost always have their roots in the client's childhood history. The seventy-year-old man or woman who is guilty about masturbating feels like a nine- or ten-year-old child caught in the act by a punitive parent. This is the main reason why elderly clients, or for that matter any client, cannot feel free to discuss sexuality with the practitioner: they feel like children discussing a transgression that they think can only be considered awful by any listener. Here, again, it is important for the helping person to be a benign superego who does not judge or condemn. As clients begin to appreciate the big difference between their introjected voices, which punish them for childish sexual fantasies, and the practitioner's actual voice, which attempts to understand and ease discomfort, clients over time can become more accepting of their own sexuality. When this occurs there is almost always a rise in the client's self-esteem, a diminution of guilt, and an increased capacity for pleasure in general.

Mrs. Gold, a seventy-year-old widow, was in a Widows' Group in a social agency. The group had been formed for lonely women who had just lost their husbands and who were having a lot of difficulty coping with their interpersonal and intrapsychic lives.

When the group discussions got around to sex, Mrs. Gold grew progressively more anxious, talked less in the group, came late for sessions, and canceled several. When the group therapist noted that the group was making Mrs. Gold uncomfortable and asked the group members what they could do to help her, Mrs. Gold said, "It's not their fault. I just feel guilty about my sexual practices." In response to Mrs. Gold's "confession" the other group members talked about their masturbating, fetishist practices, and other childish sexual activities. As they discussed their sexual fantasies, desires, and guilts, they became for Mrs. Gold a permissive parent who helped her be less harsh on herself and like herself more.

Whether it be Mrs. Gold in the above vignette or any aged person, society must help older people to have more opportunities to physically and emotionally express their sexual passion, affection, and love for one another (Waltzman and Korasu, 1979). While it is encouraging to witness an increasing number of helping professionals devoting more attention to the psychosexual problems of the elderly (Murphy, 1979), a great deal more work needs to be done in helping practitioners, society at large, and the aged themselves to overcome their biases about the aging process. The older person will be ensured a more enjoyable psychosexual life when senescence is viewed as a developmental phase comparable to latency or adolescence (Jackel, 1975) rather than as a time to become a celibate, vegetate, and die.

In a recent book, *Growing Young*, the anthropologist Ashley Montagu (1981) pointed out that in our society we tend to rush into what we call "maturity"—which he describes as "psychosclerosis," or hardening of the psyche. It appears, according to the author, as if we can hardly wait to get rid of our spontaneity and our sense of wonder in order to acquire the restrictive lineaments of sophistication or "maturity." Montagu prescribes what should be the unique and most outstanding human trait, namely, "remaining in an unending state of development." Like Woody Allen, who was referred to at the beginning of the chapter, Montagu would probably concur with the notion that "sex should be confined to one's life-time."

Chapter 9

An Overview of the Sexual Therapies

HELPING PEOPLE with their sexual problems is a professional activity that does not exist in every society. Perhaps it is somewhat of a paradox to find that where the institution of marriage is valued, where love between the sexes is esteemed, and where equality between men and women is championed is where sexual therapies are in abundance. Conversely, where the institution of marriage is repudiated, where love between the sexes is not an important value, and where equality between men and women is derogated is where sexual therapies are few in number or nonexistent (Stern and Stern, 1981). While statistics are not plentiful to fully substantiate these notions, a comparison of sexual practices in the United States with those in the Soviet Union might shed some light on the matter.

Although there is ambivalence toward marriage in the United States, marriage is still considered a highly valued institution (Hunt, 1974). According to Masters and Johnson (1970), approximately 50 percent of married people in the United States report consistent sexual satisfaction, participate in sexual activity at least once a week, utilize a diversity of sexual positions, and have no sexual problems such as impotency or frigidity. In the Soviet Union, where the institution of marriage is frequently held in low esteem, only 10 percent of

197

married people report consistent sexual satisfaction and spouses participate in sexual activity about once a month; the modal sexual position is one in which the man enters the woman from the rear; and over 90 percent of Russian married men and women report serious sexual problems (Stern and Stern, 1981). Although there are a few professionals in the United States who repudiate the notion of therapy for sexual problems, e.g., Szasz (1980), by and large such therapy in the United States is a frequent occurrence. By contrast, in the Soviet Union an extremely limited amount of therapy is available for the many people who have sexual problems.

Currently there are two major orientations to the assessment and treatment of sexual problems. One is a behavioral approach introduced by Masters and Johnson (1966; 1970), and the other is a psychodynamic one, the approach utilized in this text. Adherents of both perspectives utilize many different treatment modalities.

This chapter will present and critique the Masters and Johnson approach and will also briefly discuss and evaluate the treatment modalities that have not been discussed very much in this text: conjoint treatment, group treatment, short-term treatment, and the sensitivity and encounter movement.

The Masters and Johnson Program*

When Masters and Johnson completed the first part of their research study of human sexuality, which was essentially an examination of the physiology of the human sexual response (Masters and Johnson, 1966), they then embarked on the second aspect of their research: an eleven-year controlled study which aimed to develop a rapid treatment of human sexual dysfunction. This study is described in detail in their popular book, *Human Sexual Inadequacy* (1970).

According to Masters and Johnson, the crucial dimensions of their program are as follows:

1. A sexual dysfunction in a marital unit is the responsibility of both partners. Consequently, both partners have to be seen in therapy and take responsibility for the sexual problems and the treatment, regardless of who is suffering from a lack of sexual satisfaction and what form it takes.

*This section is a summary of a chapter by the author entitled "Psychosexual Disorders," which appears in *Adult Psychopathology: A Social Work Perspective*, ed. Frank Turner (New York: The Free Press, 1984).

2. Sexual problems are not always the result of psychic conflict. They are frequently the consequences of faulty learning. Therapy, therefore, should be heavily laden with education and information.

3. In addition to providing education and information, Masters and Johnson focus on some of the "superficial causes" of sexual disorder: performance anxiety, fear of failure, and excessive need to please the partner.

4. Enjoyable sexual interaction depends on the capacity to communicate. Consequently, there is a strong emphasis in the therapy on enhancing the communication between the partners.

5. The dual sex-therapy team is one of the integral aspects of the approach; each patient is provided with a role model. This procedure is based on the assumption that no woman or man can fully comprehend the other gender's sexual functioning or dysfunctioning.

6. The basic treatment approach is a behaviorally oriented one. A key ingredient is the assignment of progressive tasks and behavioral prescriptions.

The sexual problems that Masters and Johnson treat are premature ejaculations, impotence, frigidity and orgasmic dysfunctions, vaginismus, and painful intercourse in the female. In addition to the behavioral tasks used by all patients, specific techniques are utilized for dealing with specific dysfunctions. For example, in the treatment of premature ejaculation, the "squeeze technique"—a procedure in which the female partner squeezes the man's penis to delay his ejaculation—is used (Semans, 1956); for vaginismus, dilators of gradually increasing size are employed.

The Masters and Johnson treatment program consists of a two-week phase of rapid education and treatment. All couples are seen daily. Inasmuch as 90 percent of them live outside the St. Louis area, where the program is located, the daily treatment program requires a two-week "vacation" for most couples. This isolation from everyday demands is considered advantageous in that it provides the opportunity of reviving communication between the marital partners without external intrusions. An advantage of the daily conference, according to Masters and Johnson, is that it allows for immediate discussion of sexual events and feelings instead of permitting mistakes to go uncorrected or fears to intensify.

An important technique used by the sex team is that of "reflective teaching," whereby the therapists restate in objective terms what the problems are and how the couples are failing to communicate with each other. By holding up the "mirror of professional objectivity" to reflect the couple's sexual attitudes and practices, the therapists attempt to aid the couple in understanding what it reveals.

Recognizing that performance fears cannot be removed by merely exhorting people not to have them, Masters and Johnson developed a highly structural behavioral conditioning approach, referred to as "sensate focus." The sensate-focus exercises are designed to permit a gradual learning or relearning of sensual and sexual feelings under authoritative direction. Sensate focus involves a hierarchy of behavioral prescriptions in the form of mutual body exercises. First the partners are instructed to take turns "pleasuring each other" by caressing, touching, and massaging each other's bodies—avoiding the genital areas and refraining from intercourse. The focus is continually on the process and not on the goal. Next the partners are instructed to give feedback to each other and to indicate their preferences about the kind and location of touch desired. Experiences, mistakes, feelings, and reactions are discussed in detail during the sessions with the therapists the following day. When one step has been successfully negotiated, the next step is introduced—and gradually, as the couples progress, they move into genital stimulation.

According to Masters and Johnson, their program has been extremely successful in that they report over 80 percent of their subjects have sustained considerable improvement over five or more years.

Modifications of the Masters and Johnson Program

Because the results of Masters and Johnson were considered very impressive, their methods were quickly adopted by hundreds of practitioners in clinics, agencies, and private practice. As the program moved into various settings, modifications took place. According to Karasu, Rosenbaum, and Jerrett (1979), the most important modifications that have evolved can be summarized as follows:

1. Tailoring the time allotted for therapy to fit the needs of individual patients—contracting or expanding the time commitment as deemed necessary for optimal results.
2. Making the therapy available to patients in their home community, allowing for continuous integration of the treatment experience with the everyday life of the individuals.

3. Developing methods for working with the single patient, if necessary.
4. Using a single therapist instead of the dual sex-therapy team approach.
5. Making the therapy available to low-income populations and special-patient populations.
6. Integrating the specific "sex therapy" techniques with other forms of therapy.

Hartman and Fithian (1974) are representative of the many sex therapists who have been influenced by Masters and Johnson but who have modified their approach in many ways. First, they themselves (or any other therapists working with a couple) actively participate in the sexual training procedures. During the "sexological" examination given to all patients at the onset of therapy, the therapists stimulate the patients' body parts, specifically the genitals. Then the patients are requested to carry out foot, face, and body-caress exercises in the presence of the therapists. The rationale is that the therapists can observe a couple's physical interactions, instead of relying solely on their verbal reports. In addition, the therapists can teach the couple more effective techniques by direct "coaching."

Lobitz and LoPiccolo (1972) have fused the general program of Masters and Johnson with behavior techniques developed by Wolpe (1969) and others. In addition to homework assignments, they include a nine-step masturbation program designed to enhance the couple's arousal of each other, building on progressively more comfortable autoerotic experiences. Just prior to orgasm by masturbation, the patient is instructed to switch his or her focus to fantasies of sexual activity with the partner.

Helen Kaplan (1974) has expanded on the Masters and Johnson method at the Cornell Medical Center. Her approach involves a combination of prescribed sexual exercises and psychotherapeutic sessions. According to Kaplan this new sex therapy is a "task-centered form of crisis intervention which presents an opportunity for rapid conflict resolution. Toward this end the various sexual tasks are employed, as well as the methods of insight therapy, supportive therapy, marital therapy, and other psychiatric techniques as indicated" (p. 199).

In the area of behavior modification therapy, desensitization techniques have been reported to be successful for premature ejaculation (Dengrove, 1967; Ince, 1973), frigidity (Brady, 1975; Glick,

1975), and impotence (Dengrove, 1973). A modified systematic desensitization technique, used within a multivariate behavior approach, has been described by Obler (1975). Because it was found that some patients are unable to imagine situations that cause extreme anxiety, Obler (1975), instead of asking patients to fantasize, has substituted erotic films and slides portraying experiences with the potential to produce such anxiety.

Integrating the behavioral approach with cognitive and emotive methods in a systemic framework, Ellis (1975) has described the Rational-Emotive approach (RET) to sex therapy. The main premise of RET is that humans feel disturbed and act dysfunctionally in sexual as well as in other areas when they escalate any desire or wish into an absolute: "should," "ought," or "must." To exemplify this, Ellis has described the ABC's of emotional disturbance. "A" is the activating experience (e.g., a sexual failure) and "C" is the emotional consequence (e.g., feelings of shame and guilt). The mediating "B" is the belief system, which consists of rational and irrational beliefs (e.g., "How awful that I failed!"). The aim of RET is to dispute these irrational beliefs and remove the individual's guilt about sex. The cognitive aspect of RET is designed to change the individual's "awful-izing" and "absolutizing" philosophies so that he or she can think and act differently. The emotive aspect of RET aims at changing irrational beliefs by altering emotions. This is accomplished through unconditional acceptance by the therapist, shame-attacking exercises, risk-taking exercises, and emotive feedback. The behavior phase includes assertion training, homework assignments, and operant conditioning.

A Critique of Masters and Johnson's Program and Their Modifiers

There is now a vast literature which criticizes the Masters and Johnson program and the programs of their modifiers. The many critics of these programs have questioned their research methodology, therapeutic procedures, theroretical underpinning, and conceptions of the human being (Karasu, Rosenbaum, and Jerrett, 1979; Zilbergeld and Evans, 1980; Fine, 1981; Strean, 1980; Hogan, 1978; Levay and Kagle, 1977; Wright, et al., 1977; Karasu and Socarides, 1979). This section will summarize the major questions about the sexual therapies that have just been reviewed.

Regarding the Masters and Johnson program, Karasu, Rosenbaum, and Jerrett (1979) offer the following criticisms:

1. The expense involved, not only in the commitment to spend two weeks in St. Louis, but also in paying for the services of two therapists, limits the accessibility of this particular treatment to a select affluent population.

2. A biased sample has been seen as one of the reasons for the impressive results. The patients had to be highly motivated in order to go to the lengths required.

3. The program is designed for married couples who have relatively stable and secure relationships and who are willing to work together. This omits all single individuals with sexual problems and those with partners who refuse to participate.

4. The two-week commitment in Masters and Johnson's original approach is not only difficult because of the expense, but is of questionable efficacy. Do results obtained in the ideal climate of a vacation atmosphere carry over into the everyday existence of a couple, with all the stresses and demands of their regular lives?

5. The need for two therapists has not been established. Although Masters and Johnson (1970) believe that dual therapy teams are necessary, they have never proved the need for them.

6. Masters and Johnson do not allow time for the assimilation of character or intrapsychic change. To the extent that an individual has neurotic and character problems, there is concern about backsliding when the co-therapists are no longer present.

7. In evaluating the program, there seems to be a lack of careful controls. For example, the degree of improvement among nonfailures is not specified, and there is a lack of information concerning treatment failures.

Zilbergeld and Evans, in a comprehensive study entitled "The Inadequacy of Masters and Johnson" (1980), have pointed out that "Masters and Johnson's sex-therapy research is so flawed by methodological errors and slipshod reporting that it fails to meet customary standards—and their own—for evaluation. This raises serious questions about the effectiveness of the ten-year-old discipline they created" (p. 29). The authors further aver that the claims of Masters and Johnson were accepted with very little critical scouting; no one can replicate their findings. Masters and Johnson report only failure rates, but since they do not define failure, the failure rates mean nothing. Furthermore, we do not learn precisely how many hours of therapy each patient received because information is incomplete. Masters and Johnson say nothing about dropouts. Were there none? Were those patients who asked to leave counted as failures? The authors conclude that "sex therapy is still uncritically accepted for the most part, but the fact is that the evidence for the effectiveness of Masters and Johnson's therapy—and therefore that of almost all sex therapy—is less solid than has generally been believed" (p. 43).

The sexual therapies that have been reviewed here must be seriously questioned by the clinician for reasons that most critics have not presented. As this text has tried to demonstrate throughout, any therapist who maintains an objective eye, a neutral ear, and an empathetic heart knows that what gets people into conflict, particularly into sexual conflict, are unconscious wishes, irrational and childish fantasies, and unresolved psychosocial tasks. All the sexual therapies that have just been discussed operate under the unscientific premise that the human being is completely rational, always conscious, and a victim of external forces. It is now well known by many clinicians that people who are in sexual conflict are not aware of their own childish fantasies, superego admonitions, and ego defenses, which unconsciously "work together" to create their difficulties.

Masters and Johnson and their modifiers fail to take into consideration what many experienced clinicians accept as an axiom: The man or woman who cannot spontaneously, warmly, comfortably, enjoyably, and successfully have a sustained sexual relationship with a member of the opposite sex is full of large quantities of hatred, fear, and revenge of which he or she has no conscious awareness or control. These maladaptive responses are part of the individual's dynamic personality—a personality that fears intimacy because the individual is not able to trust, be autonomous, or take initiative (Erikson, 1950). As has been reiterated, the clinician who works with the total person recognizes that a sexual dysfunction is a sign of internal distress, and that a happy person is sexually free whereas an unhappy person is sexually dysfunctioning.

It can be anticipated that as behavior therapists who subscribe to the practices of Masters and Johnson become more sophisticated and more experienced with the practical problems of handling clients and patients, they will recognize the significance of transference, will deal with resistances, and will pay much more attention to how an assessment of the client's psychosocial development is crucial to understanding his or her sexual conflicts (Fine, 1981). Furthermore, as they come to appreciate transference, countertransference, and unconscious motivation as ever-present variables inherent in any treatment relationship, they will be more able to evaluate objectively the results of the interpersonal experience that sexual therapy always is.

Conjoint Therapy

In the late 1950s, Dr. Nathan Ackerman (1958) introduced family therapy. He believed that the existence of problems in a child always implied that there was a disturbance in the entire family network. If the child was to be helped, Ackerman contended, all the family members had to confront the ways in which each of them were contributing to making the child a scapegoat. Since the entire family became the unit of diagnosis and the unit of treatment, the therapy became focused on interpersonal problems rather than intrapersonal ones; on the here and now, rather than the past; on family defenses, rather than individual pathology; on reality, rather than fantasy; and on action, rather than understanding.

Conjoint therapy, or couple therapy, derives from family therapy and is an attempt to study a married couple's interactions and transactions rather than their individual, idiosyncratic personalities (Ables, 1977; Paolino and McCrady, 1978). When husband and wife are seen in conjoint therapy the therapist attempts to show them, on the basis of their interactions with him and with each other, how they are conjointly aiding and abetting their sexual and interpersonal problems.

Regardless of the presenting problem—e.g., the wife's frigidity or the husband's impotence—the assumption in conjoint therapy is that both parties are in unconscious collusion to sustain the particular sexual problem (Jackson, 1965) and both parties are needed for the therapy to be successful. For example, if the husband was impotent, the therapist would show both husband and wife, on the basis of their interactions and communication patterns, how each was helping to maintain a dysfunctional marital balance (Zilbach, 1968).

In conjoint therapy there is "shared blame" (Pollak, 1956), so that a husband or wife is less likely to feel impelled to carry the burden of the marriage's difficulties alone. By locating how and when husband and wife fail to express what they feel toward each other and how they misunderstand each other, the therapist can eventually help their sexual and interpersonal interaction become smoother. One of the major tasks of the therapist in conjoint therapy is to help husband and wife become aware of their "double-bind" messages, in which an individual says one thing and means another, contradicting the verbal message by behavior (Ruesch, 1961; Spiegel, 1960).

Sanford and Sheila Alt, a couple in their early thirties, were in conjoint therapy because neither of them was sexually satisfied in the marriage. Although they had been married for over four years, they had completed sexual intercourse no more than six or seven times during this entire interval, and most of the time they just avoided each other sexually.

In their treatment they both professed a great deal of concern and love for each other, and it was obvious to the therapist that there was a superficial accommodation on the part of each partner to the other. They never expressed disagreement or hostility to each other, but always agreed.

As the therapist studied the Alts' interaction, it became quite clear that each of them was in unconscious collusion to avoid expressing any hostility toward the other. When there was the possibility of disagreement, each changed the subject. Sometimes the Alts expressed mutual agreement when it was obvious that they were internally fuming at each other. In one session Sheila said, "I'm sure we'd enjoy sex more if Sanford didn't snore so much." Sanford nodded his head in agreement, but it was obvious from his facial expression and darting eyeballs that he was covering up a great deal of rage. At another point in the session, when Sanford said that sex would be better if Sheila wasn't so obese, Sheila agreed. However, her fists were clenched as she did so, and it was clear that she, too, was holding back a great deal of anger.

When the therapist pointed out that the Alts were both frightened of their angry feelings toward each other, and that by avoiding facing these feelings they were avoiding improving their sexual lives, both Sheila and Sanford tried to repudiate this observation. For the first time in their three months of therapy, each became much more animated, and they jointly expressed much resentment toward the therapist. Taking turns, they chastised him for his "professional" and "pedantic" approach, his "smug" attitude, and his "lack of warm spontaneity."

Blasting the therapist was a turning point in the Alts' therapy. When they saw that he was not destroyed by their barrages, they could begin to inform each other of their mutual dissatisfactions and mutual distrusts. Since they did not have to use so much energy defending against their hostility, they could both feel more liberated, and with that their sexual lives improved.

Double-bind messages induce much confusion in the recipient, create tension in communication, exacerbate distrust, and alienate husband and wife from each other. Conjoint therapists, as was done with the Alts, try to expose double-bind messages when they work with married couples and try to examine their causes and eliminate their use as much as possible.

The concept of "pseudo-mutuality," which is commonly used by therapists who work with couples, refers to a seeming accommodation by a married couple at the expense of the enhancement of each individual (Wynne et al., 1958). As with the Alts, each member of the dyad is forced to give up much individuality to maintain the marital balance (Zilbach, 1968), and unfortunately, each member's pleasure is sacrificed.

Many practitioners who do conjoint therapy point out that this type of therapy also has the advantage that a spouse is seldom able to remain silent and uninvolved. It is felt that the presence of the mate serves as a catalyst for working on problems and that the couple's customarily maladaptive ways of coping with one another come into full view. Frequently the therapist requires husband and wife to substitute different communication lines—such as listening more to one another and trying new modes of coping with conflict. In this type of treatment, there is less reflective discussion by any one person and more shared reflection about current interaction (Stamm, 1972).

Conjoint therapy requires some capacity in each member to identify with the other, expose anxieties and imperfections, and tolerate some frustration in order to listen to the other's complaints. Many couples that seek help for their sexual problems do not have the ego functions necessary to participate in shared responsibility; usually each spouse must fix blame on the other. Such a spouse also tends to lack the frustration tolerance necessary to participate in the cooperative effort of conjoint treatment, finding it too trying to take note of the mate's anxieties and wishes, and particularly the mate's complaints about the marriage. These clients need a therapeutic experience tailored to their maturational level, and this would probably be a one-to-one therapeutic relationship in which the client has exclusive access to a parental figure.

From a theoretical point of view, when a couple has strong defenses against communicating and interacting with each other, conjoint therapy might very well seem to be the treatment of choice. However, the individuals involved may not be able to bear the anxiety of sharing. Hence, a one-to-one relationship with the therapist should probably be considered initially, so that each spouse can receive enough protection and understanding while communicating with the therapist to eventually develop the strength to share problems with the mate.

Conjoint therapy is not only a valuable form of treatment when the mates have the capacity to trust, identify with, and share with each other, but with certain symbiotic couples who cannot stand any separation from each other, it would seem to be the treatment of choice. Such couples might cease to be in treatment if they were seen individually.

Conjoint treatment of sexual problems can help many couples understand how they are participating in sustaining these problems. It can enhance their communication, which eventually can help them become psychologically closer and sexually more intimate. However, for many clients the roots of their sexual conflicts are so unconscious, their resistances to facing childish fantasies are so great, and their distrust of their spouses is so intense that only long-term, one-to-one treatment will be effective. In the one-to-one treatment, when they see how their sexual anxieties and inhibitions manifest themselves with a stranger, they can gain an inner conviction about their own role in their sexual problems in marriage.

Group Treatment

There seems to be little question that society, particularly in the past two or three decades, has isolated people from one another. Paradoxically, the increased popularity of such communication devices as television appears to help decrease the intimacy of personal relationships. It may be that the growth of group therapy and group counseling represents a correction against the social isolation engendered by technological improvement. A strong need has developed for people to get closer together, and it is met to some extent by participating in small groups (Corsini, 1964). Groups satisfy the basic human need to belong—what Slavson (1943) has termed "social hunger." According to Tropp (1968):

> The group . . . is not only an alliance through which normal needs can be met; it can also be a natural healer of hurts, a supporter of strengths, and a clarifier of problems. It may serve as a sounding board for expressions of anxiety, hostility or guilt. It often turns out that group members

learn that others in the group have similar feelings weighing them down in their aloneness, that they are not so different or so alone—and learning this in live confrontation with one's peers is a most powerful change-inducing experience. (p. 267)

Group treatment, like family therapy, is a "here and now" experience, with the group usually experienced by its members as a symbolic family. In the group the individual member repeats patterns of interaction that he learned in his original family. As he interacts with "siblings" in the here and now, he learns what he typically does to alienate and isolate others and also what he does and can do to bring others closer to him.

The use of group therapy for the treatment of sexual problems is not a new concept. As early as 1943, Slavson demonstrated how group discussions with a mature leader could help children and adolescents reduce their anxiety and guilt about sex and increase their acceptance of it (Slavson, 1943). In 1950 Stone and Levine reported on their use of group sessions for women with orgasmic difficulties. Discussions centered on the underlying causes of the difficulties and what measures could be taken to correct them; a number of women showed marked improvement.

Powell et al. (1974) have described a program integrating the principles of Masters and Johnson (1970) into a group-therapy framework. The program, designed for couples, incorporates dual sex-therapy teams, self-administered questionnaires to shorten intake, and group techniques in an intense two-and-a-half-day sexual workshop. After the initial intake, each individual couple meets with the co-therapists for a round-table discussion, when the specific problems are crystalized and the details of the workshop are explained. Several couples meet together with the therapeutic team at the workshop, where slides as well as movies are shown and explicit instructions are given for homework exercises. After practicing the exercises, the couples meet again the next day for group discussions, and share their feelings, attitudes, and experiences. In general, "these discussions serve to facilitate great progress since success in the group is contagious" (Powell et al., 1974, p. 93).

A couple group-therapy approach has been described by LoPiccolo and Miller (1975). The design is to teach basic sexual skills to "normal," nondysfunctional couples who, despite the absence of specific dysfunctions, join the group because "they are dissatisfied with their sexual lives." Both encounter-group techniques and specific behavioral exercises are used. Each group consists of three patient couples plus a dual sex-therapy team and meets for three exercises lasting three hours each. Between the sessions, the couples carry out homework exercises. Using a no-treatment control group, the authors reported significant gains in sexual interaction for the couples.

Other couples' groups described in the literature have included time-extended therapy in resort settings (Reckless et al., 1973), nude marathons (Bindrin, 1968), and sexual attitude restructuring groups (Mann, 1975; Vandervoort and Blank, 1975). The information on these groups is vague, and the results are not described fully.

Group therapists contend that their approach to the treatment of sexual dysfunctions offers several advantages over individual or couple treatment. First, they point to the fact that group treatment is usually less expensive than individual therapy. Second, they aver that peer understanding in a group atmosphere offers a mutual support and encouragement which transcends on individual therapist's understanding. A third advantage is that the group provides for vicarious learning from the successes and failures of others (Zilbergeld, 1975). Finally, an advantage can lie in the impetus supplied when other group members resolve their problems, because group members do identify with each other as they strive for more maturity (Powell et al., 1974).

Some of the limitations of group treatment of sexual problems are similar to the limitations of conjoint treatment of marital problems. In a group, men and women might be able to learn that they are avoiding the opposite sex and are repressing their own sexual fantasies; however, in a group it would be difficult to fully come to grips with the exact nature of their inhibitions, particularly those unconscious wishes that propel them. That is why many group therapists advise "conjoint treatment"—group treatment plus individual treatment (Ormont and Strean, 1978)—so that the individual can have the unique opportunity to study both intrapsychic and interpersonal problems which interfere with psychosexual functioning.

Many individuals liken group treatment to "getting undressed" in front of a whole assembly of people. Their anxiety about their exhibitionistic and voyeuristic wishes can result in considerable shame and they become "tongue-tied" in the group setting (Rosenthal, 1971). The same phenomenon can occur with aggressive fantasies. If individuals are frightened by their own sadistic or murderous wishes, they fear that the group members and the leader might retaliate and this fantasy can inhibit the working through of their sexual conflicts.

Group treatment, like couple therapy or family therapy, seems to be an effective modality for those clients who have the capacity to share their interpersonal and sexual problems with others. To share constructively, they must have some capacity to empathize, listen, and identify with their peers. If they are very narcissistic or impulsive, or have poor frustration tolerance, group treatment would seem contraindicated.

The Sensitivity and Encounter Movement

In the United States today, only 16.3 percent of the population lives in a setting consisting of father, mother, and children (Howard, 1978). Many natural families are broken up, extended family members are frequently unreachable, and because we are a mobile population, social groups are constantly being disbanded. It has been reported that over 40 million Americans change residence each year (Packard, 1972).

A great many Americans feel an inarticulate sense of loss, unrelatedness, and lack of connection, and have an urgent need for remedies that will reduce their feelings that they are in the midst of strangers (Packard, 1972). Catering to their social hunger are encounter and sensitivity groups. These groups take a variety of forms such as twenty-four-hour marathons, EST lectures, primal-scream sessions, and exercises in hand-holding and other types of sexual foreplay. Proponents of these groups want people to relax more and enjoy more emotional intimacy (Kovel, 1976).

In order to resolve barriers and reduce emotional distance from peers, clients are usually persuaded to take some action in the group setting. They might be encouraged to hand-wrestle so that they can overcome their fear of sexual assertiveness; they might be helped with holding hands so that they can resolve some of their fears of intimacy and tenderness; or they might be directed to "tell somebody off" so that they can feel more secure in taking sexual initiative.

A great deal of what occurs in sensitivity and encounter groups might be likened to sexual foreplay. Some clients, particularly those who are very sexually inhibited and feel very alienated from others, derive some support and encouragement from their peers as they become more action-oriented in the group. This support from the group can assist them as they sexually experiment outside the group.

The sensitivity and encounter groups with their action-orientation do bypass a number of crucial issues which seem quite pertinent to the resolution of sexual conflicts. Some of the therapeutic issues that the adherents of this approach seem to overlook are the role of motives, particularly unconscious motives, in the etiology of sexual disorders; the crucial significance of transference and countertransference; the importance of resistance and the influence of the client's past on present maladaptive sexual functioning. Nonetheless, for the very alienated person who can respond to direction from a group and is action-oriented rather than reflective, the experience can be beneficial (Kovel, 1976).

Short-Term Treatment

In consonance with the mores of our "future shock" society (Toffler, 1971), in which we all want a great deal and pronto, are therapies that reflect the type of modus vivendi we champion: "short-term treatment," "crisis intervention," "quick-response therapy," "brief treatment," and "time-limited treatment." Regardless of the label attached to these therapies, their advocates aver that clients can be helped in a short period of time if both therapist and client participate in "problem solving" and utilize their conscious, rational thinking to tackle the presenting problems. Reactive depressions in adults, school phobias in children, and certain situational problems such as homesickness and vocational distress, as well as certain sexual problems, have been reported to respond well to short-term treatment (Mann, 1973; Parad, 1965; Goldring, 1980; Golan, 1978; Lang, 1974; Reid and Epstein, 1972).

Brief treatment was initiated and became popular as a response to the dearth of therapists at many mental health clinics and social agencies in the late 1950s. It was viewed as a partial solution to the manpower problem in the mental health field. However, many practitioners began to view it as a treatment of choice for many clients, and some see it as the appropriate therapy for most clients.

Influenced by the psychoanalyst Franz Alexander (1948), who coined the term "the corrective emotional experience," many therapists began to believe that if clients were provided with unique relationships, different from what they had experienced with their parents when they were children, they could be appreciably helped and helped quickly. For example, it was suggested that if the adult patient

had an authoritarian father, the therapist should behave democrati-
cally and permissively. According to Alexander and his followers, the
patient would then be relieved of self-hatred and other problems
much faster than would be the case in long-term treatment.

Stimulating the popularity of brief treatment are research reports
which suggest that clients and therapists have found this form of therapy much more beneficial than long-term treatment (Masserman,
1965; Phillips and Weiner, 1967; Wolberg, 1965; Goldring, 1980). In
reaction to research results many clinics, agencies, and private practitioners have stopped providing long-term treatment altogether and
have substituted short-term therapy.

In the field of marital counseling and sexual therapy, short-term
treatment has become particularly popular among those clinicians
who utilize the behavioristic approach of Masters and Johnson
(1970). Dorothy Freeman (1981), in her recent book *Marital Crisis
and Short-Term Counseling*, has summarized what are alleged to be
the advantages of short-term counseling in marital and sexual therapy. First she cites the research of Eysenck (1952), who attacked the
efficacy of conventional depth psychology in the early 1950s. She
also quotes Michael Balint, the English psychoanalyst, who referred
to "the highly embarrassing observation, recorded from all over the
psychiatric world, that a very high percentage of patients . . . drop
out from their treatment in the very early stages" (Balint, 1961,
p. 42). Freeman also refers to the findings of other researchers (Reid
and Shyne, 1969; Hepworth, 1979) that most changes take place during the early sessions of open-ended treatment.

Further justification of short-term treatment is that it enhances
client motivation, obviates undue dependence and regression, and
helps clients feel that they have much more control (Masserman,
1965; Wolberg, 1965; Mann, 1973). Finally, "the short-term counselor cannot become sidetracked into the leisurely relationship building, the passive listening, or the detailed and lengthy history taking
that are characteristic of long-term therapy and that often confuse
clients, who may not see the relevance of what is going on" (Freeman, 1981, p. 3).

From the psychodynamically oriented perspective utilized in this
text, short-term treatment can be viewed as the treatment of choice
for *some* individuals who suffer from psychosexual problems. There
are those clients who are so frightened of exposing themselves to a
therapist and so terrified of the possibility of depending on a parental
figure that when they are assured that they can come for treatment

for just a few sessions, they often feel very comforted. Not feeling coerced or controlled, some of these clients eventually become long-term participants in therapy as they begin to feel more trust in the helping professional. Also, there are certain clients who, for various reasons (including the fear of dependency and control), genuinely believe that a few consultations are all that they want and need; they insist on this format. If the therapist respects their wishes, these clients can gain a great deal from the consultations, and some of them, experiencing less pressure, go into long-term treatment to learn more about themselves (Strean and Blatt, 1969).

Short-term therapists, in their enthusiasm to assist many individuals quickly, have tended to overlook some of the requisites needed to help people resolve their psychosexual problems and sustain their therapeutic gains. The notion of the "corrective emotional experience" in the therapy that takes place over a few sessions disregards much that clinicians know about the nature of help. A sexual problem such as chronic masturbation or chronic exhibitionism is a result of many disturbing interpersonal experiences that have transpired over many years. Consequently, the client inevitably needs a long-term interpersonal experience to correct distortions about self and body image, to understand childish fantasies and fears that propel sexual conflicts, and to resolve maladaptive defenses. For example, if a client has had an authoritarian father and is still influenced by the image of the father, what this client usually needs is to experience the parental introject in the transference relationship with the therapist and learn why he *unconsciously wishes* to sustain a relationship with an authoritarian father. It is somewhat naive to believe that the therapist's enactment of a role that is different from the client's introjected image is going to rid the client of the introject. Frequently, short-term therapists tend to overlook the fact that if people are negatively influenced in the present by past experiences with parental figures, they still wish, albeit unconsciously, to be so influenced. As has been stated several times in this text, for effective treatment to take place clients should experience the therapist in the many ways they have experienced parents, siblings, lovers, and spouse, so that they can learn that their current psychosexual conflicts stem from wishes to stay a child.

A statement by short-term therapists that a client shows many gains early in treatment is true. This is what Dr. Reuben Fine (1971) has called the "honeymoon" phase of treatment. However, these gains are rarely ever sustained (Strupp et al., 1977; Karasu, Rosenbaum, and Jerrett, 1979; Fine, 1971; Hogan, 1978), as the findings from the Masters and Johnson program so convincingly demonstrate (Zilbergeld and Evans, 1980). A honeymoon in treatment is not too different from a honeymoon in marriage: The client, like the new spouse, has "fallen in love," and the sharp rise in his or her self-esteem and self-confidence is being nourished by false romantic ideals which inevitably get punctured.

Finally, the research on short-term therapy has to be questioned because of its lack of scientific accuracy. To rely on the self-reports of clients and therapists that are gathered from questionnaires or from one research interview does not capture the myriad variables in operation. When an individual responds to questions either in an interview or on a questionnaire, transferential factors, defenses, superego admonitions, and childish wishes all influence the response. The only way that one can really study the effects of therapeutic intervention is to observe the client over time and carefully watch the fluctuating transference responses, shifting defenses, voices from the superego, and other reactions. This type of research takes much time and effort but seems to be mandatory in studying the effects of any treatment (Fine, 1971).

Regardless of the orientation utilized—behavioristic or psychodynamic—and regardless of the preferred modality—short-term, long-term, group, individual, or conjoint—therapy and counseling should be regarded as a learning situation. Learning, as most clinicians and educators know, is never a completely smooth process. Every learner moves forward and backward, has impasses with the teacher, and invariably gets stuck at crucial times. Both therapist and client must allow these processes to take place for therapeutic learning to be effective.

As more therapists and counselors recognize the crucial factors that interfere with sexual pleasure and absorb the salient issues inherent in disciplined therapeutic intervention, more and more children, adolescent, and adults will be able to enhance their psychosexual functioning.

References

ABLES, B. 1977. *Therapy for Couples.* San Francisco: Jossey-Bass.

ACKERMAN, N. 1958. *The Psychodynamics of Family Life.* New York: Basic Books.

ADAMS, M. 1976. *Single-Blessedness.* New York: Basic Books.

AICHORN, A. 1935. *Wayward Youth.* New York: Viking Press.

ALEXANDER, F. 1948. *Fundamentals of Psychoanalysis.* New York: W. W. Norton.

———, AND H. ROSS. 1952. *Dynamic Psychiatry.* Chicago: University of Chicago Press.

ANTHONY, E. 1981. "The Paranoid Adolescent as Viewed Through Psychoanalysis." *Journal of the American Psychoanalytic Association* 29, no. 4: 745–788.

———. 1975. "The Reactions of Adults to Adolescents and Their Behavior." In *The Psychology of Adolescence,* ed. A. Esman. New York: International Universities Press.

ARLOW, J., AND C. BRENNER. 1964. *Psychoanalytic Concepts and Structural Theory.* New York: International Universities Press.

ATKIN, E. 1982. *In Praise of Marriage.* New York: Vanguard Press.

BACH, G. 1969. *The Intimate Enemy: How to Fight Fair in Love and Marriage.* New York: Avon Books.

BALINT, M. 1961. *Psychotherapeutic Techniques in Medicine*. London: Tavistock Publications.

BARBARA, D. 1958. *The Art of Listening*. Springfield, Ill.: Charles C. Thomas.

BARTUSIS, M. 1978. *Every Other Man*. New York: E. P. Dutton.

BELL, A. 1961. "The Role of Parents." In *Adolescence: Psychoanalytic Approach to Problems and Therapy*, ed. S. Lorand and H. Schneer. New York: Hoeber.

BERGLER, E. 1969. *Selected Papers of Edmund Bergler*. New York: Grune and Stratton.

_____. 1963. "Marriage and Divorce." In *A Handbook of Psychoanalysis*, ed. H. Herma and G. Kurth. Cleveland: World Publishing Co.

BERMAN, G., AND M. EISENBERG. 1971. "Psychosocial Aspects of Academic Achievement." *American Journal of Orthopsychiatry* 41: 406–415.

BERNARD, J. 1972. *The Future of Marriage*. New York: World Publishing Co.

BERON, L. 1944. "Fathers as Clients of a Child-Guidance Clinic." *Smith College Studies in Social Work* 14: 351–366.

BERTHELSDORF, S. 1976. "Survey of the Successful Analysis of a Young Man Addicted to Heroin." In *The Psychoanalytic Study of the Child*, Vol. 31, ed. K. Eissler. New Haven: Yale University Press.

BETTELHEIM, B., AND K. ZELAN. 1981. *Learning to Read*. New York: Alfred A. Knopf.

BIEBER, I. 1962. *Homosexuality*. New York: Basic Books.

BINDRIN, P. 1968. "A Report on a Nude Marathon." *Psychotherapy: Theory, Research and Practice*, 5, pp. 180–188.

BLANCK, R., AND G. BLANCK. 1974. *Ego Psychology*. New York: Columbia University Press.

_____. 1968. *Marriage and Personal Development*. New York: Columbia University Press.

BLOCK, J. 1978. *The Other Man, The Other Woman*. New York: Grosset and Dunlap.

BLOS, P. 1967. "The Second Individuation Process of Adolescence." In *The Psychoanalytic Study of the Child*, vol. 22, ed. K. Eissler. New York: International Universities Press.

_____. 1961. "Delinquency." In *Adolescence: Approach to Problems and Therapy*, ed. S. Lorand and H. Schneer. New York: Hoeber.

_____. 1953. "The Contribution of Psychoanalysis to the Treatment of Adolescents." In *Psychoanalysis and Social Work*, ed. M. Heiman. New York: International Universities Press.

BOLTON, C. 1961. "Mate Selection as the Development of a Relationship." *Marriage and Family Living* 23: 234–240.

BONAN, A. 1963. "Psychoanalytic Implications in Treating Unmarried Mothers with Narcissistic Character Structures." *Social Casework* 44, no. 6: 323–330.

BOWLBY, J. 1969. *Attachment and Love.* New York: Basic Books.

————. 1951. *Maternal Care and Mental Health.* Geneva: World Health Organization.

BRADY, J. 1975. "Behavior Therapy of Sexual Disorders." In *Comprehensive Textbook of Psychiatry*, vol. 2, ed. A. Freedman, H. Kaplan, and B. Sadock. Baltimore: Williams and Wilkins.

BRAZELTON, T. 1969. *Infants and Mothers: Differences in Development.* New York: Delacorte Press.

BRENNER, C. 1955. *An Elementary Textbook of Psychoanalysis.* New York: International Universities Press.

BRILL, L. 1981. *The Clinical Treatment of Substance Abusers.* New York: The Free Press.

BROZAN, N. 1982. "Lark-Owl Marriages." *The New York Times*, January 24, 1982, p. 48.

BROWN, G. 1980. *The New Celibacy.* New York: McGraw-Hill Book Co.

BULLOUGH, V. 1978. "Variant Life Styles: Homosexuality." In *Exploring Intimate Life Styles*, ed. B. Murstein. New York: Springer Publishing Co.

BURGUM, M. 1942. "The Father Gets Worse: A Child-Guidance Problem." *American Journal of Orthopsychiatry* 12: 474–486.

BURK, M. 1978. "Coming Out: The Gay Identity Process." In *Exploring Intimate Life Styles*, ed. B. Murstein. New York: Springer Publishing Co.

BUTLER, S. 1978. *Conspiracy of Silence: The Trauma of Incest.* Houghton Mifflin Co.

CAMERON, N. 1963. *Personality Development and Psychopathology.* Boston: Houghton Mifflin Co.

CHRISTENSON, C., AND J. GAGNON. 1965. "Sexual Behavior in a Group of Older Women." *Journal of Gerontology* 20: 351–356.

CHRISTENSON, C., AND W. JOHNSON. 1973. "Sexual Patterns in a Group of Older Never-Married Women." *Journal of Geriatric Psychiatry* 6: 80–98.

COEN, S. 1981. "Sexualization as a Predominant Mode of Defense." *Journal of the American Psychoanalytic Association*, 29, no. 4: 893–920.

COHN, D. 1943. *Love in America,* New York: Simon and Schuster.

COLBY, K. 1960. *An Introduction to Psychoanalytic Research.* New York: Basic Books.

COOPER, S., AND L. WANERMAN. 1977. *Children in Treatment.* New York: Brunner-Mazel.

CORSINI, R. 1964. *Methods of Group Psychotherapy.* Chicago: William James Press.

CRIST, T. 1971. "Contraceptive Practices Among College Women." *Medical Aspects of Human Sexuality* 5: 168–178.

DEBURGER, J. 1978. *Marriage Today.* Cambridge, Mass.: Schenkman.

DELUCCIA, I. 1981. "Facing Up to the Problem of Drug Abuse." *The New York Times*, October 15, 1981, p. 38.

DEMAUSE, L. 1981. *Foundations of Psychohistory.* New York: Creative Roots Press.

DENGROVE, E. 1973. "The Mechanotherapy of Sexual Disorders." *Current Psychiatric Therapy* 13: 131–140.

_____. 1967. "Behavior Therapy of Sexual Disorders." *Journal of Sexual Research* 3: 49–61.

DENNY, T., J. FELDHAUSE, AND C. CONDON. 1965. "Anxiety, Divergent Thinking and Achievement." *Journal of Educational Psychology* 56: 40–45.

DESPERT, L. 1965. *The Emotionally Disturbed Child—Then and Now.* New York: Robert Brunner.

DICKES, R. 1979. "The New Sexuality: Impact on Psychiatric Education." In *On Sexuality*, ed. T. Karasu and C. Socarides. New York: International Universities Press.

DRABBLE, M. 1966. *The Millstone.* New York: Alfred A. Knopf.

DULIT, E. 1975. "Adolescence." In *Personality Development and Deviation*, ed. G. Wiedeman. New York: International Universities Press.

DULLEA, G. 1975. "Marriage Tax: It Has Couples in a Rage." *The New York Times*, March 27, 1975, p. 26.

DURBIN, K. 1977. "On Sexual Jealousy." In *Jealousy*, ed. G. Clanton and L. Smith. Englewood Cliffs, N.J.: Prentice-Hall.

EASLEY, E. 1974. "Atrophic Vaginitis and Sexual Relations." *Medical Aspects of Human Sexuality* 2: 32–47.

EIDELBERG, L. 1956. "Neurotic Choice of Mate." In *Neurotic Interaction in Marriage*, ed. V. Eisenstein. New York: Basic Books.

EISENSTEIN, V. 1956. "Sexual Problems in Marriage." In *Neurotic Interaction in Marriage*, ed. V. Eisenstein. New York: Basic Books.

EISSLER, K. R. 1953. "The Effect of the Structure of the Ego on Psychoanalytic Technique." *Journal of the American Psychoanalytic Association* 1:104–143.

ELLIS, A. 1975. "The Rational-Emotive Approach to Sex Therapy." *Counseling Psychologist* 5:9–13.

ELLIS, H. 1907. *Studies in the Psychology of Sex.* New York: Random House.

220   THE SEXUAL DIMENSION

ENGLISH, O., AND G. PEARSON. 1945. *Emotional Problems of Living.* New York: W. W. Norton.

———. 1937. *Common Neuroses of Children and Adults.* New York: W. W. Norton.

ERIKSON, E. 1956. "The Problem of Ego Identity." *Journal of the American Psychoanalytic Association* 4:56–121.

———. 1950. *Childhood and Society.* New York: W. W. Norton.

ESMAN, A. 1979. "Adolescence and the New Sexuality." In *On Sexuality,* ed. T. Karasu and C. Socarides. New York: International Universities Press.

———. 1975. *The Psychology of Adolescence.* New York: International Universities Press.

EVANS, R. 1964. *Conversations with Carl Jung.* Princeton, N.J.: Van Nostrand Reinhold.

EYSENCK, H. 1952. "The Effects of Psychotherapy: An Evaluation." *Journal of Consulting Psychology* 16:319–323.

FEDERN, P. 1952. *Ego Psychology and the Psychoses.* New York: Basic Books.

FEINSTEIN, S., P. GIOVACCHINI, AND A. MILLER. 1971. *Adolescent Psychiatry,* vol. 1. New York: Basic Books.

FELDMAN, Y. 1958. "A Casework Approach Toward Understanding Parents of Emotionally Disturbed Children." *Social Work* 3: 23–29.

FENICHEL, O. 1945. *The Psychoanalytic Theory of Neurosis.* New York: W. W. Norton.

FINE, R. 1981. *The Psychoanalytic Vision.* New York: The Free Press.

———. 1979a. *The History of Psychoanalysis.* New York: Columbia University Press.

———. 1979b. "The Love Life of Modern Man." In *Modern Man: The Psychology and Sexuality of the Contemporary Male,* ed. G. Goldman and D. Milman. Dubuque, Iowa: Kendall-Hunt Publishing Co.

———. 1975a. *Psychoanalytic Psychology.* New York: Jason Aronson.

———. 1975b. "The Bankruptcy of Behaviorism." *The Psychoanalytic Review* 62, no. 3:437–452.

———. 1971. *The Healing of the Mind.* New York: David McKay.

FINKLE, P., AND A. FINKLE, 1975. "Urologic Counseling Can Overcome Male Sexual Impotence." *Journal of Geriatric Counseling* 30:119–129.

FISHEL, D., AND N. ALLEN. 1972. "Urban Courting Patterns: Singles Bars." Paper presented at the American Sociological Association Annual Meeting, July 1973. New York.

FORREST, T. 1966. "Paternal Roots of Female Character Development." *Contemporary Psychoanalysis* 3, no. 1:21–31.

FOUNTAIN, G. 1961. "Adolescent into Adult: An Inquiry." *Journal of the American Psychoanalytic Association* 9: 417–433.

FOX, V., AND M. QUITT. 1980. *Loving, Parenting and Dying: The Family Circle in England and America, Past and Present.* New York: Psychohistory Press.

FRAIBERG, S. 1977. *In Defense of Mothering.* New York: Basic Books.

FRANCE, A. 1933. *Penguin Island.* New York: The Modern Library.

FREEDMAN, A., H. KAPLAN, AND B. SADOCK. 1976. *Modern Synopsis of Psychiatry*, vol. 2. Baltimore: Williams and Wilkins.

FREEMAN, D. 1981. *Marital Crisis and Short-Term Counseling.* New York: The Free Press.

FREEMAN, L., AND J. ROY. 1976. *Betrayal.* New York: Stein and Day.

FREEMAN, L., AND H. STREAN. 1981. *Freud and Women.* New York: Ungar.

FREUD, A. 1965. *Normality and Pathology in Childhood.* New York: International Universities Press.

―――. 1958. "Adolescence." In *The Psychoanalytic Study of the Child*, vol. 13, ed. K. Eissler. New York: International Universities Press.

―――. 1951. "Observations of Child Development." In *The Psychoanalytic Study of the Child*, vol. 6, ed. K. Eissler. New York: International Universities Press.

―――. 1937. *The Ego and the Mechanisms of Defense.* New York: International Universities Press.

FREUD, S. 1939. *An Outline of Psychoanalysis. Standard Edition*, vol. 23. London: Hogarth Press.

―――. 1917. *Mourning and Melancholia. Standard Edition*, vol. 14. London: Hogarth Press.

―――. 1916. *Some Analytic Character-Types Met in Psychoanalytic Work. Standard Edition*, vol. 14. London: Hogarth Press.

―――. 1910. *A Special Type of Choice of Object Made by Men. Standard Edition*, vol. 11. London: Hogarth Press.

―――. 1909. *Analysis of a Phobia in a Five-Year-Old Boy. Standard Edition*, vol. 10. London: Hogarth Press.

―――. 1905. *Three Essays on the Theory of Sexuality.* Standard Edition, vol. 7. London: Hogarth Press.

―――. 1900. *The Interpretation of Dreams. Standard Edition*, vol. 4. London: Hogarth Press.

Frontiers of Psychiatry: A Roche Report. 1981. Vol. 2, no. 9, p. 3.

FROSCH, W., G. GINSBERG, AND T. SHAPIRO. 1979. "Social Factors in Symptom Choice: The New Dynamics of Impotence." In *On Sexuality*, ed. T. Karasu and C. Socarides. New York: International Universities Press.

FURSTENBERG, F. 1976. *Unplanned Parenthood.* New York: The Free Press.

GALENSON, E., AND H. ROIPHE. 1979. "The Development of Sexual Identity." In *On Sexuality*, ed. T. Karasu and C. Socarides. New York: International Universities Press.

GARRETT, A. 1951. *Interviewing: Its Principles and Methods*. New York: Family Service Association of America.

GAYLIN, W. 1976. *Caring*. New York: Alfred A. Knopf.

GELEERD, E. 1957. "Some Aspects of Psychoanalytic Technique in Adolescents." In *The Psychoanalytic Study of the Child*, vol. 12, ed. K. Eissler. New York: International Universities Press.

GILDER, G. 1973. *Sexual Suicide*. New York: Quadrangle Books.

GLICK, B. 1975. "Desensitization Therapy in Impotence and Frigidity: Review of the Literature and Report of a Case." *American Journal of Psychiatry* 132:169–171.

GLOVER, E. 1960. *The Roots of Crime*. New York: International Universities Press.

———. 1949. *Psychoanalysis*. London: Staples Press.

GOCHROS, H., AND J. GOCHROS. 1977. *The Sexually Oppressed*. New York: Association Press.

GOCHROS, H., and D. KUNKEL. 1979. "Sexual Evolution and Social Work Practice." In *Sexual Issues in Social Work*, ed. D. Kunkel. Honolulu: University of Hawaii.

GOLAN, N. 1978. *Treatment in Crisis Situations*. New York: The Free Press.

GOLDRING, J. 1980. *Quick Response Therapy: A Time-Limited Approach*. New York: Human Sciences Press.

GOLDSMITH, J. 1957. "The Unmarried Mother's Search for Standards." Social Casework 48, no. 2:69–73.

GRANICK, S., and R. PATTERSON. 1971. *Human Aging: An Eleven-year Follow up*. Rockville, Md.: National Institutes of Mental Health.

GREENACRE, P. 1971. "Considerations Regarding the Parent-Infant Relationship." In *The Capacity for Emotional Growth*, ed. E. Zetzel. New York: International Universities Press.

GREENSON, R. 1967. *The Technique and Practice of Psychoanalysis*. New York: International Universities Press.

GREGORY, M. 1974. *Sexual Adjustment: A Guide for the Spinal Chord Injured*. Bloomington, Ill.: Accent on Living, Inc.

GRUNEBAUM, H. 1962. "Group Psychotherapy of Fathers: Problems of Technique." *British Journal of Medical Psychology* 35:147–154.

———, and J. CHRIST. 1976. *Contemporary Marriage*, Boston: Little, Brown.

GRUNEBAUM, H., and H. STREAN. 1970. "Some Considerations on the Therapeutic Neglect of Fathers in Child Guidance." In *New Approaches in Child Guidance*, ed. H. Strean. Metuchen, N.J.: Scarecrow Press.

GUTTMACHER INSTITUTE, 1981. *Teen Age Pregnancy: The Problem That Has Not Gone Away*. New York: Guttmacher Institute.

HALPERN, H. 1964. "Work Inhibition in Children." *Psychoanalytic Review* 51:5–21.

HARLEY, M. 1961. "Masturbation Conflicts." In *Adolescents: Psychoanalytic Approach to Problems and Therapy*, ed. S. Lorand and H. Schneer. New York: Hoeber.

HARRISON, D. 1979. "Sexuality and the Physically Handicapped: Some Guidelines for Social Workers." In *Sexual Issues in Social Work*, ed. D. Kunkel. Honolulu: University of Hawaii.

HARTMAN, W., and M. FITHIAN. 1974. *Treatment of Sexual Dysfunctions*. New York: Jason Aronson.

HARTMANN, H. 1964. *Essays on Ego Psychology*. New York: International Universities Press.

———. 1958. *Ego Psychology and the Problem of Adaptation*. New York: International Universities Press.

HENDIN, H. 1975. *The Age of Sensation*. New York: W. W. Norton.

HEPWORTH, D. 1979. "Early Removal of Resistance in Task-Centered Casework." *Social Casework* 69, no. 7:317–322.

HESLINGA, K., A. SCHELLEN, and A. VERKUYL. 1974. *Not Made of Stone: The Sexual Problems of Handicapped People*. Springfield, Ill.: Charles C. Thomas.

HITE, S. 1976. *The Hite Report*. New York: Macmillan.

HOGAN, D. 1978. "The Effectiveness of Sex Therapy: A Review of the Literature." In *Handbook of Sex Therapy*, ed. J. LoPiccolo and L. LoPiccolo. New York: Plenum.

HONIGMAN, J. 1944. "A Cultural Theory of Obscenity." *Journal of Criminal Psychopathology* 5:715–733.

HOOKER, E. 1957. "The Adjustment of Male Homosexuals." *Journal of Projective Techniques* 21:17–31.

HOWARD, J. 1978. *Families*. New York: Simon and Schuster.

HUNT, M. 1977. "Is Marriage in Trouble?" In *Marriage Today*, ed. J. Deburger. New York: John Wiley & Sons.

———. 1974. *Sexual Behavior in the 1970's*. New York: Dell.

———. 1969. *The Affair*. New York: World.

———. 1959. *The Natural History of Love*. New York: Alfred A. Knopf.

———, AND B. HUNT. 1977. *The Divorce Experience*. New York: McGraw-Hill.

INCE, L. 1973. "Behavior Modification of Sexual Disorders." *American Journal of Psychotherapy* 27: 446–451.

JACKEL, M. 1975. "Senescence." In *Personality Development and Deviation*, ed. G. Wiedeman. New York: International Universities Press.

JACKSON, D. 1965. "The Study of the Family." *Family Process* 4:1–20.

JACOBS, J. 1971. *Adolescent Suicide*. New York: Wiley Interscience.

JACOBSON, E. 1964. *The Self and the Object World*. New York: International Universities Press.

————. 1961. "Adolescent Moods and the Remodeling of Psychic Structures in Adolescence." In *The Psychoanalytic Study of the Child*, vol. 16, ed. K. Eissler. New York: International Universities Press.

JOHNSON, A. 1975. "Drifting on the God Circuit." In *The Psychology of Adolescence*, ed. A. Esman. New York: International Universities Press.

JONES, E. 1922. "Some Problems of Adolescence." In *Papers on Psychoanalysis*, ed. E. Jones. London: Bailliere, Tindall, and Cox.

JOSSELYN, I. 1948. *Psychosocial Development of Children*. New York: Family Service Association of America.

JUDGE, J. 1951. "Casework with the Unmarried Mother in a Family Agency." *Social Casework* 32, no. 1:7–14.

JUSTICE, B., and R. JUSTICE. 1979. *The Broken Taboo: Sex in the Family*. New York: Human Sciences Press.

KADUSHIN, A. 1972. *The Social Work Interview*. New York: Columbia University Press.

KAPLAN, H. 1974. *The New Sex Therapy*. New York: Brunner-Mazel.

KARASU, T., AND C. SOCARIDES, 1979. *On Sexuality*. New York: International Universities Press.

KARASU, T., M. ROSENBAUM, AND I. JERRETT. 1979. "Overview of New Sex Therapies." In *On Sexuality*, ed. T. Karasu and C. Socarides. New York: International Universities Press.

KARLEN, A. 1971. *Sexuality and Homosexuality*. New York: W. W. Norton.

KERNBERG, O. 1967. "Borderline Personality Organization." *Journal of the American Psychoanalytic Association* 15:641–685.

KESTEN, J. 1970. "Learning for Spite," in *New Approaches in Child Guidance*, ed. H. Strean, Metuchen, N.J.: Scarecrow Press.

KESTENBERG, J. 1956. "Vicissitudes of Female Sexuality." *Journal of the American Psychoanalytic Association* 4:453–476.

KIELL, N. 1964. *The Universal Experience of Adolescence*. New York: International Universities Press.

KINSEY, A., W. POMEROY, C. MARTIN, AND P. GEBHARD. 1953. *Sexual Behavior in the Human Female*. Philadelphia: W. B. Saunders.

————. 1948. *Sexual Behavior in the Human Male*. Philadelphia: W. B. Saunders.

KLEIN, M. 1957. *Envy and Gratitude*. New York: Basic Books.

KOVEL, J. 1976. *A Complete Guide to Therapy*. New York: Pantheon Books.

KNUPFER, G., W. CLARK, and R. ROOM. 1966. "The Mental Health of the Unmarried." *American Journal of Psychiatry* 122:841–851.

KRAFFT-EBING, R. VON. 1892. *Psychopathia Sexualis*. New York: G. P. Putnam's Sons.

KRANTZLER, M. 1975. *Creative Divorce*. New York: New American Library.

KÜBLER-ROSS, E. 1969. *On Death and Dying*. New York: Macmillan.

LAMPE, H. 1961. "Diagnostic Considerations in Casework with Aged Clients." In *Casework with the Aging*, ed. B. Diamond. New York: Family Service Association of America.

LANG, J. 1974. "Planned Short-Term Treatment in a Family Agency." *Social Casework* 55, no. 6:369–374.

LANGLEY, R. AND R. LEVY, 1977. *Wife Beating: The Silent Crisis*. New York: E. P. Dutton.

LAUGHLIN, H. 1970. *The Ego and its Defenses*. New York: Appleton-Century Crofts.

LEDERER, W., AND D. JACKSON. 1968. *The Mirages of Marriage*. New York: W. W. Norton.

LEVAY, A., AND A. KAGLE. 1977. "A Study of Treatment Needs Following Sex Therapy." *American Journal of Psychiatry* 134:970–973.

LEVIN, S. 1963. "Depression in the Aged." *Journal of Geriatrics* 18:302–307.

LIBBY, R. 1978. "Creative Singlehood as a Sexual LIfe Style." In *Exploring Intimate Life Styles*, ed. B. Murstein. New York: Springer Publishing Co.

LICHT, H. 1932. *Sexual Life in Ancient Greece*. London: The Abbey Library.

LIFSCHUTZ, T., T. STEWART, AND A. HARRISON. 1958. "Psychiatric Consultation in the Public Assistance Agency." *Social Casework* 39, no. 1:3–8.

LIFTON, R. 1971. "Protean Man." *Archives of General Psychiatry* 24:298–304.

LINN, L. 1975. "Neurologic Aspects of Aging." In *Personality Development and Deviation*, ed. G. Wiedeman. New York: International Universities Press.

LINTON, R. 1936. *The Study of Man*. New York: D. Appleton-Century.

LOBITZ, W., AND J. LOPICCOLO. 1972. "New Methods in the Behavioral Treatment of Sexual Dysfunction." *Archives of Sexual Behavior* 2: 163–171.

LOPICCOLO, J., AND V. MILLER. 1975. "A Program for Enhancing the Sexual Relationship of Normal Couples." *Counseling Psychologist* 5: 41–45.

LORAND, S. 1961. "Treatment of Adolescents." In *Adolescents: Psychoanalytic Approach to Problems and Therapy*, ed. S. Lorand and H. Schneer. New York: Hoeber.

LUSTIG, N. 1966. "Incest: A Family Group Survival Pattern." *Archives of General Psychiatry* 14:32–39.

LUTZ, W., 1964. "Marital Incompatibility." In *Social Work and Social Problems*, ed. N. Cohen. New York: National Association of Social Workers.

LYNCH, J. 1977. *The Broken Heart*. New York: Basic Books.

LYNESS, J. 1978. "Androgyny." In *Exploring Intimate Life Styles*, ed. G. Murstein. New York: Springer Publishing Co.

MAHLER, M. 1968. *On Human Symbiosis and the Vicissitudes of Individuation*. New York: International Universities Press.

_____. 1963. "Thoughts About Development and Individuation." In *The Psychoanalytic Study of the Child*, vol. 18, ed. K. Eissler. New York: International Universities Press.

_____. 1952. "On Child Psychosis and Schizophrenia." In *The Psychoanalytic Study of the Child*, vol. 7, ed. K. Eissler, New York: International Universities Press.

MAISCH, H. 1973. *Incest*. London: Andre Deutsch.

MALINOWSKI, B. 1922. *Argonauts of the Western Pacific*, New York: E. P. Dutton and Co.

MANN, J. 1975. "Is Sex Counseling Here to Stay?" *Counseling Psychologist* 5:60–63.

_____. 1973. *Time-Limited Psychotherapy*. Cambridge, Mass.: Harvard University Press.

MARASSE, H., AND M. HART. 1975. "The Oedipal Period." In *Personality Development and Deviation*, ed. G. Weideman. New York: International Universities Press.

MARCUS, I., AND J. FRANCIS. 1975. *Masturbation: From Infancy to Senescence*. New York: International Universities Press.

MASSERMAN, J. 1965. "Short-Term Therapy." In *Short-Term Therapy*, ed. L. Wolberg. New York: Grune and Stratton.

MASTERS, W., AND V. JOHNSON. 1970. *Human Sexual Inadequacy*. Boston: Little, Brown.

_____. 1966. *The Human Sexual Response*. Boston: Little, Brown.

McINTYRE, K. 1981. "Role of Mothers in Father-Daughter Incest: A Feminist Analysis." *Social Work* 26:462–467.

MEAD, M. 1967. "Sexual Freedom and Cultural Change." Paper delivered at Forum, "The Pill and the Puritan Ethic," San Francisco State College, February 10, 1967.

MEERLOO, J. 1969. "The Contribution of Psychoanalysis to Problems of the Aged." In *Psychoanalysis and Social Work*, ed. M. Heiman. New York: International Universities Press.

MEISSNER, W. 1978. *The Paranoid Process*. New York: Jason Aronson.

MILLER, E. 1962. "Individual and Social Approach to the Study of Adolescence." *British Journal of Medical Psychology* 35:211-224.

MONTAGU, A. 1981. *Growing Young*. New York: McGraw-Hill.

_____. 1956. "Marriage: A Cultural Perspective." In *Neurotic Interaction in Marriage*, ed. V. Eisenstein. New York: Basic Books.

MUESTERBERGER, W. 1961. "The Adolescent in Society." In *Adolescents: Psychoanalytic Approach to Problems and Therapy*, ed. S. Lorand and H. Schneer. New York: Hoeber.

MURDOCK, G. 1949. *Social Structure*. New York: Macmillan.

MURPHY, G. 1979. "Human Sexuality and the Potential of the Older Person." In *Sexual Issues in Social Work*, ed. D. Kunkel. Honolulu: University of Hawaii.

MURSTEIN, B. 1976. "The Stimulus-Value-Role Theory of Marital Choice." In *Contemporary Marriage*, ed. H. Grunebaum and J. Christ. Boston: Little, Brown.

NEUBAUER, P. 1960. "The One-Parent Child and His Oedipal Development." In *The Psychoanalytic Study of the Child*, vol. 15, ed. K. Eissler. New York: International Universities Press.

NEUBECK, G. 1969. *Extramarital Relationships*. Englewood Cliffs, N.J.: Prentice-Hall.

NIEDERLAND, W. 1965. "The Role of the Ego in the Recovery of Early Memories." *The Psychoanalytic Quarterly* 24:564-571.

NIXON, R. 1962. *My Six Crises*. New York: Doubleday.

OBLER, M. 1975. "Multivariate Approaches to Psychotherapy with Sexual Dysfunction." *Counseling Psychologist* 5:55-60.

OFFER, D. 1971. "Attitudes Toward Sexuality in a Group of 1,500 Middle-Class Teen-Agers." *Journal of Youth and Adolescence* 1:81-91.

_____, AND J. OFFER. 1975. *From Teenage to Young Manhood*. New York: Basic Books.

O'NEILL, N., AND G. O'NEILL. 1972. *Open Marriage*. New York: M. Evans.

ORMONT, L. 1964. "The Resolution of Resistances by Conjoint Psychoanalysis." *The Psychoanalytic Review* 51:89-101.

_____, AND H. STREAN. 1978. *The Practice of Conjoint Therapy*. New York: Human Sciences Press.

OSTFELD, A., C. SMITH, AND B. STOTSKY. 1977. "The Systemic Use of Procaine in the Treatment of the Elderly: A Review." *Journal of the American Geriatric Society* 25:1-20.

OSTOW, M. 1974. *Sexual Deviation: A Psychoanalytic Insight*. New York: Quadrangle Books.

PACKARD, V. 1972. *A Nation of Strangers*. New York: David McKay.

PAOLINO, T., AND B. McCRADY. 1978. *Marriage and Marital Therapy*. New York: Brunner-Mazel.

PARAD, H. 1965. *Crisis Intervention*. New York: Family Service Association of America.

PEARSON, L. 1980. "Changes Wrought by Death." In *Loving, Parenting, and Dying: The Family Cycle in England and America, Past and Present*, ed. V. Fox and M. Quitt. New York: Psychohistory Press.

PERLMAN, H. 1964. "Unmarried Mothers." In *Social Work and Social Problems*, ed. N. Cohen. New York: National Association of Social Workers.

PHILLIPS, E., AND J. WEINER. 1967. *Short-Term Psychotherapy*. New York: Basic Books.

POLLAK, O. 1956. *Integrating Sociological and Psychoanalytic Concepts*. New York: Russell Sage Foundation.

POSNER, W. 1961. "Basic Issues in Casework with Older People." In *Casework with the Aged*, ed. B. Diamond. New York: Family Service Association of America.

POWELL, L., P. BLAKENEY, H. CROFT, AND G. PULLIAM. 1974. "Rapid Treatment Approach to Human Sexual Inadequacy." *American Journal of Obstetrics and Gynecology*, 119:89–97.

PROCHASKA, J., AND J. PROCHASKA. 1978. "Twentieth-Century Trends in Marriage and Marital Therapy." In *Marriage and Marital Therapy*, ed. T. Paolino and B. McCrady. New York: Brunner-Mazel.

RADO, S. 1933. "The Psychoanalysis of Pharmacothymia." *Psychoanalytic Quarterly* 2:1–23.

RAPAPORT, D. 1942. *Emotions and Memory*. New York: International Universities Press.

RECKLESS, J., D. HAWKINS, AND A. FAUNTLEROY. 1973. "Time-Extended Group Therapy Sessions in a Remote Setting." *American Journal of Psychiatry* 130:1024–1026.

REID, W., AND I. EPSTEIN. 1972. *Task-Centered Casework*. New York: Columbia University Press.

REID, W., AND A. SHYNE. 1969. *Brief and Extended Casework*. New York: Columbia University Press.

REIK, T. 1949. *Listening with the Third Ear*. New York: Farrar, Straus.

ROBINSON, I., K. KING, AND O. BALOWICK. 1972. "The Premarital Sexual Revolution Among College Females." *The Family Coordinator* 6: 189–195.

ROGERS, C. 1951. *Client-Centered Therapy.* Boston: Houghton Mifflin.

ROHEIM, G. 1952. *The Gates of the Dream*, New York: International Universities Press.

ROSENTHAL, L. 1971. "Application of Small Groups to Casework Theory and Practice." In *Social Casework: Theories in Action*, ed. H. Strean. Metuchen, N.J.: Scarecrow Press.

ROSS, N. 1979. "On the Significance of Infantile Sexuality." In *On Sexuality*, eds. T. Karasu and C. Socarides. New York: International Universities Press.

RUESCH, J. 1961. *Therapeutic Communication.* New York: W. W. Norton.

RYDER, R. 1978. "Androgynous and Contract Marriage." In *Exploring Intimate Life Styles*, ed. B. Murstein. New York: Springer Publiching Co.

SALINGER, J. 1945. *Catcher in the Rye.* Boston: Little, Brown.

SAUL, L. 1976. *Psychodynamics of Hostility.* New York: Jason Aronson.

SCHAFER, R. 1960. "The Loving and Beloved Superego in Freud's Structural Theory." In *The Psychoanalytic Study of the Child*, vol. 15, ed. K. Eissler. New York: International Universities Press.

SCHMIDEBERG, M. 1951. "Psychiatric-Social Factors in Young Unmarried Mothers." *Social Casework* 32. no. 1:3–7.

SCHMIDT, G., AND V. SIGUSCH. 1972. "Changes in Sexual Behavior Among Young Males and Females Between 1960–1970." *Archives of Sexual Behavior* 2:27–45.

SEMANS, J. 1956. "Premature Ejaculation: A New Approach," *Southern Medical Journal* 9:353–357.

SERBAN, G., 1981. Interview in *Frontiers of Psychiatry*, 11, no. 9, October 15, 1981.

SHAINESS, N. 1979. "Gender Stereotypes, Identity, Sexual Concepts, and Behavior Today." In *Psychosexual Imperatives*, ed. M. Nelson and J. Ikenberry. New York: Human Sciences Press.

SHLAKMAN, V. 1966. "Unmarried Parenthood: An Approach to Social Policy." *Social Casework* 2:27–45.

SIPORIN, M. 1981. "Moral Philosophy in Social Work Today: Are Social Workers Immoral?" Paper Presented at National Association of Social Workers Professional Symposium. Philadelphia, November 19, 1981.

SLAVSON, S. 1943. *An Introduction to Group Therapy.* New York: Commonwealth Fund.

SMITH, J., AND L. SMITH. 1974. *Beyond Monogamy.* Baltimore: The Johns Hopkins University Press.

SOCARIDES, C. 1978. *Homosexuality.* New York: Jason Aronson.

SORENSEN, R. 1973. *Adolescent Sexuality in Contemporary America.* New York: World.

SPIEGEL, J. 1960. "The Resolution of Role Conflict with the Family." In *The Family*, ed. N. Bell and E. Vogel. Glencoe, Ill.: The Free Press.

SPITZ, R. 1945. "Hospitalism: An Inquiry into Psychiatric Conditions in Early Childhood." *The Psychoanalytic Study of the Child*, vol. 1, ed. K. Eissler. New York: International Universities Press.

SPOTNITZ, H. 1961. "Adolescence and Schizophrenia: Problems in Differentiation." In *Adolescents: Psychoanalytic Approach to Problems and Therapy*, ed. S. Lorand and H. Schneer. New York: Hoeber.

————, AND L. FREEMAN. 1964. *The Wandering Husband*. Englewood Cliffs, N.J.: Prentice-Hall.

STAMM, I. 1972. "Family Therapy." In *Casework: A Psychosocial Therapy*, 2nd edition, ed. F. Hollis. New York: Random House.

STARR, J., AND D. CARNS. 1973. "Singles in the City." In *Marriages and Families*, ed. H. Lopata. New York: Van Nostrand.

STEARNS, G. 1974. "Declining Testicular Function with Age-Hormonal and Clinical Correlates," *American Journal of Medicine*, 57:761–766.

STERN, M., AND A. STERN. 1981. *Sex in the U. S. S. R.* New York: Times Books.

STERNBACH, O. 1947. "Arrested Ego Development and Its Treatment in Conduct Disorders and Neuroses of Childhood." *The Nervous Child* 6:306–317.

STOLLER, R. 1975. *Perversion: The Erotic Form of Hatred*. New York: Pantheon Books.

STONE, A., AND J. LEVINE. 1950. "Group Therapy in Sexual Maladjustment." *American Journal of Psychiatry* 107:195–202.

STREAN, H. 1982. *Controversy in Psychotherapy*. Metuchen, N.J.: The Scarecrow Press.

————. 1980. *The Extramarital Affair*. New York: The Free Press.

————. 1979. *Psychoanalytic Theory and Social Work Practice*. New York: The Free Press.

————. 1978. *Clinical Social Work*. New York: The Free Press.

————. 1976. *Crucial Issues in Psychotherapy*. Metuchen, N.J.: The Scarecrow Press.

————. 1972. *The Experience of Psychotherapy*. Metuchen, N.J.: The Scarecrow Press.

————. 1970. *New Approaches in Child Guidance*. Metuchen, N.J.: The Scarecrow Press.

————. 1970. "Reconsiderations in the Casework Treatment of the Unmarried Mother." In *New Approaches in Child Guidance*, ed. H. Strean. Metuchen, N.J.: The Scarecrow Press.

————, AND A. BLATT. 1969. "Long or Short-Term Therapy: Some Selected Issues." *Journal of Contemporary Psychotherapy* 1, no. 2:114–122.

STRUPP, H., S. HADLEY, B. SCHWARTZ, AND B. GOMES. 1977. *Psychotherapy for Better or Worse*. New York: Jason Aronson.

SZASZ, T. 1980. *Sex by Prescription*. Garden City, N.Y.: Anchor Press.

TANNAHILL, R. 1980. *Sex in History*. New York: Stein and Day.

TERMAN, L. 1938. *Psychological Factors in Marital Happiness*. New York: McGraw-Hill Book Co.

Time magazine, November 23, 1981.

TOFFLER, A. 1971. *Future Shock*. New York: Random House.

TROPP, E. 1968. "The Group in Life and Work." *Social Casework* 49:265–273.

TURNER, F. In press. *Adult Psychopathology for Social Workers*. New York: The Free Press.

United States Bureau of the Census, 1974.

VANDERVOORT, H., AND J. BLANK. 1975. "A Sex Counseling Program in a University Medical Center." *Counseling Psychologist* 5:64–67.

VANGGAARD, T. 1972. *Phallas*. New York: International Universities Press.

VITALIANO, P., J. JAMES, AND D. BOYER. 1981. "Sexuality of Deviant Females: Adolescent and Adult Correlates." *Social Work* 26, no. 6:468–473.

WALLERSTEIN, J., AND J. KELLY. 1980. *Surviving the Breakup: How Children and Parents Cope with Divorce*. New York: Basic Books.

WALTZMAN, S., AND T. KARASU. 1979. "Sex in the Elderly." In *On Sexuality*, ed. T. Karasu and C. Socarides. New York: International Universities Press.

WEINBERG, M., AND C. WILLIAMS. 1974. *Male Homosexuals*, New York: Oxford University Press.

WERMER, H., AND S. LEVIN. 1967. "Masturbation Fantasies: Their Changes with Growth and Development." In *The Psychoanalytic Study of the Child*, vol. 22, ed. K. Eissler. New York: International Universities Press.

WERTHAM, F. 1966. *A Sign for Cain*. New York: Macmillan.

WIEDEMAN, G. 1975. *Personality Development and Deviation*. New York: International Universities Press.

WIEDER, H., AND E. KAPLAN. 1969. "Drug Use in Adolescents: Psychodynamic Meaning and Pharmacogenic Effect." In *The Psychoanalytic Study of the Child*, vol. 24, ed. K. Eissler. New York: International Universities Press.

WILLIAMSON, D. 1977. "Extramarital Involvements in Couple Interaction." In *Counseling in Marital and Sexual Problems*, ed. R. Stahmann and W. Hiebert. Baltimore: Williams and Wilkins.

WOLBERG, L. 1965. *Short-Term Psychotherapy*. New York: Grune and Stratton.

WOLFE, T. 1976. *Mauve Gloves and Madmen, Clutter and Vine and Other Stories, Sketches and Essays.* New York: Farrar, Straus, and Giroux.

WOLPE, J. 1969. *The Practice of Behavior Therapy.* New York: Pergamon Press.

WRIGHT, J., R. PERREAULT, AND M. MATHIEU. 1977. "The Treatment of Sexual Dysfunction: A Review." *General Psychiatry* 34:881–890.

WYNNE, L. I. RYCKOFF, J. DAY, AND S. HIRCH. 1958. "Pseudomutuality in the Family Relations of Schizophrenics." In *A Modern Introduction to the Family*, ed. N. Bell and E. Vogel (revised edition). New York: The Free Press.

YANKELOVICH, D. 1974. *The New Morality.* New York: McGraw-Hill.

ZELNIK, M., AND J. KANTNER. 1971. "Sex and Contraception Among Unmarried Teenagers." In *Toward the End of Growth*, ed. C. Westcoff. Englewood Cliffs, N.J.: Prentice-Hall.

ZILBACH, J. 1968. "Family Development." In *Modern Psychoanalysis*, ed. J. Marmor. New York: Basic Books.

ZILBERGELD, B. 1975. "Group Treatment of Sexual Dysfunction in Men Without Partners." *Journal of Sex and Marital Therapy* 1:204–214.

————, AND M. EVANS. 1980. "The Inadequacy of Masters and Johnson." *Psychology Today*, April, pp. 29–43.

ZINBERG, N., AND I. KAUFMAN. 1963. *Normal Psychology of the Aging Process.* New York: International Universities Press.

ZISKIN, J., AND M ZISKIN. 1973. *The Extramarital Arrangement.* London: Abelard-Schuman.

Index

Ables, B., 127, 205
Ackerman, N., 54, 205
Adams, M., 151, 152, 153
Adolescence, 24–27, 88–122
  adult reactions to, 92–95
  celibacy, 108–110
  compulsive sexual activity,
    106–107
  countertransference problems,
    96–97
  drug use, 119-122
  educational difficulties, 114–117
  homosexuality, 26, 90, 92, 93,
    98, 110–112, 114, 120
  masturbation, 117–119
  paranoia, 112–114
  rebelliousness, 95, 97–101
  sexuality and new morality, 91
  treatment in, 95–96
  unmarried mothers, 101–105
Aged, 176–196
  aging process, 181–183
  cultural issues, 177–179
  impact of physical changes on
    sexuality, 183–185
  psychosexual problems,
    185–189
  research on sexual behavior of,
    179–181
  in treatment, 189–196
Aichorn, A., 80
Alcoholism, 12
Alexander, F., 87, 90, 212–213
Allen, W., 176, 196
Allon, N., 153
Anal state of psychosexual
    development, 15–18, 121,
    139–142
Anorgasmia, 8, 21, 92, 134–137,
    199, 201
Anthony, E., 93, 94, 112, 113
Asexual marriages, 137–139
Atkin, E., 124

Autonomy vs. self-doubt, 15–18

Bach, G., 7
Balint, M., 213
Barbara, D., 34
Bartusis, M., 145
Battered husbands and wives, 7
Bed-wetting, 77–79, 87
Behavior modification therapy,
    201–202
Bell, A., 93
Bergler, E., 10, 113, 161
Berman, G., 69
Bernard, J., 153
Beron, L., 58
Berthelsdorf, S., 120
Bettelheim, B., 70–71
Bieber, I., 162, 163, 166
Bindrin, P., 210
Bisexuality, 3, 155
Blanck, G., 126
Blanck, R., 126
Blank, J., 210
Blatt, A., 214
Block, J., 145
Blos, P., 25, 89, 97, 99, 102
Bolton, C., 126
Bonan, A., 102
Bowlby, J., 14, 54, 80
Boyer, D., 171
Brady, J., 201
Brazelton, T., 15
Brener, C., 40
Brief treatment, 212–213
Brill, L., 120
Brown, G., 151, 152
Brozan, N., 137
Bullough, V., 152
Burgum, M., 58
Burk, M., 152
Butler, S., 82

Calvin, J., 4

Cameron, N., 85, 188
Carns, D., 153
Castration anxiety, 19, 118, 165, 168
Celibacy, 3–4, 151, 152, 154
  in adolescence, 108–110
  in marriage, 137–139
  in widowhood, 157–160
Children, 52–87
  answering questions on sex, 53–57
  compulsive masturbation, 74–77
  depression, 84–86
  enuresis, 77–79
  incest, 82–84, 93
  infantile sexuality, 52–53, 89, 163
  learning problems, 68–71
  parents in treatment, 61–63
  phobias, 71–74
  psychosomatic problems, 86–87
  role of parents in sexual problems of, 57–61
  sexual identity problems, 64–68
  sexual provocativeness, 59, 79–82
Christ, J., 125
Christenson, C., 180, 181
Civil rights, 155, 164
Clark, W., 153
Client's history, 37–38
Coen, S., 107
Cohabitation, 1, 152
Cohn, D., 53
Compulsive masturbation, 74–77
Compulsive sexual activity, 29, 106–107
Condon, C., 92
Conjoint therapy, 205–208
Conscience, 17, 41
Contract marriages, 152
Cooper, S., 65
Coprophiliac, 168–169

Corsini, R., 208
Countertransference, 50–51, 96–97, 187–189
Crist, T., 5
Cults, 91–92

Deburger, J., 123
Defense mechanisms, 40–41, 129
Delinquency, 98–99
DeLuccia, I., 119
DeMause, L., 52, 168
Dengrove, E., 201, 202
Denial, 40, 41, 43, 163, 175
Denny, T., 92
Dependency, love as, 27–28
Depression, 182
  childhood, 84–86
Desensitization techniques, 201–202
Despert, L., 58
Dickes, R., 2, 3, 5
Divorce, 102–103, 124, 152, 160–161
Don Juanism, 29, 90, 155, 171
Double-bind messages, 206, 207
Drabble, M., 152
Drug use, 90, 92, 119–122
Dulit, E., 90, 97
Dullea, G., 153
Durbin, K., 7

Easley, E., 186
Educational difficulties in adolescence, 114–117
Ego functions, 40–41
Ego ideal, 41
Eidelberg, L., 129, 148
Eisenberg, M., 69
Eisenstein, V., 126, 131, 132, 135, 149
Ellis, A., 202
Ejaculation, 131–132
Encounter groups, 1, 211–212

English, O., 11, 15, 52, 53, 55, 74, 75, 77, 115
Enuresis, 77–79, 87
Epstein, I., 212
Erikson, E., 11, 14, 18, 22, 24, 26, 81, 89, 98, 142, 204
Eroticism, 7
Esman, A., 88, 90, 91, 92
Estrogen-replacement therapy, 186
Evans, R., 126, 202, 203, 215
Exhibitionism, 155, 167, 168, 169–170, 194
Extramarital affairs, 1, 3, 124, 144–149
Eysenck, H., 213

Family therapy, 86, 205, 209, 211
Fees, withholding, 45–46
Feinstein, S., 92
Feldhause, J., 92
Feldman, Y., 55, 58, 59, 61
Fenichel, O., 74, 75, 77, 110, 132, 149, 165, 168, 171
Fetishism, 155, 167, 168, 194, 195
Fine, R., 5, 7, 8, 23, 26, 27, 35, 49, 50, 51, 125, 162, 163, 164, 166, 167, 185, 202, 205, 214, 215
Finkle, A., 186
Finkle, P., 186
Fishel, D., 153
Fithian, M., 201
Forrest, T., 103
Fountain, G., 89
Fox, V., 158
Fraiberg, S., 142
France, A., 127
Francis, J., 118
Freedman, A., 79, 188
Freeman, D., 213
Freeman, L., 5, 15, 146, 191
Freud, A., 25, 40, 58, 89, 90, 93, 113, 139

Freud, S., 5, 9, 11, 19, 22, 64–65, 71, 75, 80, 89, 126, 148, 159
Frigidity, 8, 21, 92, 134–137, 199, 201
Frosch, W., 8
Furstenberg, F., 101

Gagnon, J., 180
Galenson, E., 22
Garrett, A., 30
Gaylin, W., 80
Geleerd, E., 93
Genet, J., 2
Gilder, G., 9
Giovacchini, P., 92
Glick, B., 201–202
Glover, E., 79, 132
Gochros, H., 1, 174
Gochros, J., 174
Golan, N., 212
Goldring, J., 212, 213
Goldsmith, J., 102
Granick, S., 192
Greece, 2–3
Greenacre, P., 54
Greenson, R., 44
Gregory, M., 173
Group sex, 1, 152, 154
Group treatment, 208–211
Grunebaum, H., 58, 125
Guilt, 8, 22, 74–75, 82, 90, 158–160
Guttmacher Institute, 102

Halpern, H., 69
Handicapped, 173–175
Hare Krishna, 92
Harley, M., 118
Harrison, A., 102
Harrison, D., 173, 174
Hart, M., 22
Hartman, W., 201
Hartmann, H., 53
Hate affair, 125

Hate culture, 8
Helping interview, 30–37
Hendin, H., 7, 8, 91, 92, 108, 125
Hepworth, D., 213
Heslinga, K., 173
Hite, S., 7, 151, 162, 163
Hogan, D., 202, 215
Homosexuality, 1, 20, 29, 65, 152,
    154–155
  in adolescence, 26, 90, 92, 93,
    98, 110–112, 114, 120
  in ancient Greece, 3
  incidence of, 162, 164
  theories of, 162–167
Honigmann, J., 2
Hooker, E., 162, 163
Howard, J., 7, 211
Hugging therapy groups, 1
Human potential movement, 152
Hunt, B., 151, 160
Hunt, M., 1–5, 91, 127, 134, 151,
    160, 162, 197

Id, 9, 40, 49
Identity vs. identity diffusion,
    24–27
Illegitmacy, 101
Immature forms of love, 27–29
Impotence, 8, 21, 39, 92, 131–134,
    199, 202
Ince, L., 201
Incest, 82–84, 93
Infancy, 11–15
Infantile sexuality, 52–53, 89, 168
Initiative vs. guilt, 18–22

Jackel, M., 177, 178, 182, 183,
    195
Jckson, D., 123, 205
Jacobs, J., 92
Jacobson, E., 92
James, J., 171
Jerrett, I., 200, 202, 203, 215
Johnson, A., 91

Johnson, V., 2, 5, 180, 197,
    198–205, 209, 213
Johnson, W., 181
Jones, E., 89
Josselyn, I., 23, 165
Joyce, J., 88
Judge, J., 102, 103
Jung, C., 126
Justice, B., 82
Justice, R., 82

Kadushin, A., 30–31, 35
Kagle, A., 202
Kantner, J., 6
Kaplan, E., 120
Kaplan, H., 79, 184, 188, 201
Karasu, T., 1, 5, 9, 162, 176, 178,
    183, 185, 187, 195, 200, 202,
    203, 214
Karlen, A., 162
Kaufman I., 182
Kelly, J., 65
Kesten, J., 68
Kiell, N., 88
Kinsey, A., 5, 124, 134, 162,
    170–171, 179, 180
Klein, M., 14, 28, 142, 146
Knox, J., 4
Knupfer, G., 153
Kovel, J., 211, 212
Krafft-Ebing, R. von, 177
Krantzler, M., 160
Kubler-Ross, E., 159
Kunkel, D., 1

Lampe, H., 192
Lang, J., 212
Langley, R., 7
Late ejaculation, 132
Latency state of psychosexual
    development, 22–24
Lateness to therapy, 44–45
Learning problems, 68–71
Lederer, W., 123

Lesbianism, 7, 21, 151, 165–166
Levay, A., 202
Levin, S., 75, 182
Levine, J., 209
Levy, R., 7
Libby, R., 151, 153, 154
Licht, H., 2, 4
Life expectancy, 176
Lifschutz, T., 102
Linn, L., 182
Linton, R., 126
Listening, 33–36
Lobitz, W., 201
LoPiccolo, J., 201, 209
Lorand, S., 96
Lustig, N., 83
Luther, M., 4
Lutz, W., 130
Lynch, J., 153
Lyness, J., 152

Mahler, M., 14, 18, 54, 142
Maisch, H., 83
Malinowski, B., 19
Mann, J., 210, 212, 213
Mann, T., 88
Marasse, H., 22
Marcus, I., 118
Marriage, 123–150
    celibacy, 137–139
    choice of mate, 125–127
    cultural considerations, 123–125
    extramarital sex, 1, 3, 124,
        144–149
    frigidity, 8, 21, 92, 134–137,
        199, 201
    impotence, 8, 21, 39, 92,
        131–134, 199, 202
    interaction and incompatibility,
        128–131
    masturbation in, 149–150
    sadomasochism, 21, 50,
        139–142, 147, 160
Masochism, 168, 169, 170

Masserman, J., 213
Masters, W., 2, 5, 180, 197,
    198–205, 209, 213
Masturbation, 3, 49, 151, 201
    in adolescence, 117–119
    aged and, 181, 194, 195
    compulsive, 74–77
    in marriage, 149–150
McCarthy, J., 162
McCrady, B., 124, 205
McCullers, C., 88
McIntyre, K., 82
Mead, M., 144
Meerloo, J., 176, 178, 183, 185
Meissner, W., 112
Menopause, 180
Miller, A., 92
Miller, E., 94
Miller, V., 209
Milton, J., 4
Montagu, A., 4, 195, 196
Mother–infant relationship,
    11–15, 146–147
Murdock, G., 19
Murphy, G., 176, 179, 195
Murstein, B., 126

Narcissism, 89, 95, 143
National Organization For
    Non-Parents, 152–153
Negative countertransference,
    50–51
Neubauer, P., 54, 65
Neubeck, G., 127
New sexuality, 1–2, 5–10, 91
New York Times, The, 82
Nude marathons, 1
Nymphomania, 29

Obler, M., 202
Oedipal conflict, 18–22, 26, 55–56,
    71–73, 98, 110, 115–117, 121,
    132–137, 147–148, 165
Offer, D., 6, 94

Offer, J., 94
Omnipotent fantasies, 13, 14, 21,
    99, 125, 143–144
O'Neill, G., 145, 152
O'Neill, N., 145, 152
One-parent family, 64–65
"Open" marriages, 152
Oral state of psychosexual
    development, 11–15, 28, 121,
    142–144
Ormont, L., 210
Ostfeld, A., 186
Ostow, M. 171

Packard, V., 211
Paolino, T., 123, 205
Parad, H., 212
Paranoia, 112–114
Patterson, R., 192
Pearson, G., 11, 15, 52, 53, 55, 74,
    75, 77, 115
Pearson, L., 158
Pederasty, 3
Penis envy, 22, 135–137, 165–166
Perlman, H., 101
Pertinent questions, 34–37
Perversions, 155, 167–170
Phallic-oedipal stage of
    psychosexual development,
    18–22, 26, 55–56, 71–73, 98,
    110, 115–117, 121, 132–137,
    147–148, 165
Phillips, E., 213
Phobias, 71–74
Physically handicapped, 173–175
Planned Parenthood, 152
Pollak, O., 205
Positive countertranference, 50
Posner, W., 192
Powell, L., 209, 210
Premarital sex, 1, 26–27, 90–92
Premature ejaculation, 128,
    130–132, 199, 201
Prochaska. J., 124

Projection, 40, 43
Promiscuity, 102, 103, 170–173
Pseudo-mutuality, 207
Psychopathic child, 79–81
Psychosexual assessment, 37–42
Psychosexual development, 11–29
    adolescence: see Adolescence
    anal stage, 15–18, 121, 139–142
    latency stage, 22–24
    oral stage, 11–15, 28, 121,
        142–144
    phallic-oedipal stage, 18–22, 26,
        55–56, 71–73, 98, 110,
        115–117, 121, 132–137,
        147–148, 165
Psychosomatic problems, 86–87
Puberty, 24
Puritans, 4

Quitt, M., 158

Rado, S., 120
Rape, 7
Rational-Emotive approach
    (RET), 202
Reaction formation, 40, 41
Rebelliousness, 95, 97–101
Reckless, J., 210
Reflective teaching, 199–200
Regression, 16, 41, 89
Reid, W., 212, 213
Reik, T., 180
Religious groups, 91
Remarriage, 152, 158
Repression, 40, 43, 163, 175
Rescue fantasy, love as, 28
Resistance, 43–46
Retirement, 178
Robinson, I., 5
Rogers, C., 34, 82
Roheim, G., 23
Roiphe, H., 22
Romans, 3
Romantic love, 4, 126–127

Room, R., 153
Rosenbaum, M., 200, 202, 203
    214–215
Rosenthal, L., 210
Ross, H., 87, 90
Ross, N., 53, 54
Roth, P., 2
Roy J., 191
Ruesch, J., 206
Runaways, 98
Ryder, R., 152

Sadism, 28, 167–170
Sadock, B., 79, 188
Sadomasochism, 21, 50, 139–142,
    147, 160
Salinger, J.D., 88
Santayana, G., 126
Schafer, R., 80
Schellen, A., 173
Schizophrenia, 95–96
Schmideberg, M., 103
Schmidt, G., 91
Semans, J., 199
Sensate-focus exercises, 200
Sensitivity groups, 1, 211–212
Separation-individuation, 18
Serban, G., 6, 7
Serial monogamy, 91
Sex roles, 6–7
Sexual attitudes and practices,
    historical overview of, 2–6
Sexual deviancy, 154–155
Sexual identity problems, 64–68
Sexual promiscuity, 102, 103,
    170–173
Sexual provocativeness, 59, 79–82,
    192
Shainess, N., 8–9, 187
Shakespeare, W., 88
Shlakman, V., 102
Short-term treatment, 212–215
Shyne, A., 213
Sigusch, V., 91

Silence, 45
Singlehood, 151–175
    compared to marriage, 153
    divorce, 102–103, 124, 152,
        160–161
    handicapped, 173–175
    homosexuality, 162–167
    perversions, 155, 167–170
    promiscuity, 170–173
    widowhood, 152, 153, 154,
        157–160
Siporin, M., 188
Slavson, S., 208, 209
Smith, J., 7
Smith, L., 7
Socarides, C., 1, 5, 9, 162, 163,
    165, 166, 187, 202
Solon, 3
Sorenson, R., 91
Spiegel, J., 206
Spitz, R., 54
Spotnitz, H., 15, 95, 146
Stamm, I., 207
Starr, J., 153
Stearns, G., 186
Stern, A., 197, 198
Stern, M., 197, 198
Sternbach, O., 55, 60, 77
Stewart, T., 102
Stoller, R., 170, 171
Stone, A., 209
Strean, H., 1, 5, 8, 14, 37, 39, 43,
    54, 55, 58, 73, 79, 86, 92, 102,
    103, 124, 126, 129, 145, 146,
    202, 210, 214
Strupp, H., 214
Suicide, 90, 92
Sullivan, H.S., 163
Superego, 9, 17, 40, 41–42, 49, 80,
    90, 112–113, 158, 215
Swinging, 1, 24, 152
Switching, 1, 24
Symbiotic relationship, 14–15,
    27–28, 135, 142, 146, 156–157

Systemic procaine, 185–186
Szasz, T., 198

Talion principle, 19–20
Tannahill, R., 168
Terman, L., 134
Testosterone, 186
Time, 82, 84
Toffler, A., 212
Toilet training, 15, 16–18, 61,
     68–69, 77, 108, 139, 140
Transference, 46–49, 95, 187–189,
     215
Transsexualism, 155, 167, 170
Transvestitism, 168
Treatment procedures, 42–51
Tropp, E., 208–209
Trust vs. mistrust, 11–15, 98

Unattainable object, love for, 29
Unconscious wishes, 38–40, 71
U.S. Bureau of Census, 152
Unmarried mothers, 101–105
Updike, J., 2

Vagina, rejection of, 135
Vaginismus, 199
Vandervoort, H., 210
Vanggaard, T., 2, 3, 4
Verkuyl, A., 173
Vinci, Leonardo da, 64–65
Virgin, 28–29
Vitaliano, P., 171

Voyeurism, 155, 194

Wallerstein, J., 65
Waltzman, S., 176, 178, 183, 185,
     195
Weaning, 12, 13
Weinberg, M., 162, 163
Weiner, J., 213
Wermer, H., 75
Wertham, F., 162
Widowhood, 152, 153, 154,
     157–160
Wiedeman, G., 5, 176
Wieder, H., 120
Williams, C., 162, 163
Wolberg, L., 213
Wolfe, T., 124
Wolpe, J., 201
Women's liberation movement, 7,
     152
Wright, J.R., 202
Wynne, L., 207

Yankelovich, D., 91

Zelan, K., 71
Zelnik, M., 6
Zilbach, J., 205, 207
Zilbergeld, B., 202, 203, 210, 215
Zinberg, N., 182
Ziskin, J., 145
Ziskin, M., 145